Dr. Petty's Pain Relief for Dogs

DR. PETTY'S PAIN RELIEF FOR DOGS

The Complete Medical and Integrative Guide to Treating Pain

Michael C. Petty, DVM

THE COUNTRYMAN PRESS

A DIVISION OF W. W. NORTON & COMPANY

Independent Publishers Since 1923

Printed in the United States of America

For information about special discounts or bulk purchases, please contact W. W. Norton Special Sales at specialsales@wwnorton.com or 800-233-4830.

Manufacturing by QuadGraphics Fairfield
Book design by Lovedog Studio

The Countryman Press
www.countrymanpress.com

A division of W. W. Norton & Company, Inc.
500 Fifth Avenue, New York, NY 10110
www.wwnorton.com

Library of Congress Cataloging-in-Publication Data

Petty, Michael C. (Veterinarian)
  Dr. Petty's pain relief for dogs : the complete medical and integrative guide to treating pain / Michael C. Petty, DVM.
     pages cm
  Includes bibliographical references and index.
  ISBN 978-1-58157-309-1 (hardcover)
1. Pain in animals—Treatment. 2. Dogs—Diseases—Treatment. I. Title.
  SF910.P34P48 2016
  636.7089'60472—dc23
                          2015026114

10 9 8 7 6 5 4 3 2 1

PAIN has an element of blank;
It cannot recollect
When it began, or if there were
A day when it was not.

It has no future but itself,
Its infinite realms contain
Its past, enlightened to perceive
New periods of pain.

—Emily Dickinson

I would like to dedicate this book to all of the animals in pain that I didn't help but could have had I known then what I know now.

THANKS

I want to thank my family who suffered through all of my frequent and lengthy absences as I pursued my other love, pain management.

I would also like to thank all of the people who provided encouragement and support for this book, but especially Mary Ellen Goldberg, LVT, and Steven Bartlett, DVM, who unflinchingly gave me their time when it was needed. I would also like to thank my book agent, Regina Ryan, without whom this book would never have happened.

DISCLAIMER

Actual pain cases involving animals and owners are described in this book. Unless otherwise stated, the names of the animals and owners have been changed to protect their privacy. In many instances, these cases have been consolidated from two or more actual cases to further protect their privacy.

This book is not intended as a medical text for either veterinary professionals or the general public. Every dog should receive an exam and the advice of a veterinary professional prior to starting any treatment.

And finally, I would like to give an apology to cat owners. I am not ignoring you, but the treatments between cats and dogs are different enough that combining them into one book could be confusing. Why dogs? The sad fact is that the majority of cats in this country never see a veterinarian their entire lives except for getting "fixed" at the onset of sexual maturity. I felt that I could reach the largest number of animals by taking on the task of dog pain first.

CONTENTS

INTRODUCTION

ALL THE VETERINARIANS I KNOW WHO PRACTICE PAIN management have a story about their relationship with pain. Sometimes it is with an animal, sometimes a human family member or friend. My story starts with watching my mother die.

It was 1984, and I had been a veterinarian for four years. My mother was 64 years old and a 16-year survivor of breast cancer. Unbeknownst to anyone, including her doctors, the mastectomy and radiation therapy she had gone through had not cured her cancer. Instead, it had lain dormant in her bone marrow for those 16 years. Somehow awakened, the cancer snuck its way back into her life, presenting itself as vague aches, pains, and feelings of exhaustion and malaise. Eventually her physicians connected a bothersome leg pain with the previous cancer that everyone assumed had been cured almost two decades before. The pain that had started as an annoying twinge in her leg six months previous was now a metastatic disease spreading into her bones.

Her last hours of life were pure agony. As she coughed, her cancer-laden ribs fractured. These fractures made it harder for her already weakened respiratory system to function. Despite being administered oxygen, she gasped for breath, looking like a fish out of water, crying out in pain, asking for medication. I cornered the night nurse and told her to get permission to give my mother morphine. The nurse returned and said the doctor denied the request because he was afraid it would further compromise her respiratory function! The medical staff could or would not look beyond their concerns for their own protocols and instead denied my mother, who had hours if not minutes to live, any respite from her excruciating pain.

I held her hand. I watched her dying, crying out in pain, "Over, over, over." I felt her pulse slip away. My thoughts that evening were ones of concern for her and grief for myself. But the next day, her death still a fresh and raw memory, I vowed that as a caretaker and steward entrusted with an animal's health, I would never be indifferent to pain.

I learned over the years, time and again, that this vow is not an easy one to keep. Many obstacles get in the way. Not only are there things like cost of treatment and the time commitment it takes for proper treatment of pain, but also the willingness of owners to accept that their pet is in pain, the availability of effective treatments, and the limits of my own skill in helping every patient that needs to be helped. A good example comes from my own dog Abby, a Golden Retriever.

Abby was my constant companion. We had been together since 1981 when I purchased her from a litter of puppies that my coworker, a technician and dog breeder, had bred. Abby saw me through many life changes that included two jobs, a divorce, the start-up of my own clinic, and the death of both of my parents. I seldom went anywhere without her and indeed was reluctant to even consider a vacation that did not involve her. She loved the outdoors and especially liked it when we traveled to northern Michigan. As I would drive north from metro Detroit, she would fall asleep in the backseat of the car and would stir awake when we entered the conifer forests that became more common the farther north we went. Like a small child, she would press her nose against the window in excitement. When I finally opened the window for her, she would take in huge snoots-full of air, wallowing in the delight of the smell and the anticipation of our arrival.

Our destination was a piece of property purchased by my grandfather in the early part of the 20th century, located east of Mio, Michigan, on the Au Sable River in a relatively undeveloped part of Michigan. I did not have property there but could often cadge a place to stay for a night or two from one of my cousins.

The first thing that Abby would do on our arrival was to search for a "worthy" stick, look over her shoulder to make sure I was following her, and then run down a winding wooden staircase to the Au Sable. At the base of this hill was a dock that extended out into the river. Abby would drop the stick on the dock and wait expectantly for me to throw it far out into the swift-running water. She would plunge into the cold water, temporarily disappearing as she went under the surface and come back up swimming hard and sure for the stick as it was rapidly carried away by the river's current. Abby would unfailingly fetch the stick, and then back to the shore she would swim.

Dropping the stick she would shake the water from her fur, pick the stick back up, and trot back out onto the dock, dropping it at my feet with the clear expectation that this would happen over and over again. And it did, until my arm got tired or I would get concerned as her swim back upstream against the strong current got slower and slower with exhaustion. Darkness, cold weather, or hunger was no excuse to end the game. Only complete exhaustion could call a halt. This went on for our entire life together, as often as I could get away and drive the three-and-a-half hours to the river.

When Abby reached 10 years of age, I noticed a sudden decline in her ability to maintain her usual pace. I thought little of it though, as she was still willing to play and go on her walks. She just seemed to put the stick down from her games of fetch surprisingly early, or stop and look over her shoulder toward home when we would go on our walks. Then one day, I noticed that she had some abnormal wear on the tops of the nails of her back feet. I paid closer attention and, sure enough, she was starting to scuff her feet when she walked, especially when she was tired. I examined her. To my horror, I discovered that she had lost some of the sensation, called conscious proprioception, in her hind feet.

Conscious proprioception is what allows us to be able to touch a finger to our nose in the dark or with our eyes closed. In essence, through a complex feedback mechanism involving peripheral nerve receptors, the brain and spinal cord allow us to know where our body position is in our surrounding space. Loss of conscious proprioception indicates a problem somewhere in the neurological wiring, most often in the spinal cord.

With Abby, my examination showed some pain where her lower back and pelvis met, in what is called the lumbosacral junction. Radiographs of the area did not reveal the problem, but her symptoms were typical of dogs developing "lumbosacral disease," which can cause compression on the nerves at the tail end of the spinal cord.

My heart felt as though it was in my throat. At the time, there were few options for treating this issue. Surgery to relieve the compression was possible, but more often than not the procedure either did not help adequately, or even more horrifying, worsened the problem. I tried several different medications available, but none helped. And so I could do nothing but watch Abby slowly decline. Soon, even simple walks were an effort, and catching a ball or stick was almost impossible. I quit taking her to the Au Sable, as I knew she would never survive even one jump into the cold, swift water.

The disease progressed steadily. Then came early October 1991, two months after her 10th birthday. I was leaving my clinic at the end of the day, and I called out for Abby to get in the car for the ride home. I heard a strange noise and looked back to see her dragging herself down the hallway with her front legs, her back end limp and useless behind her, like a seal working its way across ice. I helped her into the car, and then went back into the clinic and drew up a syringe of euthanasia solution. We went home and had our last evening together. I fed her by hand, carried her outside to eliminate, and lay side by side with her through a sleepless night.

The next morning I cancelled my appointments and sitting with her in my sunroom at the side of my house, I injected her with the euthanasia solution. As with my mother's death, I felt her pulse stop.

Of course Abby couldn't say the words, "Over, over, over" as my mother did to describe the depths of her miseries. But had the disease run its course, Abby would have experienced terrible, relentless pain. I was relieved to know that she would no longer have to endure a paralyzed and play-free life. Weeping, I carried her in my arms and drove her to a local pet crematorium. I left the crematorium and returned a few hours later to pick up her still-warm ashes.

That Sunday, we made our last trip to the Au Sable River. This time there was no excitement in the seat behind me as the smell of the conifers suffused the car. The ceremony of choosing the "right" stick was gone. But as I opened the urn and poured her ashes into the river from the end of the dock, she did get to enter into an eternity with the river we both loved so much.

As I look back at Abby's life, her illness, and her death, I am sometimes haunted by the fact that today, with the drugs, skills, and knowledge available to me now, I could have slowed and even reversed some of the decline she experienced, the pain she suffered.

My *goal* in writing this book is to offer help for dogs like Abby, dogs that are in pain and that need and deserve the treatment she should have had. It is my *hope* that you will read this book and understand that even if you have not yet found it, *there is help if your pet is in pain.*

Abby diving off the dock for a stick.

1

RECOGNIZING SIGNS OF PAIN IN YOUR DOG

EVERY ONE OF US HAS EXPERIENCED PAIN. WHEN IT happens to ourselves, we recognize it right away, and more often than not we know its exact source. This isn't as easy to determine in another person, and it is even more difficult in a nonverbal being, such as a dog. Whether in dogs or people, the pain experience also becomes murky because almost without exception, the baggage of emotional experience also accompanies it. As aptly stated by the World Small Animal Veterinary Association, "pain is not just about how it feels, but how it makes you feel."[1]

Another confounding issue is that pain is a very personal experience, and it is impossible to anticipate the degree of pain an individual or dog will perceive as a result of a given pain-causing event. Previous pain experiences, concurrent disease, and perhaps even genetics all play a role in the level of pain your dog endures. If your dog seems to overreact to an injury, it does not mean that she is a wimp! To her the pain is very real, and her response to it is entirely appropriate.

Differentiating Acute and Chronic Pain

Pain in dogs falls into two broad categories: acute pain and chronic pain. Any discussion of pain needs to divide pain this way for a very practical reason—the differentiation and treatment of acute versus chronic pain can and often does vary considerably.

First of all, our dogs present to us both categories of pain, acute and chronic, in very different ways. Once the category of pain is identified, a distinct treatment approach for that category can be tailored to the particular physiology behind the pain. Acute pain treatment most often aims to cure the underlying cause of the pain in addition to treating the pain itself. An example of this would be the treatment of a broken leg. Chronic pain treatments, on the other hand, concentrate mostly on relieving an animal's pain rather than healing its source—they are much more focused on providing an improved long-term quality of life. An example of this would be the treatment of osteoarthritis.

Acute pain is any pain with a sudden onset, most often traumatic in origin, whether due to injury by an accident, a disease, or surgery. Acute pain occurs because it is telling your dog, "Doing that hurts." Or it is saying, "That part of you is injured—don't use it until it heals." Identification of acute pain is relatively easy, as dogs usually convey acute pain through vocalization, such as whimpering, whining, or even howling; or through their behavior, such as holding up a leg, hiding in their bed, and sometimes lashing out at the very people they love the most. Signs like these make it fairly simple to identify a dog that is suffering from acute pain.

Unlike acute pain, which serves as a form of protective mechanism allowing the body to heal, chronic pain provides no benefit to the well-being of your dog. Chronic pain says, "Don't use that arthritic limb." But protecting that limb won't heal arthritis. Indeed, not using an arthritic limb actually makes it worse. No one really understands the evolutionary advantage as to why chronic conditions cause pain and inflammation, but it is the card we have all been dealt.

Dogs in chronic pain, however, are much less likely to vocalize as the primary sign of pain. More characteristic signs of chronic pain are behavioral changes: a gradual withdrawal from social interactions, especially the decreased desire to go for walks or to initiate play in some of his favorite games. This makes the determination of chronic pain—with its subtle, gradual onset—a more formidable challenge to both the dog's caregiver and his veterinarian.

Because the diagnosis and treatment of chronic pain is more challenging, the majority of this book will be about chronic pain. This is not to undermine the importance of diagnosing and treating acute pain. Many chronic-pain states exist as a result of undiagnosed and unmanaged acute pain. This concept, and more, about acute pain will be discussed in Chapter 2.

A Pack Animal's Experience of Pain

Often an animal in chronic pain has learned how to adapt and carry on, in spite of the pain. Many go a step farther and have even learned to hide it. There are many good reasons a dog might either hide his or her pain, or adapt to it. Almost all animals are potential prey to something larger that would like to eat them. Our pets, although domesticated, still carry self-protection instincts and so do everything they can not to appear weak and vulnerable—an easy target. It follows that in the presence of other animals and people, they try as hard as possible to appear normal. This instinct becomes more apparent when they are in the presence of strangers—including their veterinarian, the very person trying to find the source of the pain and help them out.

For similar reasons, dogs also want to avoid rejection from members of their own pack. Our dogs regard us as their pack leaders, and that pack includes our families and us. This instinct, too, comes from their past. Back when dogs were undomesticated, an apparently sick pack member would be considered a risk to the rest of the pack for a variety of reasons: they might slow the pack down, or carry an infectious disease that could spread to other pack members, or, as noted previously, attract the attention of a larger predator. They might also have been seen as unlikely to contribute to the pack's needs. The harsh reality was that the well-being of the entire pack might call for the sick and injured to be expelled from the pack and left to fend for themselves. Sadly, our domesticated dogs may worry that we, as pack leaders, will force them to suffer the same fate.[2]

Avoiding Common Misconceptions of Pain

This ability of our dogs to hide chronic pain not only makes it difficult for pet owners to recognize signs of pain, and for veterinarians to diagnose it, but it also has given rise to many misconceptions. It is especially important for you, as the caregiver of your dog, to see past these misconceptions. Not only will this help you recognize the nature of your pet's pain and seek the appropriate pain treatments, but you will be better able to reassess the level of pain that your dog is experiencing. As a result, you can then better help your veterinarian determine the effectiveness of any treatments.

Misconception Number 1: Silence Means Absence of Pain.

Many pet owners assume their dog is not in pain because she is not whimpering, whining, or otherwise crying out. Consider our own aches and pains. If we experience a sudden acute pain, like a cut or burn, we ourselves may cry out and whimper. Our dogs react to these same injuries in the same way that we might. Now consider our own everyday aches and pains. When a pain is chronic, we are usually silent sufferers. Think about any chronic issues you might have: backache, arthritis, tendonitis, and so on. Although the condition might make it difficult or maybe even impossible for you to perform certain activities, you probably carry on the best you can, often without complaint. The same is true for dogs, as they possess the same nerve endings and pain centers that we do.[3] Like us, they often suffer in silence. When they do vocalize, they generally don't cry or howl like a dog in acute pain. A dog in chronic pain is instead more likely to vocalize moans and groans.

Misconception Number 2:
"My Dog Is Just Old."

As dogs age, they lose the exuberance of youth and slow down a bit, just like we do. Muscle mass naturally decreases, making it less likely they will be able to run as fast, jump as high, or play as long as they once did. But no matter the age of a dog, I've never seen a pain-free dog lose interest in playing. It is pain—not age—that shuts them down. It is pain that takes away their motivation to continue with many of their play activities.

Misconception Number 3:
Pain Medication Can Be Unsafe for
Old, Sick, or Debilitated Dogs.

Many people, and even some veterinarians, are worried about giving pain medications to old, sick, or debilitated animals, even though the need to treat them is very real. If pain is not controlled, it poses a huge threat to the well-being of a dog, as excessive pain often interferes with normal life functions. Even the most basic life requirements of eating, drinking, and elimination can become difficult or impossible to perform. The entire dilemma becomes a circular issue: Life-impairing pain is followed by a reluctance to treat that pain, causing biological dysfunction, making the pain even worse, only increasing the concern for treatment . . . and on it goes until it really becomes too late to help them.

It's important to treat pain because even old and/or sick dogs are very social creatures and need to be with their "pack." The ability to interact with their "pack" or family is often sharply curtailed in aging dogs who suffer from pain. We can't really know what a dog thinks, but it is easy to imagine that the more a dog is excluded from family activities, the less she will try to soldier on. It doesn't have to be this way for your geriatric pet. There is a pain medication or modality (procedure) for every dog, no matter what the health issues. Even severely debilitated dogs with major organ failure have pain relief options. Drugs are metabolized and excreted by different organs, and the knowledgeable veterinarian can tailor a pain-control program based on each dog's needs and condition. And for those dogs unable to take any pain medication, there are other treatment options like acupuncture and massage to help provide relief. In short, there is no excuse for not treating a sick or old dog's pain.

Misconception Number 4: "I Can't Afford It."

Cost is another concern often voiced by clients when confronted with a pet's painful condition. For certain severe and complex painful conditions, this might be a problem, but it is the exception rather than the rule. Pain treatments involving expensive drugs or time-consuming modalities may be beyond the reach of some dog owners, but there is almost always an inexpensive option available.

And let's keep this in perspective. How much money is your dog's well-being worth? Perhaps there is something you could give up to ensure your dog's health and comfort. A coffee in the morning? A drink after work? In many cases foregoing a small personal indulgence is enough to cover the cost of your dog's daily prescription. Additionally, some pharmaceutical companies offer programs to reduce the cost of medications. This topic is covered in greater detail in Chapter 23.

The Final Misconception: "Dogs Don't Feel Pain Like We Do."

This is probably true, but not in the way most people think. Over the years I have heard many excuses from both dog owners and veterinarians for not treating an animal's pain—claims such as dogs don't experience the pain we do (claiming they don't have the same nervous system as ours) or that their brains are not as developed as ours (meaning they cannot process pain signals in a way that causes them pain like it does in us). I think that all of these "excuses" are rubbish. As a matter of fact, it is my feeling that dogs actually feel pain more severely than people do.

After a lifetime of observing them, I have come to believe that most dogs look ahead only as far as the next event in their lives—when their owner comes home, when their next meal might be, when the next squirrel might walk through the yard, or maybe when their owner will take them for a walk. From this perspective, dogs probably don't ponder a "tomorrow." A lot of us might envy their ability not to think about the future and the worries it may hold, but for dogs there is a large downside to this. No concern for tomorrow also means no anticipation, or even more important in terms of pain, no hope. *They have no hope regarding what kind of pain relief the next week or month will bring.* So a dog in pain probably thinks that his current state represents the rest of his life. The pain was there yesterday, it is still here today, and it seems like it will go on for all days to come. In practical terms, what does this mean for your dog? Allow me to offer an example from my own experience.

Some years back, I ruptured a disk in my neck. It was one of the most painful and alarming events of my life. Not only was I in constant pain, but I also lost most of the use of my left arm and hand. Everything became an enormous effort. I was unable to take care of my patients, which impacted my ability to provide a living for my family. I was also unable to get more than a few hours of sleep every night, and so I was constantly exhausted and befuddled. I could not socialize or enjoy even the most basic pleasures of life. Going on seemed impossible—life did not seem worth living, and every moment, awake or asleep, was miserable. But I possessed something that we cannot give a dog, which is hope. The day after my disk ruptured, I went to the emergency room at the local university hospital. I had to wait some time to be seen. It was a busy place, especially as this was a Sunday when all doctors' offices were closed. During intake, I received pain medication (a gold star for them!) and was told that I probably had a herniated disk and could be looking at surgery and a long recovery.

I sat there, depressed and brooding, waiting to be examined when a gray-haired physician came by, looked at my chart, and said to me, "I had a ruptured disk myself, and I know what you are feeling and going through. When you go home, I want you to mark your calendar for six weeks from today, because that is the day when you are going to start to feel better." I did what he advised. Almost on cue, at the six-week mark I began to feel a drastic reduction in the level of pain. Had this kindly physician, who wasn't even my assigned doctor, not noticed my distress and taken the time to speak with me, I don't know how I would have made it through all the weeks of debilitating pain. He had given me the invaluable gift of hope.

Unfortunately, this is something that we cannot offer our pets. Do they consequently think that pain is their lot in life? Does it make them feel sad, desperate, and unwilling to cope? Does it make every day another round of hell they have to bear? It well might. This is why I agree that dogs don't feel pain like us—*for them, it is much, much worse.*

Both owners and health care providers need to remember these five things:

1. **Chronic pain is hard to measure.**

2. **Age should never be used as an excuse for an animal in pain.**

3. **There is a treatment out there for every dog.**

4. **There are affordable treatment options.**

5. **Our pets feel as much or more pain than we do.**

We cannot let ourselves slip into believing any of these common misconceptions if we want to do the best possible job of caring for our dogs and relieving their pain.

15 Signs Your Dog Is in Pain

Even for a veterinarian, diagnosing pain can be very difficult. The caregiver actually has an advantage when it comes to determining if a dog is in pain, especially chronic pain. As a caregiver, you are probably with your dog on a daily basis. You can compare the changes that accompany chronic pain by looking closely at the current abilities and behaviors of your dog and contrasting them to those of a few years before, when your dog was younger and probably experiencing less pain.

Here are the 15 indicators, both physical and behavioral, to consider as you observe your dog for possible pain. All of these signs of pain can be applied to both acute and chronic pain, but they are most helpful when looking for signs of chronic pain. Changes in physical abilities and behavioral changes sometimes overlap. For example, a dog's reluctance to run and jump can also be understood as a reduction of social interaction. So don't feel confused if you believe that, for your dog, one of these changes might fit better into the other group.

Physical Changes

First, assess your dog's physical abilities. As a general guide, when you are looking for declining abilities you should not compare what your dog can do today to what his capabilities were last week. Instead, consider what your dog can do today as compared to a year or two ago. Changes might occur over a few years. They can certainly creep up on you and your dog and seem to slowly become the "new norm" for your pet. If your dog already demonstrates one or more of these signs of pain, and if you are wondering what you can do about it, relax—I will cover that later in the book. At this point your primary concern should be discovering the existence of chronic pain in your dog. One warning: certain conditions such as cardiovascular or neurological disease also can reduce the ability of a dog to perform many of the following activities, so always consult your veterinarian if you see any of these signs.

1. **Reluctance to walk on slippery surfaces.** Some dogs may never have liked to walk on wood or vinyl flooring because it was too slippery. However, if this is a more recent issue, then pain needs to be considered as one of the possible reasons behind it. To understand why this reluctance may reveal pain, it's important to understand how dogs get traction on slippery floors. In general, dogs have very smooth pads on the bottom of

their feet. Dogs also cannot perspire out of their pads like we can from our hands and feet, which improves our grip when we need it. Because of these two factors, dogs rely on their nails for traction. But nails won't help on smooth surfaces. This isn't a big problem for the healthy dog. Strength and balance on all four legs help them to remain in an upright position, and if one limb does start to slip, it is easy enough for them to compensate with another limb. But when a dog has one or more bad limbs, problems start to occur; for instance, a leg slides out, and she doesn't have the strength to draw it back toward her body. This doesn't necessarily spell disaster—if she has three other legs to form a sturdy base and, essentially, make a triangular stance. But if she has a second bad leg, then she must suddenly ask her body to balance on only two limbs . . . easy enough for humans, but not for dogs. Out go her legs from under her, increasing her reluctance to walk on that floor. Dogs are quick learners, and it only takes a few such falls or near falls for them to become fearful of these slippery surfaces. If there is a neurological issue causing weakness or instability, this compounds the fear of walking on the slippery surface even further.

2. **Going up or down stairs.** Walking up or down a stair puts most of a dog's weight on either the front or back legs, depending on the direction the dog is moving. Some dogs in pain simply refuse outright to use stairs. Others become reluctant and will only use stairs with coaxing or assistance. Many owners describe that their dog just stands on the landing and looks up or down the stairs, not moving until they get their nerve up, or maybe just barking in frustration.

3. **Becoming selective about what to jump up onto or down from.** A reluctance to jump might be because a piece of furniture is too high or the floor is too slippery a base from which to jump. Or, you might notice this reluctance only when your

dog is trying to jump into a vehicle. The jump might be low, but he has to jump at an angle to avoid the door or seat. This reluctance to jump may happen gradually, or it might happen overnight if your dog decides "enough is enough" and no longer feels the reward is worth the effort.

4. **Attempting to stand up with the front legs first.** The vast majority of dogs stand up with their rear legs in motion first—but not dogs in pain. You may even have seen dogs start to stand up on their rear legs, and before they get all the way up, stretch their front end in what looks like a "praying" position. This is normal. When a dog has problems in its hindquarters, however, this becomes too difficult. Instead, dogs will try to gather themselves together up front first. You can actually see them pulling with their front legs as they stand. This is not normal and almost always indicates a pain-causing problem, such as hip dysplasia or arthritis (see the following image).

Dogs with hip dysplasia stand up using the front legs first; dogs without the condition stand rear legs first.

5. **The simple task of lying down may actually become difficult.** We all have seen dogs circle and circle as they look for just the right spot and angle to lie down. This normal behavior, however, might become more pronounced in the dog experiencing pain. A dog might progress through several

"false starts" where she begins to lie down, but then aborts the process and starts circling all over again. This might be a result of pain in the joints and muscles that are accustomed to the pressure of lying down, or perhaps your dog knows that it has become painful to lie on arthritic joints and is therefore reluctant to do so. In either case, it is always an indication that something is causing pain.

6. **Running and jumping activities become more limited.**
Maybe his muscle strength has decreased from months of reduced activity. Or perhaps the impact of landing is just too much for the joints to bear. In either case, the fact that your dog doesn't run or jump like before is a sign that tells you to take your dog to the veterinarian to have this checked out.

7. **Placing an abnormal amount of weight on his front legs.**
This is generally a sign that a dog is having difficulty bearing weight on his back legs. This can be due to a problem in the knee, hip, or lower back. This forward-leaning stance can be hard to detect in subtle cases, even for the trained eye. Pronounced cases can be seen more easily from the side. Instead of the front legs standing straight up and down, as demon-

Normal stance. The front legs are directly under the shoulders.

strated in the first photo, they are tucked back under the chest, as you can see in the second photo.

Hip dysplasia stance. The front legs are back under the chest to take some of the weight off the hind legs.

8. **Abnormal wear on nails.** Worn down nails can be a sign of either pain or neurological disease. Painful limbs are more difficult for the animal to pick up. This causes the nails to scuff as she walks along and tries to exert the least possible effort to pick up the limb. In cases of neurological disease, she might not even realize that she isn't lifting her feet up all the way. In either case, something is wrong and should be checked out. (See the following image.)

Notice the scuffed and worn edges of the middle two nails from the reduced ability to pick up the foot when walking.

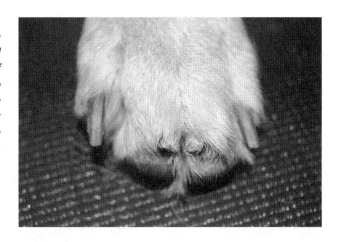

Behavioral Changes

Many behavior changes are impossible for your veterinarian to witness as they are almost always exhibited in the home environment. Yet these behavioral issues are probably more important in predicting the presence of pain than the loss of some physical abilities, as previously described. If you suspect that your dog is in pain, prepare a careful history of these behavioral points for your veterinarian.

9. **Unwillingness to initiate play or other social interactions.** This reluctance is sometimes confused with the aging process, and therefore can be hard to recognize, if only for the fact that the changes are gradual, over months or even years. Again, try to think back a few years, and compare your dog's behavior then and now. This makes it much easier to determine if some of these changes are real and represent some kind of pathology.

10. **Aggression toward other animals where no aggression existed before.** Aggression is one of the hallmarks of pain. I have had clients tell me that their dog is suddenly growling and snapping at other dogs in the same household—dogs that have lived together for years. Pain is a big motivator for your dog to let his "dog friends" understand that their previous interactions are no longer acceptable, and this is often accomplished by a showing of teeth, growling, or even snapping as if intending to bite. Successful pain treatments can sometimes be measured through observation of declining levels of aggression.

11. **Aversion to being petted or brushed.** Resistance to being touched is another strong indicator of pain. Obviously if your pet never liked these activities, this will not provide a very good yardstick. Consider if you yourself ever have had a painful shoulder, wrist, or other joint. You can often move it

around without a lot of pain, as you know exactly the toler-ance levels of that joint. But have someone grab your arm or shake your hand too hard, and the pain can almost drop you to your knees. Now think about your dog. Petting and groom-ing can have that same unwanted effect of moving joints in unexpected ways and causing a painful reaction.

12. **Disruption in sleep patterns.** Restless sleep is very common in animals experiencing pain. Painful spots might easily be ignored during waking hours, but the immobility of sleep can put pressure on joints that might not be noticed when awake. When awake, your dog is constantly shifting position to change limb and joint angles, and pressure points. This motion helps the joints stay mobile because they redistribute joint fluid through the constant flexion and extension that comes with even the subtlest movement. Dogs in pain often fall asleep for several hours, but then wake up and move around to try to get comfortable again so that they can fall back to sleep. Many of these dogs are exhausted by morning, and as a result sleep more during the day to make up for what they missed the pre-vious night. You might see the same behavior during daytime naps when your dog can't seem to get comfortable.

13. **Stiffness.** This can result from either working or playing too hard. We all overdo it from time to time and then pay the price over the next day or two. However, stiffness after rest in the absence of a known predisposing event should be cause for concern. If you've ever had plantar fasciitis, or jogger's heel, then you'll understand. You may not necessarily have walked with a limp—at least you didn't until after you put your feet up for an hour and then tried to stand up. Similar mechanisms are at play in painful conditions such as osteo-arthritis, which may cause your dog to experience the same painful stiffness.

14. **A decrease in appetite.** This change may afflict some dogs in pain. Certain breeds, such as retrievers, often maintain their appetite and interest in treats even when on death's door, so the presence of an appetite cannot always be relied upon as the best indicator of pain. However, when any dog quits eating, especially if it is outside the realm of his normal behavioral pattern, pain must be considered as one of many possible causes.

15. **House-training issues.** This problem often arises in geriatric dogs. Although many caregivers come into my clinic and joke about their dog going through its "second childhood," the reality of these accidents may be a symptom of pain. For these dogs, it might be simply too painful to come and find the owner to ask to go out, to negotiate the steps into the backyard, or to face some extremes of outdoor hot and cold. Many dogs just give up, and although they may feel shame for breaking the rules, the alternative is even more painful to contemplate.

Signs of Pain Can Be Deceptive

These 15 indicators of pain are meant to open your eyes as possible signs of pain. But you should consider pain to be potential causes for *any* change in behavior or physical activity in your dog. Finding one or more of these indicators is the first of potentially many steps toward a diagnosis that will enable proper pain treatment to begin.

2

ACUTE PAIN

ALTHOUGH THE VAST MAJORITY OF THIS BOOK IS ABOUT chronic pain, a discussion of acute pain is important for several reasons. From a practical standpoint, if your dog suffers an acute injury, there are a few things that you can do at home to relieve his pain until you can get him in for veterinary care. This chapter also contains some very important topics that you need to discuss with your veterinarian for treating either an injury your dog has sustained or the acute pain experienced in the perioperative and recovery period of surgery. Finally, I also discuss how untreated acute pain—even minor episodes, including seemingly trivial surgeries—can lead to chronic pain states, an increased sensitivity to future painful events, and a type of pain called neuropathic pain.

First Aid in the Treatment of Pain

Prior to any discussion about first aid, it would be wise to consider what protective measures you should take so that you do not receive an injury, in the form of a bite, from your dog. No matter how close of a relationship you have with your dog, and no matter how much you trust each other, an acutely painful injury can temporarily change how you and your dog interact.

The area of the brain that is responsible for managing incoming pain signals is also the same area of the brain that is responsible for certain emotions. This is true for both you and your dog, and is the reason why we cannot dispassionately look at our own injuries; as everyone knows, anger, tears, or despair commonly accompany pinched fingers, stubbed toes, or a cut finger. As the degree of injury goes up, so does the accompanying emotional response. We might cry out or maybe even kick something as a reaction. Likewise, your dog may cry out and kick in response to acute pain, but biting is common as well. For many injuries, calm reassurance is all that your dog really needs. Don't rush in and try to "fix it" but instead talk to him until he acknowledges you. Then you can give him soft strokes away from the injured area.

Protect Yourself with a Temporary Muzzle on Your Dog

In addition to your first response of comforting him, additional protection may be needed when it is time to move your dog. The degree of pain and the type of injury, along with the personality of your pet, all play a role in how likely it is that he might try to bite. There is not a simple way for me to help you predict the likelihood of a pain-motivated bite from your dog. Over the years I have had clients who know from the onset how much they can trust their dog not to bite. But I also have had many clients who are both shocked and dismayed because they never saw the bite coming. During times of injury, avoidance and biting are two big defense mechanisms. When you invade the space of your dog, maybe causing additional pain through moving him, your dog may reflexively try to bite. Don't take it personally or see it as a sign of betrayal.

Unless your dog's injury is on the face or neck, or your dog is vomiting, the easiest way to avoid a bite is to put a temporary muzzle on your dog. This can easily be done, and really only needs to stay in place until you can get your dog into a vehicle to take to your veterinarian. Once you are there, your veterinarian may want to replace it with another muzzle that will be on hand for use in the office. And don't feel bad about applying a muzzle; it protects you so that you are better able to take care of your dog. Muzzles often have a calming effect on many dogs. As a colleague of mine once said, "A muzzle relieves a dog of the obligation to bite." I have seen this often in my clinic with aggressive dogs. Many will become quite passive once they can no longer use their teeth.

Making a Homemade Muzzle

To make a homemade muzzle, the best approach is to use a length of soft fabric, hopefully with a little stretch in it. The best thing to use

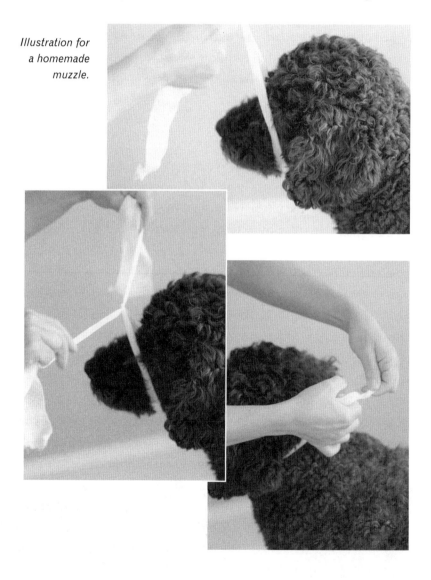

Illustration for a homemade muzzle.

is a nylon stocking. They are long, soft, and they have a bit of give in them, making it more comfortable for your dog. To create the muzzle, make a loop with a knot in the middle of the nylon, just as you might when preparing to tie a shoe. Don't tighten it down until it is over your dog's muzzle, and then only tighten it enough to make it snug. Loop the nylon below his nose from both sides and make an additional loop, tightening until snug. Finally, pass the two ends of the nylon behind your dog's ears and tie as you would a shoelace. This prevents him from reaching up with a foot and pulling the muzzle off his nose. When it is time to remove the muzzle, simply untie it from behind his ears and then gently pull forward in the direction of his nose. Unless you tied it too tight, it should slide right off. See the photos above for making a muzzle.

Moving an Injured Dog

There are a few techniques for moving an injured dog, and they vary depending on the site of the injury. If there is an injury to one or more of the extremities, the method is much different than if there is injury to the back or pelvis. One thing to keep in mind: If your dog is voluntarily lying in a specific position, he may be doing so because it is the most comfortable position he can find. For example, dogs with broken limbs almost always prefer to lie on the injured limb; pressure being preferable to having the fracture site dangle, which creates a torque force at the site of the fracture.

If only one limb is injured, your dog may be willing to move on his own. But he might still need to be moved up or down stairs and in and out of a vehicle. The size of your dog also affects how to move him. For dogs roughly 30 pounds and less, simply reach over his back and pick him up by his chest, holding him against your body. This technique allows an injured leg to dangle without putting any undue pressure on it. For dogs 45 pounds and more, this one-arm technique can be more difficult to accomplish. Instead, use both arms, one passing in front of his front legs and the other passing behind his hind legs, to pick him up and hold him against your chest. This three-point stability is more comforting for your dog and easier on you. For the in-between sizes, 30–45 pounds, you can use either method, depending on your own strength and the cooperation of your dog.

The dangling legs approach for moving an injured dog.

The three-point approach to moving an injured dog.

If your dog has an injury to his back or pelvis, the methods previously outlined could not only cause further damage, but would actually be painful to your dog. If he were a human with injuries to either of these locations, a flat board or rigid stretcher would be used. Of course you aren't going to have one of these sitting around your house waiting for an injury to occur. Moreover, for many dogs, being carried on a flat rigid surface is much too alarming. Despite their pain and injuries, many dogs will try to escape. Instead, improvise with a makeshift stretcher by using a blanket. With as many people helping as possible, place an appropriate-size blanket next to your dog and with as much support as possible, transfer him to the blanket. Then with at least two people in the case of a small dog, or four in the case of a larger dog, lift him up while keeping the blanket as rigid as possible. Although not perfectly safe for spinal injuries, this temporary stretcher has the advantage of having a "dip" in the middle, which helps secure your dog into position and makes it difficult for him to wriggle his way free.

Common Injuries

The following are common injuries and the treatments you can provide your pet at home.

Torn Nails

This is probably one of the most common injuries. It happens with great frequency in suburban areas, where it is common to have decks in the backyard. It is there where nails can get caught and broken or torn off. If a nail is torn off, soaking the foot in some ice water for ten minutes will reduce the level of pain, and allow you to put a light bandage on it, both to protect the toe and to contain the bleeding until you can get the dog to your veterinarian. It is slightly more difficult to treat a nail that has a crack in it, especially if the nail seems to be skewed to one side. You can treat with the ice water, as just noted; however, applying a bandage comes with the possibility of pushing that nail even farther to one side, causing even more pain. If you are not sure, it is best to skip the bandage in such circumstances.

Cuts and Abrasions

Many abrasions need nothing more than a cleaning and the application of an over-the-counter antibiotic ointment. As you may have found from treating your own abrasions, simply applying a petroleum-based antibiotic ointment to the wound can provide some comfort. In the case of a cut, the only treatment at your disposal while you seek veterinary attention is to wrap the cut with sterile gauze, if possible, and to apply a cold compress. You can make a compress by mixing ice and water, and sealing it in a plastic bag.

Fractures

There is not much you can do to help with the pain from a fracture. The best treatment is to get your dog to your veterinarian as soon as possible. If that is not possible, remember what I said at the start of this section: If your dog has an obvious fracture, and he wants to lie in a certain position, even if it is on the injured leg, let him do so. Trying to immobilize a dog's leg, especially when it is painful, can be quite difficult to do. However, using a towel to wrap around the leg in several layers may prevent the worst of the undesired leg movements as you get him to the veterinarian.

Burns

Cold water, not ice water, is the best first-aid treatment for burns. And the sooner it is applied the better it will be for stopping the pain and preventing further tissue damage. In the case of very hot burns from scalding, the heat can penetrate into deeper tissues, causing extensive damage. Immediate application of cold running water can help cool off the tissue. Even if you feel you have treated a burn properly, it is still a good idea to have the burn checked out, as the amount of damage from a burn can be very deceptive.

Pain Treatments at the Veterinary Hospital

For most dog owners, their first big visit to the veterinarian, after the "puppy shots" and wellness exams, is for sterilization. Unless you and your dog are very lucky, you will most likely visit the veterinarian later for more serious issues: Suspicious lumps that need to be removed, injuries such as lacerations and fractures, dental issues like broken teeth that need extraction, and so on.

Some of these procedures are minor and others more serious. Regardless, the quality of pain control can have a long-lasting and serious impact on how well your pet is going to be able to cope with future painful events.

The Power of Pain Prevention and the Consequences of Untreated Pain

In 1997, the medical journal for humans *The Lancet* published an article titled "Effect of neonatal circumcision on pain response during subsequent routine vaccination."[4] The authors described a simple experiment wherein neonatal boys were circumcised, but they were divided into two groups. The first group was pretreated at the surgical site with something called EMLA, a cream that contains a local anesthetic. The second group was not treated with anything. Both groups of boys returned for vaccinations at four and six months and it was noted that there was an increase in the pain response in the untreated group as compared to those neonates who were given EMLA cream.

This was an astounding finding. This procedure, which had been previously considered quick and practically painless, had predisposed the infants to a future of increased pain. This happened through a complex change in the spinal cord, resulting in something called hyperalgesia: A reaction to a painful stimulus that is stronger than what the expected response should be. Once hyperalgesia is in place, it is possible for it to last a lifetime.

What has this to do with your pet? Let's look at something as seemingly innocuous as a dewclaw removal. If your pet first came to you with her dewclaws (a dog's "thumbs") already removed, chances are that there was no pain control used if the breeder performed the amputation. And sad but true, there is also a good chance that there was no pain control even if a veterinarian did the procedure. Many veterinarians have been taught that, just like the infant getting circumcised, the pain pathways in three-day-old puppies are not developed and any kind of pain control is unnecessary.

This same disregard for pain control can befall a dog at any age. What about when you drop off your pet at a veterinarian to be spayed or neutered? (For that matter, what about any painful surgical procedure?) If that potential pain is not prevented and treated because the proper steps were not taken to minimize the pain, then *your* pet will pay the "pain price," and possibly will for life.

It would be comforting to think that every veterinary clinic, spaying and neutering clinic, or humane society employs proper pain control. The sad fact is that the majority does not. A 2012 study done in Australia titled "Postoperative pain and perioperative analgesic administration in dogs: practices, attitudes and beliefs of Queensland veterinarians"[5] queried veterinarians on the importance of pain control in spay and neuter operations. The majority of veterinarians agreed that pain control during these procedures was important, but a survey showed that *only 24 percent of randomly chosen veterinarians actually used postoperative pain meds!*

When you schedule your pet for any procedure that might be potentially painful, it is in your dog's best interest to ask your veterinarian exactly what she is going to use for pain control and when she is going to use it. Remember the statistics just noted, and don't assume that everything that can get done to mitigate the pain will be done. Many veterinarians (and human anesthesiologists) believe that a gas inhalant anesthetic is all that is needed for pain control. Nothing could be farther from the truth. Gas anesthesia imposes unconsciousness and amnesia, but does nothing to stop the pain signals from reaching the brain. It has been shown in study after study that there is an increase in sensitivity to pain in those patients not properly medicated immediately before, during, and after a surgical procedure.

Controlling Pain during Surgical Procedures

Many ways to control pain for surgical procedures are available, and I would like to familiarize you with some of the more common methods. Let's take a look at what I do for pain control in dogs that come to my practice for surgery.

Pain Control During a Spay or Neuter

When a dog comes in for a spay or neuter, prior to the induction of anesthesia, she or he is given an injection of an opioid, usually morphine, and a drug called dexmedetomidine (Dexdomitor), a member of the alpha-2 agonist class of drugs made by the company Zoetis. The combination of these different pain drugs work synergistically to provide both relaxation and a reduced pain state. This allows us to painlessly place an IV catheter to administer fluids and other drugs as needed. The morphine and the Dexdomitor remain in effect throughout the duration of the surgery and into the immediate postoperative period. Prior to surgery, we also inject each dog with carprofen (Rimadyl), a powerful nonsteroidal anti-inflammatory drug (NSAID). Once the dog is anesthetized, we employ the use of a local anesthetic agent. A procedure called a "line block" is administered over the area of the intended incision, and it effectively blocks 100 percent of the pain that occurs from the surgical cut. These local anesthetics normally last from one to six hours. This procedure can be enhanced by using a new product called Nocita (Bupivacaine Liposome Injectable Suspension) made by Aratana Therapeutics. This is a local anesthetic that stops the transmission of pain signals for three days! In male dogs, we then do a procedure called a testicular block where the testicle itself is numbed with additional local anesthetic. In female dogs, we block the ovarian ligaments, which contain most of the nerve fibers to the ovaries, with a local anesthetic. Finally, in the postoperative period, we use acute pain scales to monitor the level of pain and administer or re-administer drugs to help control that pain. Dogs are sent home with daily doses of carprofen for five days. And if they seem especially pained, we send them home with additional medication, most commonly a drug called gabapentin. You can read more about gabapentin in Chapter 5.

Pain Control during a More Serious Surgery

When a surgery is more serious and has the potential of causing more pain, we employ more aggressive modalities. Epidurals are used to block pain at the level of the spinal cord. Loco-regional nerve blocks might be employed to stop the pain at the level of a major nerve. We employ an IV drip of pain medications called a "constant rate infusion" that is both easy to use and very effective at allowing for moment-to-moment adjustments to the level of analgesia. And finally, we use diffusion catheters, which are small tubes that resemble the soaker hose in a garden. These can be implanted at the site of the surgical wound so that local anesthetics can continue to be injected after the surgery is finished, keeping the area pain free.

None of the procedures I described are expensive. Nor are they complicated. The only technically difficult one to perform is an epidural, but it is a procedure that can be learned in 15 minutes or so and is mastered after performing it approximately a half-dozen times. None of the drugs I mentioned are particularly dangerous when used as intended. There is no excuse for any surgeon or anesthesiologist not to employ these procedures or similar ones I described. If they do not do these things, for the sake of your pet you need to find a veterinarian who does, even if it costs a little more. This is not a time to skimp and save a few dollars, because it is your dog that will pay the price.

Neuropathic Pain

I would like to end this chapter with a brief mention of neuropathic pain. Neuropathic pain is a type of chronic pain that is difficult to understand, even for some health care professionals. This type of pain occurs when there is seemingly no injury that should be perpetuating the pain. This can occur long after the initial cause of pain has passed, be it from a surgery or injury. I mention it here because neuropathic pain *can result whenever acute pain is either not treated or is under treated.*

The earlier examples of the infant circumcision and dewclaw removal (causing pain long after the incision is healed) are examples of neuropathic pain. There are other causes of neuropathic pain in animals. Types of neuropathic pain in animals and humans can result from untreated acute pain. It can also come from certain diseases, including ones that readers of this book might suffer from, such as diabetic neuropathy and shingles.

Prevention of neuropathic pain is yet another motivation to find a veterinarian who will adequately control your dog's pain. If you are having difficulty finding a veterinary practitioner capable of providing your dog with adequate acute and perioperative pain control, please refer to Appendix A at the end of the book. Located there is information to help you find a certified pain practitioner or other veterinarian who will meet your dog's needs.

3

CAUSES OF
CHRONIC PAIN

IT MAY BE IMPOSSIBLE TO MEASURE THE COSTS OF chronic pain in our dogs. When looking at the cost in people, health economists from Johns Hopkins University, writing in *The Journal of Pain*, report the annual loss of work productivity due to chronic pain is as high as $635 billion a year, which is more than the yearly costs for cancer, heart disease, and diabetes. And this is only the financial cost. How can anyone measure the emotional costs of the suffering caused by chronic pain?

The task of measuring the different costs of pain in our animals is even bleaker than it is in humans. Dogs don't have the same self-reporting capacity as we do to discuss their emotional issues and suffering that result from chronic pain. Nor do we have the same financial statistics as on the human side, most often gathered by insurance companies, to give us any facts about the financial cost of pain. Few dogs have jobs, so we know that income lost is negligible as compared to humans. However, when looked at as a whole, and including the emotional impact to their caretakers, the totality of costs must be staggering for treating pain in dogs.

The causes of chronic pain are many, but in my practice osteoarthritis (OA) is the number one cause, followed by neuropathic pain and cancer pain. As a pet owner it is important that you have a source like this book as a reference so that you are able to sort fact from fiction. One of the downsides of the Internet is that a lot of false information about the causes, treatment, and prevention of diseases, such as chronic pain, is easily accessible. It seems like everyone online has an opinion that is based on either personal experience, information wrongly extrapolated from human medicine, or one that is completely baseless and just someone's personal theory.

I cannot possibly comment on every cause of chronic pain because real or not the many causes are legion. Instead, I have tried to keep this simple, discussing only those pain-causing conditions that make up the vast majority of what you, as your dog's caregiver, might encounter. I also have tried to keep the discussion of each condition to the point by not overwhelming you with a lot of unnecessary information. My goal is to provide you with what is most pertinent to the treatment of your dog should she have any of the following conditions. Although I may refer to an occasional treatment here in these next paragraphs, you should look to the latter chapters of this book for more in-depth discussions of actual treatment modalities.

Diseases

Anything that causes a disruption in normal body function is considered a disease. There are many different diseases that can cause pain: infections, wear and tear from normal aging, and trauma to name a few. The following list of conditions accounts for the diseases you are most likely to encounter should your dog be in pain.

Osteoarthritis (OA) is a disease of the joint and supporting joint structures. OA is sometimes referred to as Degenerative Joint Disease. It can appear in any joint. Although animals can't self-report and tell us where it hurts, veterinarians can make deductions on where it hurts based on history, observation of gait and posture, a physical exam, and X-ray films. OA can be caused by a number of factors, but the end result is essentially the same: Approximately four out of every five dogs in the United States suffer from it, meaning that the problem is epidemic.[6] Steven Fox in his book *Chronic Pain in Small Animal Medicine* writes, "OA can be defined as a disorder of movable joints characterized by: Deterioration of articular cartilage; osteophyte formation and bone remodeling; pathology of periarticular tissues including synovium, subchondral bone, muscle, tendon and ligament; and a low-grade, non purulent inflammation of variable degree."[7] In other words, it is a complex problem involving various parts of the joint and surrounding structures. The message that you as your dog's caregiver should take from this is that OA is a complex problem and almost always requires a complex, multimodal treatment. Beware of any suggestion, especially regarding more advanced cases of OA, that it can be fixed by something as easy as a dietary supplement used alone, or a single pill or injection.

Age-related OA is what most of us think of when we hear the word *arthritis*. This form of OA is the result of the natural aging process of a joint as that joint and its surrounding structures just wear out. This is considered "primary" OA and is what most of our pets experience as they age. Although the changes are gradual, they are also insidious. Our pets learn to compensate for the pain up until they reach a stage of progression when it becomes impossible to do so. This might sound a little odd, but it is why I have so many caregivers say to me, "It just happened," when really it has been happening for years. If you are fortunate enough to have either a veterinarian who is familiar with early signs of OA, or if you have caught some of the signs of pain as described in Chapter 1, you have the opportunity to actually slow the onset of OA in your dog. As I will say again and again, the early diagnosis of any disease process, especially in diseases like OA, can open up the opportunity to treat the condition with a much larger variety of treatment options and preventative measures.

Joint instability and other disorders of the joint are also a common reason for the development of OA. Common causes of joint instability include hip dysplasia, luxating kneecaps, and excessive mobility at the lumbosacral junction of the spine.

Hip dysplasia is the consequence of a poorly formed joint between the pelvis and the thighbone or femur. Hip dysplasia occurs when the junction of these two articular surfaces of the femur and pelvis are not in the best anatomical positions. This "sloppy" relationship results in excess movements and consequent wear and stresses on the joint, with the ultimate result of OA. The vast majority of dogs have hip dysplasia as a consequence of genetic predisposition; in other words, they inherited this problem from their parents.

Luxating kneecaps hold a similar fate for damage to the knee, as a consequence of the kneecap (patella) sliding off to one side of the knee joint. This abnormal movement causes instability in the knee and excessive wear on the cartilage of the patella as it abnormally moves across those ridges on the femur meant to keep it in place. Wear and tear on the knee because of a luxating patella can take years to cause damage and show signs of OA, by which time the disease is advanced and difficult to treat. Again, early diagnosis means many more possible treatment options, but especially so in the case of a luxating patella, which can essentially be "cured" if treatment is started early enough.

The lumbosacral junction of the spine is a special case in that it involves both OA and, because of its location, neurological disease. In a young dog, the lumbosacral junction may appear normal, and perhaps it is. But as some dogs age, there is excessive force and mobility on this joint and it can cause the formation of OA, sometimes with an osteoarthritic growth of bone called an osteophyte actually bridging the gap between the two vertebrae, causing arthritis pain and inflammation. This localized inflammation can then go on to irritate and inflame those nerves at the end of the spinal cord, which are located at the lumbosacral junction. This combination of conditions can result in a disease known as cauda equine syndrome (CES)[8]—Latin for "horse tail" due to a horsetail–like appearance of the spinal cord and nerves in that area. Besides OA, this syndrome can also lead to neurological dysfunction of the hind legs. In my referral practice I find that this is one of the diseases most underdiagnosed by other veterinarians. Fortunately, it can be treated, although not cured, with acupuncture and rehabilitation.

Elbow dysplasia is another inherited disease. But unlike hip dysplasia, it is less a problem of joint laxity and more a problem with something called osteochondrosis, which is a disease that occurs during development of one or more of the ossification centers of the elbow. This disease first appears most commonly in dogs between 6 and 12 months of age and is diagnosed by a combination of a physical exam and taking X-ray pictures of the affected area.

Osteochondritis dissecans (OCD) is a developmental disease, especially in large and giant breed dogs. This disease probably has a genetic component in some but not all dogs. OCD occurs during growth when something happens to the cartilage. Ultimately, it results in a thicker than normal layer of cartilage, called osteochondrosis. It becomes OCD when this abnormal cartilage separates from the underlying bone. Most commonly this occurs in the shoulder but also has been seen in the elbow, hip, and knee. Signs, primarily lameness in the affected limb, usually appear between 8 and 12 months of age. Diagnosis of OCD is made by a physical exam, X-ray films of the affected joint, and sometimes arthroscopy. Treatment of OCD involves surgical removal of the separated bit of cartilage; however, as a result of this joint defect, OA is likely to occur.

Injury is probably the most common reason for OA of the knee, although any joint can suffer from injury. Injury is an acute event, which leads to immediate pain. But injury also has long-term implications for the development of OA, as a direct result of cartilage damage that occurs at the time of the injury.

The knee is an inherently unstable joint that involves three separate bones coming together in one place. Perhaps the weakest link in this joint is a ligament called the cranial cruciate ligament. *Cranial*, because there are two cruciate ligaments, and this one is in the front or "cranial" position; and *cruciate* because it forms a cross when observed in relationship with its partner ligament. The cruciate plays an important role in the knee joint: It prevents forward and backward sliding of the knee when weight is placed on the leg. When this ligament is ruptured, the knee becomes unstable and it slides back and forth in what veterinarians refer to as "drawer movement," so named for the similar motion that occurs when opening and closing a drawer.[9] This ligament can rupture for a few reasons. The first is straightforward and involves a leg movement that puts undue stress on the ligament, causing it to rupture. Such an injury, for example, might occur from a fall due to slipping on ice. The second and more common reason for rupture is secondary to longstanding inflammatory changes in the ligament. The reasons behind this longstanding inflammation are probably multifactorial and somewhat complicated. There is also an emerging body of evidence that, for the time being, is controversial. It appears that in some dogs the cruciate ligament degrades over a period of years. As of this writing, a single cause of this longstanding inflammation has not been proven. However, it is suspected that neutering prior to puberty, especially in males, leads to bone and joint conformational abnormalities and subsequent stresses on the ligament.[10]

Repair options for animals with cruciate injuries are many. Nonsurgical repair can combine one or all of several physical modalities: acupuncture, rehabilitation, and braces. Surgical procedures abound, with no one procedure being shown as "leader of the pack." That being said, a recent paper shows a possible link between certain metal implants used for repair of the knee and bone cancer.[11] No matter which option you choose, you should not wait too long to start treatment. But that doesn't mean rushing into it either. Explore the current information on all procedures and choose the one you feel is best for your dog.

Although the knee is the most common site of injury resulting in OA, any joint can suffer. Fractures that occur near or across joint surfaces, compression of the joint surface, loss of blood to a joint secondary to injury, and other reasons can result in injury that eventually lead to OA in any joint in the body.

Myofascial pain syndrome can be both a consequence of OA and it can worsen OA. Myofascial pain results when bands within an affected muscle become shortened, resulting in joint compression.

The tight muscle draws the two bones closer together than they were meant to be, which produces abnormal joint dynamics and reduced joint functionality. Failure to treat myofascial pain can result in excessive and abnormal wear on a joint, which can either hasten or lead to OA.[12] As of this writing, myofascial pain is probably one of the least understood and most underdiagnosed pain syndromes in dogs. A detailed discussion about myofascial pain syndrome appears in Chapter 7, and so I will not go into detail here about its causes and treatment.

Dewclaw removal. The dewclaw on a dog is the equivalent of our thumb. When you look at your dog's front foot, if the dewclaw is still present, it is the digit that is the medial (inner) most toe that is shorter than the other toes and does not appear to have any significant contact with the ground as a dog walks or runs. This toe is slightly more prone to injury than the other digits, and as such it is popular to remove it within a few days of birth. Unfortunately, most people outside of sports medicine do not understand the major role that a dewclaw can play in physical activity, and see it not only as a "disposable" appendage but a possible detriment to the dog's well-being if it is not removed. This is the reason given by many dog breeders to have it amputated when the puppy is still only a few days old.

The dewclaw on a dog plays an important function in both the mechanics of the front foot and in joint stability. Slow-motion videos that study agility dogs reveal that the dewclaw plays a significant role in the placement of the front foot. Anatomically, there are many ligaments and tendons connecting it to surrounding tissue, including the "wrist" bones. Amputation of this digit results in the destruction of this network of ligaments and tendons, with resulting carpal (wrist) instability. The majority of dogs that have had their dewclaws removed as puppies have decreased range of motion of the carpal joint with or without OA by the time they are six years of age.[13] This can and often does result in painful lameness issues, necessitating treatment and/or cutting short an obedience or agility career.

We all can play a role in getting breeders to stop this barbaric, damaging, and unnecessary procedure if we all start refusing to buy "cute" puppies with their dewclaws removed.

Neuropathic pain. My friend Karol Mathews is a professor and teaches at the veterinary college at the University of Guelph in Ontario, Canada. I consider her to be the first veterinarian who *really* brought neuropathic pain to the attention of the veterinary community. Most of what I have learned about neuropathic pain came from an article she wrote called, "Neuropathic Pain in Dogs and Cats: If Only They Could Tell Us If They Hurt."[14]

Neuropathic pain is essentially "something gone wrong" between the sensory/nervous system and a region of the body. It starts as an injury or a disease that causes acute pain that under normal circumstances resolves as the injured tissue heals. Neuropathic pain emerges when there is some damage to the sensory system that occurs during the injury or disease, and then *continues long after the rest of the surrounding tissue heals.* Two common examples of neuropathic pain in humans are the pain many diabetics feel in their feet and the pain that people with shingles feel. These are chronic, painful, and sometimes debilitating types of neuropathic pain.

In animals, there is a long list of diseases that may result in neuropathic pain. I say "may" because the primary method of diagnosing neuropathic pain in people is by self-reporting the pain, which is usually described as burning, stabbing, or prickling pain. So unless our dogs start talking, the diagnosis of neuropathic pain can be high on the list but difficult to prove with absolute certainty. However, an observant veterinarian and a good case history often provide the clues necessary for a diagnosis.

Injury can cause the development of neuropathic pain, and it doesn't just have to be traumatic injury. Surgical procedures such as amputation, fracture repair, and hernia repair always mean working around nerves. Such work has the potential of damaging any of those nerves, with subsequent neuropathy as a real possibility.

The Case of the Limping Retriever

Lola was a seven-year-old Labrador Retriever that was brought to me by her owner because of lameness "somewhere" in the rear end. After a thorough examination and radiographs, I could not pinpoint the source of Lola's pain. Most dogs don't like their feet handled and Lola was no exception. But suddenly I realized it went beyond just being touched. I couldn't quite call it pain, but something about handling them made her clearly uncomfortable. I collected a blood sample, ran a quick test, and sure enough, Lola had diabetes and was having neuropathic pain as a consequence of that!

Injuries and disease of the spinal cord can also lead to this condition. A ruptured disk in the back, a spinal cord embolism, and infections of or near the spinal cord can all lead to neuropathy.

Neuropathy-related diseases can result from any condition that causes peripheral nerve damage. I mentioned diabetes in the previous case, but other diseases, including inflammatory bowel disease, pancreatitis, and many others have the potential to result in neuropathic diseases. It is my belief that the skin condition called lick granuloma, which is an area of raw skin usually on the wrist or ankle of a dog, and is usually blamed on anxiety, involves neuropathic pain. I generally treat these lesions with the assumption that neuropathic pain is present.

Treatment of neuropathic pain is difficult for two reasons. The first reason, as already mentioned, is because the condition is hard to diagnose in the first place. Even if a veterinarian makes his best medical guess at a diagnosis of neuropathy, monitoring the response to therapy is challenging because the patient cannot directly report any improvements. The second reason is because effective treatment for pain control can take months if not a lifetime of effort. In such cases, the original cause of the neuropathic pain may have healed long ago, but the nerves themselves are responsible for the perpetuation of the pain.

Treatment options for neuropathic pain often require both an ongoing daily treatment plus the treatment of acute flare-ups. Although this is considered a chronic pain problem, acute relapses could be painful enough to necessitate hospitalization, with the intravenous administration of pain medications over a two- or three-day period. This procedure is something pain practitioners refer to as a "pain vacation." The drugs that are used for this procedure are not costly; however, the treatment is labor intensive and so the costs of treatment can add up quickly.

More commonly, these cases are chronic in nature and are not so painful as to involve hospitalization. I feel that certain classes of drugs are appropriate for cases of neuropathy. But not all drugs are appropriate for all cases of neuropathic pain. Organ dysfunction, drug sensitivities, and the presence of other drugs may limit which ones can be used.

Nonsteroidal anti-inflammatory drugs (NSAIDs) provide useful treatment options because of their anti-inflammatory actions on both peripheral and central nerves. Plus, they help stop pain.

Gabapentin, a drug that stops some nerve signals from reaching the spinal cord, is very useful in the treatment of neuropathic pain. Amantadine is a drug that can suppress some of the "excessive" nerve impulses that are perpetuated by chronic pain states. Additionally, any drug that has serotonin reuptake inhibition, like tricyclic antidepressants, is useful in the suppression of neuropathic pain.

And finally, acupuncture can be extremely useful in treating neuropathic pain. When you read Chapter 9 about acupuncture, you will see that it promotes homeostasis or "normality" of the nervous system, which is exactly what the neuropathic pain patient needs.

Cancer pain. This is not going to be a discussion on how to treat cancer, but instead a discussion on how to control the pain of cancer. Treatment of cancer itself can be quite expensive and beyond the reach of many caregivers. But most owners still want as much time with their pets as they can while still maintaining a good quality of life.

This doesn't mean that treatment of cancer pain by surgery, radiation therapy, or chemotherapy should not be considered. Reduction of tumor

A Case of Peripheral Neuropathy

This case is actually about me. I earlier described my encounter with a ruptured disk and the pain that went with it. One of the sequela, or aftereffects, of that injury was that three years later I *was still* having alternating numbness and pinprick tingling in the index finger of my left hand. I had accepted this as a small but annoying issue that was probably going to be with me for life. While taking my acupuncture class, I asked the instructor, Narda Robinson, if there was anything that could be done to treat the neuropathy. Narda is both a veterinarian and a physician, and was therefore able to treat me as a patient. She showed me some acupuncture points and inserted them right then and there, asking me to leave them in for roughly 20 minutes. I did so, then removed them and promptly forgot about it. Some two hours later, I realized something was happening to my finger: the tingling had decreased and the numbness was almost gone. I could feel things with my finger again! I continued the treatment for the next six weeks and only stopped because the increasing feeling in my finger made it almost impossible for me to stick needles in and around my nail bed!

size or remission of cancer can have a profound impact on the level of pain a dog experiences. It always pays to have a discussion with a veterinary oncologist and get some ideas of what can or cannot be done. And before you worry about all of the side effects you may have seen friends or relatives suffer through as a result of treatment, be aware that dogs undergoing cancer treatments will not experience as many side effects as human cancer patients due to the differences in physiology between dogs and humans.

Cancer hurts, and it hurts for a variety of reasons that depend on the type of cancer. For the most part, although not always, treating the pain of cancer depends less on the type of cancer that is causing the pain and more on the intensity of the pain caused by the cancer.

A Case of Hospice Care

Riley was a Golden Retriever that had cancer. She was referred to me for palliative care of her pain. Because of the invasive nature of the cancer, her owner wisely opted to treat Riley's pain, as treatment of the cancer would have provided little or no benefit to her longevity or quality of life. Riley was doing so poorly that the owner sought out hospice care in the hopes of "keeping her around another week or two." She agreed to some diagnostics to determine all the sources of Riley's pain. Once we had that information, we formulated a plan that included medication, acupuncture, and massage. Instead of an extra week or two, Riley lived quite comfortably for several more months.

The book *Handbook of Veterinary Pain Management*, edited by James Gaynor and William Muir, is a terrific resource. In it, Dr. Gaynor instructs the veterinarian in what is basically hospice care for the pet. He makes several important points, and I will paraphrase them here. The first is that the veterinarian and staff must be educated in pain management. The second is that the client must have realistic expectations about the pain control, and that their involvement in treating and evaluating the pain is crucial. The third is that quality of life must constantly be assessed at regular intervals. And finally, a multimodal approach for treating cancer pain must involve the use of opioids.

Drugs commonly used in all forms of cancer are opioids, NSAIDs, NMDA receptor antagonists, and antianxiety drugs. There are other medications specific to certain types of cancers. One example is a class of drugs called bisphosphonates that are often used to ameliorate the pain of bone cancer.

Another consideration for cancer patients is the use of antianxiety drugs. Chronic pain and reduced function is a constant stress on the human cancer patient, and there is no reason to think it would be any different in our dogs.

Acupuncture can be used for pain relief and for the control of issues like nausea and anorexia, and even anxiety.

Medical massage has been shown in human medicine to provide relief of pain in cancer patients. It also seems to give the patient a sense of well-being. There is no reason to think that this is any different in our own pets.

A few types of cancer are especially painful and common enough that they deserve special attention here. In dogs, they are osteosarcoma of the bone and multiple myeloma. Both are particularly painful and always need to be put on the top of the list in the importance for pain control. Again, *any* cancer has the possibility for causing pain, and once a diagnosis of cancer is made, its pain-causing potential should be evaluated and subsequently treated.

Osteosarcoma is one type of bone cancer that is fairly common. It often initially presents itself as lameness, with no history of previous trauma or lameness. Although it can occur anywhere on the body, it seems that the limbs are the most commonly affected areas. In the front leg, it is usually in the shoulder or wrist; in the back leg it is found most frequently in the knee. This is one of the reasons that diagnostics such as X-ray films of any lameness are so important. It is a tragedy to guess at the diagnosis; treat osteosarcoma as though it is arthritis, and you lose precious time that could have been devoted to treating the cancer.

Like osteosarcoma, multiple myeloma is a cancer that has the potential for causing severe bone pain. Less common than osteosarcoma, multiple myeloma is derived from a type of cell called a plasma cell and can cause lesions in multiple sites around the body. However, when it causes something called bone lysis, which is an area where the cancer has dissolved some of the bone, this cancer becomes extremely painful. Also like osteosarcoma, X-ray films of the affected painful areas can aid in the diagnosis of this cancer, which can be mistaken for other painful disorders such as osteoarthritis and intervertebral disk disease.

Finally, in any case of cancer where the treatment is palliative and not curative, it is important to consider the "treatment" of the caregivers.

As I describe in Chapter 24, caregiver exhaustion or burnout in cancer cases seems to be more prevalent than in any other type of chronic pain issue.[15] I advise owners to get the support they need for their own emotional well-being. There are many options: from friends to clergy to social workers and support groups. And of course there is your veterinarian, who should always make you feel like he or she is there for you. Although emotional support for you is just as important as the medical care provided to your dog, such support may not be your veterinarian's area of strength. But there are veterinarians out there whose focus is in hospice care, and emotional support is one of their strengths. Hospice care is commonly utilized for cancer patients, and if you are considering it, please read Chapter 24 of this book.

4

THE PAIN EXAM: WHAT THE OWNER SHOULD EXPECT

EVERY VISIT TO THE VETERINARIAN IS ANOTHER chance for you to get confused by what is taking place and why it is happening. If you are taking your dog in for a pain issue, there are many additional procedures that might need to be performed, adding to the perplexity. Pain exams entail, by necessity, a more thorough examination process than a regular checkup. A careful case history by your veterinarian and your assessment of your dog's behavior and mobility is just the start. Your veterinarian will make a distant, hands-off observation of your dog to look for postural changes and gait abnormalities. The physical examination includes a variety of palpations (examining by touch) and tests to discover additional issues. One issue might, for example, include neurological disease, which may mimic pain conditions.

The pain exam is an extremely crucial part of the treatment for your dog. The quality of this exam has a direct impact on the outcome of a dog's pain condition. This may or may not seem obvious to you, your dog's caregiver, but it certainly should be obvious to the examining veterinarian. Too often I have had clients come into my office for a second (or third or fourth) opinion and tell me, "These medications don't work." And they are right—the medications aren't working. The unfortunate truth is that oftentimes a veterinarian will throw some pain medication at an undiagnosed problem, usually an NSAID (nonsteroidal anti-inflammatory drug). I call the condition *undiagnosed* because the dog never received a complete exam and appropriate workup. As veterinarians, we are increasingly being taught more about pharmaceuticals, interpreting laboratory tests, and performing complex surgeries while being taught less about manual therapies and hands-on diagnostics. Both the well-being of our patients and our own professional lives are worse off for it.

When confronted with complex pain issues it can be very difficult to find a diagnosis, even for someone like me who lives and breathes the subject of pain medicine. What chance is there for a proper diagnosis when a veterinarian chooses, because of lack of time or knowledge, to do an incomplete examination? Not much. Of course when a dog comes to me with a recent history of an observed injury (for example, maybe he was playing and came down hard on his front leg, which he now is slightly favoring), I might forgo the diagnostics and elect to treat the acute problem with an appropriate pain medication. But I do not prescribe this treatment without performing an exam to reassure myself that there is not an obvious serious problem. I also ask the caregiver to promise to return in a few days if all is not well. However, when it comes to signs of chronic or even short-term persistent pain, simply treating the signs of pain with medications is not enough. It is in circumstances like this when a proper diagnosis is required.

There is no one-size-fits-all approach to pain treatment.

Treatment Outcomes

Not all caregivers know what they hope to accomplish when they bring in their dog to the veterinarian for pain issues. Certainly, we all want to turn back the clock for our aging and pained pets. Sadly, some dogs are beyond the hope of ever regaining a lifestyle that allows them the mobility and social interactions, and the ability to take care of their basic biological needs, which gives them some semblance of a good quality of life. For other dogs, the problems are small enough that they need minimal intervention in order to make them feel better and their caregivers happy. No matter where your dog fits in this spectrum, every pain case needs a discussion that involves the caregiver's expectations for treatment outcomes. These expectations need to be looked at and evaluated for the purpose of both setting up a treatment program and assessing how realistic the expectations are of the caregiver.

This is extremely important for a couple of reasons. As the loving caregiver you are, your hope for treatment and recovery may have some unrealistic aspects for your dog. For example, some pain conditions may preclude the ability of your dog to go on long walks, jump and catch toys or balls, or enjoy an agility course. You as the caregiver need to express your hopes and expectations of treatment so that a conversation can be held as to both how realistic those hopes and expectations are, and how much time, money, and energy are needed for the treatments in order to achieve your goal. Such a discussion allows everyone to understand what is desired and what the course of treatment entails, and to come to an endpoint that is both reasonable and agreeable to everyone concerned.

Some caregivers come to me thinking that they will see me a time or two and that will be the end of the treatment. However, these well-meaning people often fail to consider the condition that is causing that dog's chronic pain. More than likely, the underlying ailment took months or years to develop. In such cases it is probably unrealistic to expect that the problem can be "fixed" in a week or two. On top of that, most problems that have put that dog in a pain state are permanent. This is to say, even though the pain might be controlled, the underlying cause will not be cured. Almost without exception, lifelong treatment of some type will be necessary in cases like these.

A final treatment outcome question that you should ask your veterinarian is, "How long will it take to get results?" This is often a hard question to answer, but an experienced pain practitioner can suggest the usual time frame necessary to treat before reevaluation. If reassessment shows progress being made, then it is easier to make a treatment plan based on the positive results. If there is no progress, then it is almost always prudent to start a different course of treatments, with a new date for reevaluation.

I remember one case where I forgot to have the "outcome" discussion with the owner. This dog was presented to me as having difficulty walking on anything "but the shortest of walks." An examination revealed some muscle pain, which I decided was probably secondary to an orthopedic issue. Sure enough, when the X-ray films were taken, the dog turned out to have hip dysplasia with secondary osteoarthritis. I placed him on pain medications and started acupuncture for the OA and trigger point therapy for the muscle pain. I sent the owner home with some fun strengthening exercises. By the time this dog came in for his third visit, he was noticeably walking better, seemed much more secure on the clinic's slippery floor, and seemed to have a better attitude overall. I said to the owner, "You must be happy with his progress!" She replied, "He is no better!" I was floored. I pointed out all the ways he was improving and asked her where she saw the problem. "Dr. Petty, I used to take him on an 18-mile hike every weekend. This past weekend, the most he could handle was about three miles. That is better than what we started with three weeks ago, but not anywhere near what both he and I want." Obviously, her disappointment and confusion was completely my fault. I had never once asked her what she hoped to see her dog accomplish as treatment progressed. So, almost a month after we should have had the original discussion, we talked about treatment outcomes and what was realistic for a dog with his condition. Suddenly, although the treatment didn't change, the owner adjusted her expectations and she viewed the treatment program as a success!

Since that experience I have never concluded a pain exam without discussing treatment outcomes. During this discussion, we set goals, such as, "If by the third acupuncture treatment, your dog isn't doing a, b, and c, we will reassess and adjust our treatments." This way we have an outcome we can measure, a time frame for our expectations, and a built-in plan that allows us to tweak treatments and try something different if there is no progress.

Any veterinarian who does not do this with you is already doing a less than adequate job. Her willingness to involve you in the discussion and treatment considerations makes you one of the team players in treating your dog's pain. By only following "doctor's orders" you are probably dooming the treatment to failure, as there is nothing in place for meeting your dog's needs if things don't work out as expected. And honestly, even if the treatments work some caregivers may stop therapy because they had an altogether different treatment outcome in mind.

Where Does It Hurt? The Importance of Getting a Physical Exam

Asking the question, "Where does it hurt?" does not pass for a pain exam for humans, much less for dogs. Even though a dog may "tell you" where it hurts by holding up a leg, he isn't always correct! For example, a ruptured disk in the neck can cause radicular pain. (You may have known someone with sciatica, which is a type of pain that starts in the lower back but feels as though there is something wrong with the leg.) If a dog has this type of pain in the neck, he perceives the pain to be in the forelimb. Consequently, your dog could be holding that leg up or crying and licking at it even though the source of the pain is not in the leg at all.

Many other problems can also look incredibly similar: A ruptured cruciate ligament in the knee, bone cancer, severe muscle injury, spinal arthritis, disk disease, and so on, all can make their way into the exam room looking the same and cannot be distinguished from each other by observation only. Even a physical exam may not reveal every painful area. Indeed, if one area is painful enough at that moment, it might overshadow pains felt elsewhere that to your dog may seem mild by comparison.

Furthermore, taking radiographs of the affected limb is not enough! A dog may have pathology in several places that show up when an X-ray is taken. However, not all of these issues might be causing a significant amount of pain. Again, a thorough exam must be conducted.

Watching Him Walk:
The Importance of Distant Observation

When a veterinarian examines a dog by observation, it is important that he does not "zero in" on the most apparent issue. Sure, it may be obvious that there is something wrong with the left hind leg, but what else is going on? Is the dog's back kyphotic (arched), indicating possible spinal issues? Is he scuffing his toenails as he walks, indicating possible neurological involvement? And looking carefully, although the left hind limb has the most pathology, does one of the other legs have something going on as well?

When I look for a gait abnormality I try to use the trip that the patient takes from the waiting room to the exam room as an opportunity to spy on them unobserved. And I say spy because dogs get "white coat syndrome" just like people. They can see they are being scrutinized and they try their hardest to tell the owner, "See, I'm just fine! Whatever was bothering me at home has steadily improved since we pulled into the vet's parking lot. Now I can't even recall what all the fuss was about!"

Some dogs are too unsteady or scared to walk on a tile or vinyl floor, making it become almost impossible to determine which leg is affected. With these dogs, we take them outside and walk on the sidewalk, or if there is inclement weather we roll out a 25-foot length of yoga mat. In either case, the footing is secure and allows for a better evaluation. Additionally, dogs that are taken back outside to the sidewalk think, "This was the easiest trip to the vet ever" and begin looking for their car (and a ride home) and so are less likely to hide their limp.

Some dogs have personalities that make them difficult to observe properly. These are the dogs that show no obvious sign of limping (usually while the owner tries to assure me, "Honest Doc, he barely has been able to put the foot down at home for the past week!"). With these dogs we videotape their movements, and if necessary, use gait analysis software to assist in the diagnosis. Videotaping the patient allows us to look at the same motions over and over, slow them down if necessary, and hopefully locate the problem area.

Hands On

Careful palpation of the entire dog is mandatory. Muscle pain, limited range of joint motion, painful palpation, and the dog's reactions throughout the exam all tell a story. It takes an astute practitioner to sort out all of the reactions from a dog and interpret them properly. The easiest dogs to examine are those that cry out when you hit the sore spot. The hardest dogs to diagnose are those that don't react by vocalizing but instead give body clues, such as a change in their respiration rate, or maybe licking their lips or turning their head to look at you. Some of them even start wagging their tail harder and harder as you close in on the sore spot.

The hardest category for me to diagnose through palpation are the dogs that cry out at everything. Some of these dogs have a condition called allodynia, where everything really does hurt. But many of these dogs are just so tired of their pain, or so scared of the situation, that they start vocalizing preemptively to stop the exam before it reaches the painful spot.

Neurological Examination

More than once I have had owners bring in their dog for pain issues, sometimes sent on referral by their primary care veterinarian for my diagnosis of the supposed pain issue, only to discover that the source of the limping is neurological. It is human nature to focus on the most obvious sign of an issue and to assign it the most obvious diagnosis, and for this reason many people presume that limping almost always equates with the pain of injury or OA. Even in veterinary and medical schools they teach students the "hoof beat test."[16] They are told, "If you are walking down a city block, and you hear hoof beats coming from around the corner, expect to see a horse. Don't expect to see a zebra." In other words, when you see certain signs of disease, look for the obvious not the bizarre. This "test" might get you by if you practice in a high patient–volume clinic where you can't take the necessary time to explore other possibilities. You need to save time, cut costs, and bet on the odds. And for some of the cases, the assessment is correct. But sometimes it is a zebra. And sometimes a limp is caused by a neurological problem, a vision problem, or some other unexpected condition.

Listen to the Caregiver

I teach other veterinarians to always take a careful history and to really listen to what the owner has to say. Behavioral changes often occur because of pain. A dog might become more guarded when approached by other dogs, or she might not seem as enthused by life as usual. If someone says, "Something is not right" despite the fact that all appears well, I start my exam over again and consider even more advanced diagnostics. Sometimes the owners were worrying about nothing, but it is my obligation to take every concern seriously. If I don't, proper diagnoses will be missed. This is where you need to be your dog's advocate. Your dog can't tell the veterinarian what is wrong, so tell her yourself, even if you have to make a list at home so you don't forget anything.

Listen to the Dog

Sometimes an owner will come in for a routine exam and vaccinations. But as I "listen" to the dog by observing his behavior, I might detect subtle behaviors that might indicate various diseases that produce pain: getting up from the floor front feet first, matted fur because he no longer likes to get brushed, abnormal body posture, or even an indifference to being at the vet's office. Some dogs have dealt with chronic pain issues for so long they just no longer care and, as a result, act befuddled. This has its parallel in human medicine and has been described as "fibro fog" in patients with fibromyalgia. If a person has this fibro fog, the world becomes hard to negotiate through. The brain of an afflicted person in such cases shuts out a lot of the world and instead expends all of its mental energy and concentration trying to deal with the pain. I have seen this parallel in dogs that are experiencing chronic pain.

The average person in pain has to visit about seven physicians before finding someone who can adequately understand and treat his pain. I can't even begin to imagine what it takes for a dog's caregiver to find a veterinarian who can help. But persevere, keep trying, and don't be satisfied with poor results. Talk to your veterinarian. If she ultimately cannot help you, look for someone else. Please see Appendix A for assistance in finding a veterinary pain practitioner.

5

COMMON PAIN MEDICATIONS FOR YOUR DOG

IT IS IMPORTANT FOR YOU, AS YOUR DOG'S CAREGIVER, to understand the medications that might be prescribed to treat your dog's pain. You might wonder, "Why is it important for me, a layperson, to know any information beyond how often I need to give each medication? After all, don't medications fall under the purview of my veterinarian?" They do and they don't. Your veterinarian is who first makes a diagnosis and prescribes medical treatments, including medications. But you are the one who must purchase the drugs, give them to your pet, and be prepared to deal with any side effects.

In my practice, I encourage all of my clients to understand what I am giving to their dog and why I am dispensing it. The relationship between veterinarian and pet owner should be one of cooperation and consent, and should not be like the old days of medicine where the veterinarian dictated and the owner was expected to obey. I actually knew of one veterinarian who refused to put the names of the medication he prescribed on the packets in which they were dispensed! Luckily for his patients, he is no longer practicing medicine.

In addition to discussing with my clients the "what and why" behind dispensing medications, I also talk with them about the most common side effects and adverse events, and how to be on the lookout for them. The side effects I tell clients to look for are usually some minor, non-harmful effects that come about from taking a medication. If you ever have taken a motion-sickness drug, for example, then you are probably aware that a common side effect is drowsiness. This is a common and not unexpected event that has no serious impact on your health. Adverse events, on the other hand, are quite different. An adverse event usually refers to an event that can cause a mild to serious health problem, maybe even lead to death. If you were to take that same motion-sickness drug and broke out in hives, or had trouble breathing, that would be considered an adverse event. It is important that you have a discussion with your veterinarian about both side effects and adverse events prior to buying and administering medications to your dog.

Not every client who walks through my door is interested in this information, of course. And I don't expect every reader to be interested in this chapter. But should you wonder exactly why a particular medication is being prescribed, or if you see a side effect or adverse event, reading this chapter can help you more effectively consult with your veterinarian. In any event, knowledge about these common pain medications can help you better understand why your veterinarian is giving (or not giving) a particular medication to your dog. Look at the end of this chapter for a quick reference guide that lists some of the most common concerns about familiar pain medications. Use it to help form a plan of action to either prevent or observe a problem in its early stages before anything serious can happen.

I visit veterinary practices all of the time, and I often meet veterinarians who misunderstand the proper use of many of these medications. Most pain drugs we utilize were meant for human use. The use of these drugs in dogs has been extrapolated from human data, meaning that sometimes little or no research has been done on dogs. Since there are no dog labels on some of these medications, only the practitioner who actively seeks information and has discussions with other pain professionals will grasp why a certain drug might be used (or not used) for pain treatment. Don't be afraid to ask your veterinarian about the drugs noted in this chapter—some of which might be appropriate for treating your dog. But at the same time, know that there are thousands upon thousands of drugs out there, and your veterinarian may have to look into it and follow up with you should she be unfamiliar with a drug you mention.

It is beyond the scope of this book to describe every pain medication that is available for use in dogs. Every year, there is some new discovery made. Routinely, medications that were not designed to treat pain are found to have anti-pain benefits. New potential pain medications are continually being discovered and begin the long road toward FDA approval. Instead of trying to discuss every pain medication on the market, I am going to discuss pain medications that are either FDA approved or have the backing of some research trials and a preponderance of clinical experience. There are, however, many new pain drugs on the horizon. Some of them are only a year or so away from FDA approval, and others are many years out. I will discuss some of these drugs in Chapter 17, Future Pain Treatments.

Interestingly, for chronic pain the only FDA-approved medications are the NSAIDs (nonsteroidal anti-inflammatory drugs), and another drug called Adequan, which I discuss in Chapter 13, Diets and Nutraceuticals. As such, this class of medication (NSAIDs) should always be considered first for cases of chronic pain. But as you will find as you read along, many other medications are out there that can be used alongside NSAIDs because, in most cases, one drug is not enough.

It should be noted that a discussion of these drugs does not suggest that you, the caregiver, should administer any of these medications without the supervision and approval of the veterinarian who is caring for your dog. Just as a discussion about brain surgery would not be tacit approval for you to go home and try it on your pet, so it is for administering these medications. The discussion that follows is a very basic one and as such it lacks important information necessary for the layperson to safely combine drugs or to treat dogs that might have certain medical conditions.

NSAIDs

The following discussion is important for understanding the side effects and adverse events of nonsteroidal anti-inflammatory drugs (NSAIDs). The first NSAID approved for use by the FDA in dogs was carprofen, made under the trade name Rimadyl by the pharmaceutical company Pfizer Animal Health (now called Zoetis) on October 25, 1996. Since then several other NSAIDs have appeared on the veterinary market. Some of these NSAIDs for dogs have stayed and some have come and gone. For the purposes of a broad discussion about NSAIDs, it is enough to know that, in general, they all have similar benefits, contraindications, side effects, and adverse events.

Stick with me for a moment while I provide a brief, and I hope not too boring, explanation about how this class of drugs works. I've done my best to be succinct—even veterinarians start to get all glassy-eyed if I lecture on this topic too long!

All veterinary NSAIDs currently on the market have their primary effect on something called the cyclooxygenase (COX) pathway.[17] The COX pathway is a set of chemical reactions in a dog that result in making something called prostanoids. Prostanoids cause both pain and inflammation at the site of the nerve ending and in the spinal cord.[18] NSAIDs can help block this reaction and, as a result, less of the prostanoids end up in a dog's body. Why do you need to know this? Because, unfortunately, some of the agents made through this COX pathway by the dog are also important to maintaining essential body functions, including proper kidney function and protection of the gastrointestinal tract. The loss of these protective functions is the reason behind most of the adverse events of NSAIDs.

What are the benefits of NSAIDs? These drugs are powerful pain-killers. Anyone who has taken Motrin, Aleve, or Celebrex for head-ache or arthritis pain knows how quickly they work to dampen the pain. The same is true for pain in dogs. In my patients I depend on an NSAID to be the first pharmaceutical option for treating arthritis and for mild to moderate surgical pain. In the case of osteoarthritis, less pain means more joint mobility and better return to normal function. The anti-inflammatory effect can remove some inflammatory agents, which in turn may slow the progression of the arthritis. In addition, when NSAIDs are used daily without interruption, they have been shown to steadily lessen pain scores with each passing month.[19]

Some NSAID-causing contraindications, unfortunately, prevent those NSAIDs from being administered to certain animals. Especially unfor-tunate is that much of the time these contraindications occur in aged dogs, the population that needs NSAIDs the most. If a dog has moder-ate to severe kidney disease, administering NSAIDs can put a dog into a full-blown case of kidney failure. Because the liver metabolizes NSAIDs, dogs with liver disease may not be able to handle the drug and could end up in liver failure.[20] There are some dogs, although the number is very low, in which NSAIDs can cause liver problems even though there were no liver issues prior to taking the medication. NSAIDs should never be given with aspirin or with a class of drug called corticosteroids or with other NSAIDs, because any of these combinations can interact and cause life-threatening problems, including gastric ulcers. Since NSAIDs remove the COX properties that help protect the stomach, dogs with preexisting gastrointestinal (GI) issues should probably not use NSAIDs. This includes dogs that are on NSAIDs and must undergo intestinal surgery. In these cases the NSAID should probably be stopped until everything is healed. Even if your dog never has had a preexisting prob-lem, ulcers still can develop. Finally, many herbal supplements either can prevent the function of NSAIDs or make their side effects worse. The most commonly used herbs that interfere with NSAID function are ginkgo, ginseng, garlic, chamomile, ginger, and devil's claw. Always tell your veterinarian about any herbal supplement you might be giving. Just because it is herbal doesn't mean it is safe.

As previously mentioned, the side effects of NSAIDs usually involve the gastrointestinal tract, the liver, or the kidneys. We can't see these organs, of course, so we have to rely on lab tests. In the case of the gastrointestinal tract, however, we monitor by watching for certain signs and behaviors because we can't monitor the gastrointestinal tract with lab tests. Proper monitoring depends on the ability of you the caretaker to watch closely for signs of GI upset. These signs include slight or total appetite loss, vomiting with or without blood, diarrhea, and dark tarry-looking stool. This task is even more difficult if your dog is a picky eater that regularly skips a meal or two. In such a case, it's hard to know if the dog is just not hungry or is developing an ulcer. If any of these things occur, it is best to stop the NSAID and consult with your veterinarian.

Discovering the presence of an ulcer is difficult, and usually involves looking into the stomach with an endoscope under general anesthesia.

Because ulcers can be serious, I make sure clients understand the possible signs of ulcer formation in order to monitor the gastrointestinal tract. I also monitor liver and kidney function, and I insist that every dog that is starting on long-term NSAIDs get a blood test to look for problems prior to administering the first pill. Assuming the results are normal, the patient is started on the NSAID. The blood values are then rechecked after two to three weeks. If your dog is put on NSAIDs, do not balk at returning for this important follow-up blood test. If it shows a developing problem with the liver or kidneys, the NSAID should be assumed guilty until proven otherwise, and the medication should be stopped. With early intervention, most issues are reversible. Wait too long and you can easily reach the point of no return, resulting in unnecessary pain, expensive veterinary care, and maybe even death. If, however, the blood test is normal, the patient gets to continue on the NSAID. Even then, monitoring the organs every 6 to 12 months with a follow-up blood testing is prudent.[21]

Is there anything you can do to lessen the chances of one of these three things (ulcer, liver problems, and kidney problems) from happening? No. Many owners (and veterinarians) think that by giving the NSAID with food, or administering an antacid, that ulcers can be avoided. There is no evidence for this because the problem is inhibition of the "good" COX enzymes (discussed in the first part of this section); and except in very rare cases, NSAIDs do not have a direct effect on the lining of the stomach.

Have I scared you off of NSAIDs? I hope not. My own dog receives them every single day, and she greatly benefits from their anti-inflammatory and anti-pain actions.

Gabapentin

Gabapentin is a drug that was developed in human medicine to treat epilepsy and, more recently, to treat neuropathic pain. It is not approved for use in dogs, but as there are no similar veterinary drugs, the FDA allows its use in veterinary medicine.

In dogs, gabapentin is most commonly used for both chronic and neuropathic pain. Its mode of action seems to be its ability to block pain signals as they travel at the point where the nerve crosses over into the spinal cord.

Imagine some wires that are connected on one end to a pain nerve ending and on the other end to the spinal cord. When the nerve ending is stimulated by something like osteoarthritis, it sends a signal up the wire to the spinal cord. This does not cause perceived pain in the dog's mind, at least not yet. The spinal cord must then accept the signal, and then send its own signal up to the brain where it connects with a part of the brain that then causes your dog to experience pain. There are many opportunities to stop pain along this entire path. Gabapentin works by preventing *some* of the pain signals from making the jump from that peripheral pain nerve at the exact point where the signal enters the spinal cord. If you can block half of the signals from getting through, you can decrease the amount of pain by half. In my experience, gabapentin does not seem to work as well alone as it does when used alongside other pain medications, NSAIDs in particular.

Contraindications for the use of gabapentin are few. The only contraindication for gabapentin is any prior sensitivity to gabapentin or other drugs of the same class, such as pregabalin. However, careful administration must be observed in giving gabapentin to dogs with kidney disease. A dog depends on its kidneys to clear the drug from his system by essentially filtering it out. If a dog has kidney disease, the rate at which the drug is filtered and removed is decreased. This does not mean that these patients can't have gabapentin; it just means your veterinarian must use a reduced dose.

Side effects from gabapentin are uncommon; the most reported ones being sleepiness and diarrhea.[22] Both of these side effects will often, but not always, dissipate over time. I try to avoid the sleepiness by prescribing it for the first week at bedtime only; then I increase the dose when the dog has gotten somewhat used to it. If your dog just seems too sleepy, ask your veterinarian if you can give a lower dose or reduce the frequency until he is more used to it. Then work with your veterinarian to move back up to the original dose.

Another cause for concern is from stopping the gabapentin abruptly. Forgetting to give a few doses can cause something called rebound pain, which can be as bad or worse than the original pain you were trying to treat. Always work with your veterinarian if for some reason you need to stop giving gabapentin. He will set up a regimen for slowly stopping the drug to avoid the rebound pain.

Amantadine

Amantadine belongs to a class of drugs called N-methyl-D-aspartate (NMDA) antagonists (they antagonize or block NMDA receptors, and thereby stop some of the pain). The NMDA is one pathway whereby the spinal cord transmits pain signals to the brain. (Recall the explanation I used for gabapentin where I described the journey a painful stimulus must take to get to the brain and actually cause pain.) This pathway can become very active in chronic pain. In such cases, the spinal cord becomes sensitized to the pain in a pathological state that is called hyperalgesia or allodynia.

Hyperalgesia means that when a painful stimulus is applied to a nerve, the pain that is felt by the dog is much greater than what would be expected by the stimulus. For example, we all probably have stubbed a toe or slammed a finger in something. Of course it hurts at the time of the injury, but in many cases, just a small bump of the same area at a later time, often within an hour or two, causes as much if not more pain than the original injury. This is hyperalgesia or "wind-up" pain.

I had something similar happen to me in college. I reached into my pocket and jabbed myself with a pencil I had in there. The lead of the pencil went under my fingernail and broke off. Of course it hurt terribly, and it was too far under the nail to easily retrieve. By the time I was able to get to my doctor seven hours later, not only did my finger throb, it was actually painful to touch my arm.

An even more serious overreaction to pain is called allodynia. Allodynia is a condition wherein a light, normally non-painful stimulus such as touch causes pain. Both hyperalgesia and allodynia are conditions that involve, in part, the NMDA pathway. It is therefore important that this pain path be considered when deciding on the course of treatment.

Think of the poor dog with osteoarthritis, or some other chronic painful condition. The constant barrage of pain signals from the affected area to the spinal cord may eventually cause hyperalgesia in the spinal cord (we don't know why some dogs get it and others don't). Because hyperalgesia is in part supported by that NMDA pathway, it needs to be treated with drugs that can help shut down this pathway.

Amantadine, one of the few oral drugs we have to treat hyperalgesia, is a medication that was originally licensed to treat cases of the flu in humans. However, it was discovered that it also helped "squeeze tight" this NMDA pathway, thus preventing some of the pain signals from reaching the brain. It is not sufficient on its own to stop pain, and I would never prescribe it by itself. However, in cases of chronic pain, amantadine can be used in addition to the two classes of drugs I already mentioned, NSAIDs and gabapentin. Some dogs seem to need to be on amantadine for long term, where other dogs respond after a three- to four-week course of the medication and can stop taking it without an immediate return to the previous level of pain.

Contraindications are limited to a known sensitivity to amantadine. Side effects are few, but some dogs do become nervous, even hyperactive on the medication. I have had some clients report that their dogs pant constantly while taking amantadine. Unfortunately, these side effects may not dissipate over time and if they are profound enough, the dog must be taken off of the medication.[23]

Amitriptyline

Amitriptyline belongs to a class of drugs called tricyclic antidepressants. They are antidepressants because they help slow the reuptake of a substance called serotonin. For this very same reason, they work on chronic pain. Receptors for serotonin are in both a dog's brain and in the peripheral tissues where the pain nerves are located. Serotonin modulates pain signals, so if its reuptake is decreased, thereby making serotonin more available in peripheral tissues, it can modulate or reduce the pain signals even more. Several drugs belong to this class, but amitriptyline is the most commonly used because it is relatively inexpensive and it requires dosing of only once or twice a day in most dogs. Unfortunately, not all dogs respond to amitriptyline or similar drugs with the same mode of action.

Contraindications for use of this drug include combining it with other drugs that are serotonin reuptake inhibitors. Tramadol is one such drug used for pain (and will be covered later in this chapter), and it should never be given at the same time as amitriptyline. Some flea, tick, and mange products also contain a serotonin reuptake inhibitor called amitraz, and should not be given with amitriptyline. Other drugs such as fluoxetine, which is used for separation anxiety in dogs, also has serotonin reuptake inhibition. SAMe, a popular over-the-counter drug, increases levels of serotonin. St. John's wort, an herbal supplement, also increases levels of serotonin. This is all very important, because if levels of serotonin are too high, it can result in something called serotonin syndrome in which seizure-like activity occurs. This can be irreversible, leading to death or euthanasia.

I am not trying to discourage the use of this medication. But it is important that both you and your veterinarian must be cognizant of using any other product along with amitriptyline, even pet store products and dietary supplements. Make sure your veterinarian checks those products for compatibility and safety. The other contraindication for amitriptyline is using it at the same time as St. John's wort. This herbal remedy can both increase the likelihood of serotonin syndrome while at the same time decreasing the levels of amitriptyline, making it ineffective.

Side effects are not common. One possible side effect is that amitriptyline can make it difficult for some animals to urinate by tightening up the detrusor muscle, which is the muscle that normally keeps urine from leaking out.[24] For an old dog that has become "leaky" with age, I use this side effect to my advantage to both decrease pain and to stop urinary incontinence! If your dog has incontinence issues, and is in pain, you might ask if amitriptyline is appropriate to use for your dog.

Tramadol

There is a lot of confusion about the action of oral tramadol. In humans (and cats and horses), it is known to pass through the liver to become metabolized, and one of its metabolites is morphine, or at least a morphine-like metabolite. This metabolic process does not happen in dogs, at least not to the degree it does in people and cats. In dogs, tramadol's main action seems to be that it is a serotonin reuptake inhibitor (see previous section on amitriptyline). It is also a norepinephrine reuptake inhibitor. Norepinephrine, like serotonin, plays a part in modulating pain; so like serotonin, its reuptake inhibition can help stop pain even more.

Tramadol is one of my least favorite drugs to use for treating cases of chronic pain. There are several studies out there that look at its effectiveness for long-term use. One study showed that its metabolite was no longer detectable in the urine after as little as five days.[25] Is this a problem with absorption from the stomach? Perhaps a decrease in the liver's ability to utilize it? No one knows as of yet. We do know that there are detectable levels in the blood for at least the first five days, probably making it okay for use in acutely painful situations, but making it questionable for long-term chronic pain control.

Contraindications are similar to those for amitriptyline: avoiding the use of any other drug, herbal preparation, or insecticide that has known serotonin reuptake inhibition.

Side effects of using tramadol are not common but could include either sleepiness or excitability.[26] Rarely, it causes stomach upset. This medication is extremely bitter tasting and will cause drooling and even vomiting if your dog should taste it on its way down. I have had a few owners tell me that when they pick up the vial of tramadol, their dog runs off to avoid getting medicated. Make sure that you either place the pill in the very back of the mouth, or that you hide it in something tasty that he will eat in one gulp.

Acetaminophen

Although this drug has been around since it was discovered at Johns Hopkins in 1877,[27] not a lot is known about its mode of action. The best information says it probably works in dogs by attaching to endocannabinoid receptors, but the truth is no one really understands its complex mode of action. It is well known to be extremely toxic in cats, but many laypeople and veterinarians believe it to be toxic in dogs as well. This simply isn't true. It is probably a myth perpetuated by incidents where dogs ate an entire jar of acetaminophen and overdosed on it. There are published safe doses of this drug for the treatment of pain in dogs. Unfortunately, it is not a strong analgesic and should not be the sole source of medication for severe pain, including postsurgical pain. It is often used in veterinary medicine in combination with codeine.

Contraindications would be use of this drug in any dog with moderate to severe liver disease because the liver metabolizes it. This makes it important to check with your veterinarian, and maybe even get a blood test prior to using this easy-to-get, over-the-counter medication. Although not common, some dogs can develop a blood disorder called methemoglobinemia that, if discovered early, can be reversible.

QUICK REFERENCE CHART

No doses are given or suggested with these medications. All of these medications should be given only under the strict supervision of a veterinarian.

Medication	Concern	Action	Contraindications
NSAIDs	Liver and kidney. Ulcers.	Test both before and after its use. Stop medication and call your vet if there is more than one missed meal, vomiting, or dark tarry stool.	Moderate to severe kidney or liver disease. Aspirin and corticosteroids. Preexisting gastrointestinal problems. Herbal supplements: ginkgo, ginseng, garlic, chamomile, ginger, and devil's claw.
Gabapentin	Sleepiness upon starting medication. Diarrhea.	Ask your veterinarian if you can give it at bedtime only for the first week or so, then slowly increase to the prescribed dose. Try stopping the medication for a few days, then try again.	Known sensitivity to gabapentin. Use with caution in dogs with kidney disease.

Amantadine	Nervousness, excitability.	Ask your veterinarian if you can give a lower dose.	Known sensitivity to amantadine.
Amitriptyline	Difficulty urinating.	This might be remedied by a lower dose, but if your dog cannot urinate at all, then this is an emergency and you should contact your veterinarian.	Use with other serotonin reuptake inhibitor drugs. Use with insecticides that contain serotonin reuptake inhibitors. SAMe. St. John's wort.
Tramadol	Sleepiness or excitability. Serotonin syndrome. Stomach upset.	Make sure your veterinarian is aware of all drugs your dog is on. Reducing the dose often reduces the side effects. Call your veterinarian, especially if your dog is also taking an NSAID.	Use with other serotonin reuptake inhibitor drugs. Use with insecticides that contain serotonin reuptake inhibitors. SAMe. St. John's wort.
Acetaminophen	Liver disease.	Blood work prior to use.	Moderate to severe liver disease. Methemoglobinemia.

6

IN THE PAIN WORLD: 1+1+1=10

WOULDN'T IT BE GREAT IF THERE WERE A SINGLE PILL or treatment that was a "silver bullet" to take care of every pain problem? Unfortunately there are very few conditions that benefit from a single stand-alone treatment. Most pain conditions require a combination of pain treatment modalities: pills plus acupuncture, acupuncture plus rehab, and even a combination of three or more modalities. This chapter will explain why this is so and encourage you to seek out a veterinarian who can provide a variety of pain treatment modalities.

Unfortunately, the pain of osteoarthritis is never caused by one single mechanism, and therefore cannot be completely controlled by one single type of treatment. However, if one or more of the key components of pain can be eliminated, doing so might be enough to vastly improve your dog's quality of life. Let me explain.

Imagine that it is the middle of winter and you are going to enjoy a relaxing weekend at a cabin in the woods. The only way to get there is by a long walk through the snow, and you must pull a sled loaded with all of your supplies. The burden is light and the sled moves easily through the snow. But what if something changes and you need to pile ever-increasing loads onto the sled? The job of moving the sled through the snow would become more and more difficult until it reached a point where it would become impossible for you to budge the sled even an inch.

Keep that image in mind, but instead of adding more weight on the sled think in terms of ever-increasing inflammatory substances on an arthritic joint that eventually add up to the point at which movement becomes almost impossible. For a time, the inflammation is so low that the pain is easy to ignore. But the inflammation keeps building and at some point it becomes a burden. And eventually that burden becomes so large that it prevents movement.

What if your veterinarian could give your dog something that removed one or two of those inflammatory substances? It might be enough to make that arthritic joint tolerable. This is the aim of most pain treatments: to provide enough pain control measures to return a good quality of life to your dog.

The Pain Signal Pathway

In the 1600s, a man named René Descartes proposed that a single filament from a point of injury to the brain carried pain signals. Although this simplistic idea is not true, it was groundbreaking in its time and brought into medicine the idea of nerves as the messengers of pain.

Modern medicine now has a much better idea about this pain signal pathway. We know that it is not a single filament but a series of interconnections that make their way from the point of injury up to the brain. Knowing how the pain signal reaches the brain gives the pain practitioner many opportunities to either stop or modify that pain signal during its journey. In explaining this pathway, it is my hope to give you a better sense of how important it is to treat pain with multiple treatments, and the benefits of doing so for your dog.

It might help you to think about this pathway by comparing its actions to that of a commuter leaving work and heading home for the day. The end of the workday starts with a signal. In this case let's call it the clock reaching quitting time, but in your dog let's think of it as the stimulation of a nerve ending. The worker must now leave his place of employment and walk to a metro stop, the equivalent of the signal traveling along a nerve. Upon entering the metro stop, the commuter must now get on the appropriate line that will take him home, the equivalent of traveling through the spinal cord. At the end of the line, he arrives at home, the equivalent of the brain. In medical terms, the pathway the commuter just took consists of transduction (the clock), transmission (the trip to the metro stop), spinal modulation (the subway ride), and pain perception (home).

What follows is a description of each stage that a nerve impulse takes from the point of injury to its perception as pain in the brain and how that signal can be either stopped or modulated along each step of the way. I don't intend this to be a complicated how-to manual for you to follow; your veterinarian should already know this discourse. Instead, I am trying to take a complicated idea and put it into terms and concepts that will allow you to have a conversation about your dog's pain treatment, should the need arise.

Treatment of Transduction Pain

Transduction of the pain signal is what happens to the nerve ending at the point of injury. (This is the clock signaling the end of the day in the example of the commuter.) Whether it is a burn, cut, surgery, a blunt force, or some other injury, it all starts at the nerve ending. If the pain could be 100 percent stopped at this point, there never would be a need for any other pain medications! But as you will see, this is not practical or possible for the vast majority of pain situations.

Local Anesthetics

Local anesthetics block pain. When pain can be anticipated, such as prior to a surgery, a local anesthetic can be given by injection that will completely stop the pain signal from going any farther. Of course, the effects of that medication will not last throughout the entire healing time and so other steps must be taken to manage this pain.

Unfortunately, surgery only represents a small percentage of pain causes. Most acute pain (such as injuries or burns) cannot be anticipated, so preemptively administering a local anesthetic is not possible. However, it is possible to apply local anesthetics to closed areas of trauma such as a burn or superficial abrasion in order to stop the pain signal. Applying local anesthetics to open wounds, such as a cut, can cause problems with proper healing and should not be done.

Corticosteroids

Corticosteroids work differently than local anesthetics in that they have the ability to reduce inflammation, a component of pain, and so make your dog more comfortable. As is the case of local anesthetics, applying corticosteroids to an open wound on your dog's skin can cause some problems with healing. This class of drugs also can be given by mouth or injection; however, when given by these routes they have the potential to cause many unwanted side effects, making topical administration the best route.

Nonsteroidal Anti-Inflammatory Drugs (NSAIDs)

NSAIDs are not useful when applied topically except in a few specific cases, such as in the eye. However, when given by injection or orally, they can have a strong effect on the transduction of pain. Almost without exception, they should be given both before and after surgery, or when there are particular areas of pain and inflammation such as ear infections and anal sac disease.

Capsaicin

Capsaicin is the compound in chili peppers that makes them hot. The reason capsaicin creates a hot sensation is that it stimulates a type of nerve called a C fiber. C fibers are responsible for detecting heat, chemicals, and slow throbbing pain. They are the culprits that turn a painful cut on your finger into a deep throbbing pain a short time after the cut occurs.

Why would I want to put something on your dog's skin that causes pain in its mouth? Capsaicin not only stimulates C fibers but over time they also "burn off" the nerve endings, making them less reactive to pain. This is why people are able to tolerate hot foods. They are not building up their ability in some kind of macho way; they are merely destroying the nerve endings responsible for perceiving the heat that capsaicin imparts to the

C fibers. Doing so then allows people to eat foods with even greater concentrations of capsaicin. (Don't worry if I am describing you. The C fibers
will eventually grow back if you stop eating spicy food.)

Applying capsaicin to the skin can temporarily kill off those C nerve
fiber endings, just as in the case of eating spicy foods, and so reduce the
amount of pain felt in the skin and in any structures immediately under the
skin. Care must be taken that the capsaicin does not get somewhere it is not
wanted, either on your dog or a family member. If you have ever rubbed your
eyes after chopping a hot pepper, you know how much it can hurt.

Ice

Ice at the site of injury can slow the rate of transduction of the pain signal. This works in the case of acute injuries, as mentioned in Chapter 2,
but also can be applied in chronic conditions.

Acupuncture

I am going to talk a lot more about acupuncture in Chapter 9, but I want
to mention here its ability to help stop the transduction of pain signals.
Very simply put, an acupuncture needle that is properly inserted at or
near a point of injury has the ability to cause our bodies to release local
anti-inflammatories.

Laser

Laser therapy will be discussed more in Chapter 11 when I discuss its use
in rehabilitation. Here I would simply like to note that laser treatments can
increase both blood flow and mitochondrial activity in superficial tissue,
thereby speeding the healing process and reducing pain and inflammation.

Opioids

Opioids, such as morphine, cannot be rubbed onto an area of injury.
However, during surgical procedures they can be injected into joints
where nerves originate, just as they do in the skin. Opioids by their
nature attach to "pain receptors" and help shut down their pain-causing
activity.

Treatment of Transmission Pain

Transmission of pain occurs when the nerve endings have emitted a pain signal (transduction) and that pain signal travels up the nerve toward its next stop in the pain pathway. (This is the equivalent of the commuter walking to the metro station.) There are only a few drugs that can stop the transmission of pain, and unfortunately they must be given by injection. This makes them impractical for chronic use, but very helpful in stopping acute pain. If this were the commuter on his way home from work, these drugs would be the equivalent of a barricade put up across the route that he must walk to reach the metro station.

Local Anesthetics

Just as local anesthetics can block the transduction of pain at the nerve ending, they also can be used to stop the pain as it travels along the path toward the spinal cord, or from the spinal cord toward the brain. In the first action, injecting a local anesthetic in the vicinity of the nerve numbs an entire nerve trunk. This is usually called a regional block or a loco-regional block and is used just prior to surgery. In the second instance, a local anesthetic can be injected around the spinal cord in procedures known as spinals or epidurals. These procedures numb all of the nerves that are distal or "downstream" from the point of injection. Doing so can be very useful when it is desirable to numb an entire rear leg or the pelvis. You can't do an epidural up high on the spinal cord because this unfortunately would stop a lot of other useful functions, like the ability to breathe!

Alpha-2 Agonists

Drugs such as dexmedetomidine can have an action on the transmission of nerves when given by injection. Its agonist action on receptors in the spinal cord is very effective for modulating the pain signal.

Opioids

Most commonly, opioids are used in the spinal and epidural blocks, as described previously. However, they can be injected near any nerve and similarly help modulate or stop the intensity of the pain signal.

Acupuncture

Acupuncture needles, when placed near a major nerve trunk, can help stop the transmission of pain by encouraging the brain to send down inhibiting pain signals. These inhibitory signals occur naturally. This natural process is why, for example, a cut finger does not keep hurting with the same intensity it does during the first few minutes after the cut. Acupuncture enhances the brain's own ability to inhibit pain.

Treatment of Spinal Modulation Pain

Spinal modulation involves several different complex reactions that differing components of the spinal cord have when confronted with a pain signal. (In our commuter model, this is his ride on the subway.) A part of this spinal pathway is responsible for both hyperalgesia and allodynia. Remember that hyperalgesia is when a painful stimulus hurts more than it should, and allodynia is when a non-painful or light touch stimulus hurts when it shouldn't.

There are different areas involved in the spinal cord during modulation. Something called the NMDA pathway, alpha-2 delta ligand sites, and the dorsal horn are just a part of the complexities of the spinal cord and pain modulations. This complexity is somewhat akin to our commuter arriving at his metro station and choosing the right train line to get on for his ride home. Stopping these pathways for our commuter would be the equivalent of a breakdown of the train as it travels on the line toward its final destination.

Pharmaceuticals

Fortunately, we have several drugs that can be used to help suppress or down regulate the expression of pain that occurs in the spinal cord. Those drugs belong to several classes: opioids, local anesthetics, NSAIDs, alpha-2 agonists, tricyclic antidepressants, NMDA antagonists, and alpha-2 delta ligand antagonists. It would be too long of a list to mention the individual drugs here, although the big players in chronic pain are listed in the previous chapter.

Acupuncture

Once again, acupuncture is a big player in pain control, utilizing the modulation of spinal pathways. Acupuncture needles that are strategically placed near structures (called dorsal root ganglia) on either side of the spinal cord can help modify the way the spinal cord perceives and reacts to pain.

Treatment of the Perception of Pain

Perception of pain is exactly what it sounds like: how our dog's brains perceive or interpret pain signals coming from the body. (For our commuter, he has finally arrived at home.) Without perception, your dog has no awareness or knowledge of the pain. This doesn't mean bad things can't happen if he happens to be unconscious during a painful event, it just means he is not aware of it at the moment. Life-threatening physiologic changes, hyperalgesia, allodynia, and more can occur if pain perception is stopped, but the other parts of the pain pathway remain intact and running. If our commuter arrives at home but his cable service is out, then he will merely be unaware of the fires, crimes, and floods that are still happening and causing damage in the outside world.

Anesthetics

I mention anesthetics first because it is the impression by many people that a general anesthetic is all that is needed during a painful surgical procedure. This simply is not true. Although anesthesia knocks out perception and provides amnesia for the procedure, tissue trauma and your dog's reaction to that trauma can have an effect on your dog's well-being for weeks, months, or years after the anesthesia wears off. As such, it is imperative that you insist on pain control measures beyond a general anesthetic.

Pharmaceuticals

Certain drugs, mentioned previously for their use elsewhere in the body, also have an effect on pain perception. Opioids are considered the gold standard when it comes to treating acute pain, and their primary action occurs at the level of perception in the brain. Alpha-2 agonists and NSAIDs also can play an important role in the perception of pain and should be considered as options for treating acute or chronic pain states.

Acupuncture

Is there anywhere acupuncture doesn't work? I can't think of a single type of pain that won't respond, at least in part, to acupuncture. Ascending signals from the placement of acupuncture needles farther down the body can help modulate the brain's perception of pain. Endorphin release (often described as the long-distance runner's high) also results from the placement of acupuncture needles.

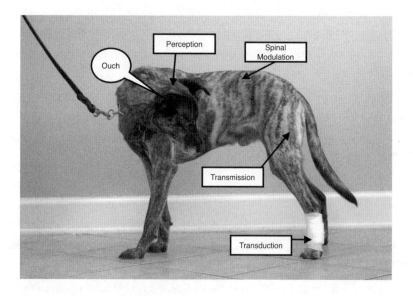

Putting It All Together

The knowledgeable pain practitioner can look at these four pain pathways and formulate a treatment strategy based on where the pain originates, the type of pain that needs to be treated, involvement of any special pain receptors, and the appropriateness and ability to deliver these pain treatments. In other words, a skilled practitioner can stop our

The Case of the Arthritic Dog: Treating a Chronic Pain Case

Buddy was a 12-year-old Labrador Retriever with severe hip dysplasia and osteoarthritis. He was brought to me by his caregiver because he refused to go on his walks and had trouble walking across the hardwood floors. He had quit climbing the stairs to his caregiver's bedroom almost a year previously.

Buddy was a big guy and as I thought about treating him by a pain pathway approach, I knew that topical medications such as corticosteroids and capsaicin would never reach his joints and stop the **transduction** of the pain signal. In order to help modulate that pain signal, I chose acupuncture as a treatment. I also chose to put him on carprofen (Rimadyl), one of several NSAIDs I had available to me. This helped reduce the pain and inflammation at the site of the osteoarthritis and slow the **transduction** of the pain signals.

Like all chronic pain cases, it was impractical to block the **transmission** by an injection of a local anesthetic because the effect would only last a few hours. Indeed, I was already treating that when I chose to use acupuncture.

Fortunately, for Buddy, I had several drugs available to me that could help with the **spinal modulation** of his pain. I chose to use gabapentin, which inhibited the pain signals through antagonism of

(continued)

the alpha-2 delta ligand receptors. I also gave Buddy amantadine, which helped slow the transmission of pain signals through the NMDA pathway. Additionally, I chose some supplemental acupuncture points near the portion of the spinal cord that reads pain signals from the hips. This further helped modulate his pain.

When it came to Buddy's **perception**, I didn't have to add an additional drug. The NSAID I put him on had an effect on his pain perception, as did the acupuncture.

It took about three weeks to realize the full benefits of his treatment, but at the end of that time Buddy was going for walks, crossing the hardwood floors, and with a little help was making it up the stairs.

The Case of the Ruptured Cruciate Ligament: An Acute Pain Case

Gizmo was a middle-age male mixed-breed dog. While playing in the park, Gizmo screamed in pain and quit using his right hind leg. His owner rushed him in and upon examination I discovered that he had torn his cruciate ligament, an essential ligament that is in the knee and that is prone to injury in dogs. Choosing from several treatment options, the owner opted to have it surgically repaired.

Prior to surgery, Gizmo was given an opioid, which helped stop the **transduction**, **spinal modulation**, and **perception** of his pain. A local anesthetic was given at the site where I was going to make my surgical incision, stopping the possible **transduction** of the pain signal. I also performed an epidural using an opioid and a local anesthetic to stop the **spinal modulation** of the pain signal through the spinal cord. Finally, he was given an injection of an NSAID in order to help stop the **transduction**, **spinal modulation**, and **perception** of his pain.

During surgery, I gave Gizmo something called a constant rate infusion of two drugs: one was an opioid and the other was a drug called ketamine. The opioid helped with the **transduction**, **spinal modulation**, and **perception** of the pain, while ketamine, an injectable NMDA antagonist, helped with the **spinal modulation** of pain.

After surgery, the constant rate infusion was continued for its pain-relieving benefits. I also applied ice to the surgical site to reduce inflammation and to stop the **transduction** of the pain signals. Acupuncture needles were also put in locally to stop the **transduction** of the pain signals.

Gizmo woke up from his surgery, happy and comfortable and ready for a meal. Palpation of his surgery site did not elicit any pain, and within a few hours he was taken for a walk outside to relieve himself.

commuter from leaving work, impede his walk to the metro station, slow the train ride home, and once he gets home, make him unaware of what is happening in the outside world.

As the two cases above show, knowledge of pain pathways can help the pain practitioner make good decisions in the treatment of pain cases. These examples are not the final word on pain management: Medications and physical treatments can be added or subtracted depending on the type of case being treated, existing medical conditions the dog may have, and the skill set of the veterinarian. However, employing a pain pathway approach gives your dog, as the title of this chapter suggests, a treatment that is greater than the sum of its parts.

7

MUSCLE PAIN AND TRIGGER POINTS

MYOFASCIAL PAIN SYNDROME IS UNDOUBTEDLY THE most common problem associated with orthopedic issues such as hip or elbow dysplasia, injuries from accidents or surgeries (especially limb amputation where the dog compensates for the missing limb by abnormal body posture and head position), and repetitive strain injuries. This syndrome also can result from internal problems like irritable bowel syndrome (IBS).

So what is myofascial pain syndrome, and how does it develop? First of all, what does myofascial mean? The "myo" part of the word refers to muscles, and the "fascial" part refers to the tissue that is either surrounding or separating the muscles. Put together, myofascial pain literally means pain of the muscles and their surrounding tissues. Whether a dog is protecting a painful limb by holding it partially or completely off the ground (the most usual cause), or compensating for a missing limb, or repeating a specific activity (an issue for working and agility dogs that practice the same moves over and over again), a muscle contraction will occur that lasts an extended period of time. This lengthy contraction results in the formation of tiny, sensitive areas within the muscles called trigger points. In turn, these painful areas of contracted muscle within the entire muscle become unable to let go of the contraction by themselves, thus forming the basis of myofascial pain syndrome.

Almost everyone who has worked at a computer or sat hunched over a book for an extended period of time sooner or later develops trigger points. When we sit for any length of time doing either one of these activities, there is a natural tendency to lean slightly forward to find the best distance for reading what is on the screen or page. Although this posture helps us to see the written word more clearly, it is not the best posture for the muscles in our neck that have to constantly work to keep our heads from falling forward. If we keep at it long enough, we might feel a painful tightness in the muscles on either side of our neck when we finally sit up straight or stand. This is a trigger point. Usually some massage or stretching will quickly dissipate these trigger points, but for people who work at a computer for a living, these painful spots turn up more frequently with each workday and last longer, even when the individual is no longer in front of the computer. Eventually these trigger points become permanent, and can even become debilitating.

Why is it so difficult for us to hold our head at an incline for any length of time? Our system of muscles have developed in such a way that only as many muscle fibers as needed for the job at hand are employed. For small tasks, that means only a few muscle fibers are put to work.

If you were to use the entirety of a single muscle, for example your bicep, for small tasks, not only would it be a waste of energy, it would result in exaggerated movements that more than likely would result in disaster. Say you want to pick up a small glass of water to drink, but instead of using just enough strength to lift it, you use all the strength in your bicep. More than likely, the water would go flying all over the place. Using a limited number of muscle fibers presents a problem only when the task involved is repetitive or goes on for an extended period of time. No matter how tired those few muscle fibers get, no other muscles are going to step in to help the exhausted ones. For this reason, the act of these few muscle fibers taking on a fatiguing task has been compared to Cinderella's daily toil,[28] because she was always the first one up in the morning to start a job, the last one to get to bed, and no matter how tired she was, none of her sisters ever offered any help!

Two Typical Cases: Myofascial Pain after Surgery and Linked to Osteoarthritis

Case 1

Many of the dogs I see with myofascial pain have had surgery but never really have recovered to the satisfaction of either the owner or the surgeon. The following case is typical.

Becky was a nine-year-old West Highland White Terrier who was an American Kennel Club Earthdog. (Earthdog events are designed by organizations such as the American Kennel Club to test a dog's ability to run through underground tunnels in search of rodents.) She had undergone surgery for a ruptured cranial cruciate ligament in her knee, and, although the operation had been a complete success, as time went on it became increasingly difficult for her to walk, let alone resume her Earthdog career. When I examined Becky, I found she had very painful and contracted bands of muscles in the front of her thigh and in a muscle in her abdomen called the iliopsoas. These muscles have a combined responsibility for flexing the hind leg, something Becky was continuously doing following the surgery in an effort to take some weight off the leg and knee. It was a subtle action and neither the owner nor the veterinarian who referred the case to me had noticed it. Even this slight contraction over the five weeks following her surgery was enough to induce myofascial pain that continued long after the surgical site had healed. In other words, because of post-operative pain she kept weight off her leg by keeping the muscles slightly contracted, and this allowed trigger points to develop. The surgery site had healed, but the trigger points had come to stay and were now the primary source of pain. After only a single treatment for her myofascial pain, there was a noticeable improvement. With a series of treatments, Becky was walking normally once again and able to return to her Earthdog events.

Case 2

Myofascial pain caused by arthritis is another common problem I see in my practice. This case involves my own dog, Joy.

Joy was a three-year-old Portuguese Water Dog with hip dysplasia. I kept close tabs on her condition as the disease and accompanying osteoarthritis progressed. I used acupuncture, a nonsteroidal anti-inflammatory drug, PSAG injections (a drug that helps increase the amount and function of joint fluid), and rehabilitation exercises to keep her leg and core muscles strengthened. For a while she was able to get around and to perform most activities that a dog without her hip problem might be expected to handle. After a year or so, it became obvious that these treatments were no longer working; she was having difficulty jumping into the car, and her enthusiasm for play and walks had declined. I reexamined her and found that she had developed myofascial pain not only in the muscles of her rear legs, but also in the triceps and infraspinatus muscles of the front legs, all of which I discovered by careful palpation. She had been increasing the weight on her front end in an effort to remove some of the weight from her painful hips, as dogs with hip dysplasia often do. Treatment of her myofascial pain in both areas allowed her to return to a more normal weight-bearing pattern.

In both of these cases, although the dogs had received the proper treatment for their diseases, the development of trigger points in their muscles was not a surprise. Myofascial pain is a common secondary issue. No matter how well the original pain is managed (for some causes, such as osteoarthritis, cruciate injury, and so forth), no treatment alleviates 100 percent of that underlying pain. As the dogs' bodies compensated for this unresolved underlying pain, their muscles soon became affected. For both Becky and Joy, the subsequent myofascial pain became more painful than the conditions that had originally caused it.

Treating Myofascial Pain

Although myofascial pain syndrome can be quite painful, it is easily treated. In humans, there are numerous options for treating myofascial pain, including massage, stretching, physical therapy, injections, and dry needling. In dogs, dry needling is the preferred method of treatment. Knowing proper massage technique also can be helpful in dogs, but the results are not as quick or satisfying as dry needling.

Dry needling uses an acupuncture needle, but it is not acupuncture because the needle is not actually placed in an acupuncture point. (While some acupuncture points are found in muscles, the vast majority of points are associated with nerves and blood vessels.) Rather, the acupuncture needle is placed directly into the painful trigger point within the muscle. This action results in a complex cascade of events that affect the muscles. These events include some signaling from the spinal cord to the muscle, increased blood flow to the treated area, and an increase in energy in the form of adenosine triphosphate (ATP, the basic energy molecule in all living things). These events cause the trigger point to relax. When the trigger point relaxes, the pain relief is immediate.[29]

Multiple sessions are usually required to provide complete relief. But most important, as mentioned previously, unless the underlying cause of the myofascial pain can be located and fully treated, the pain eventually returns and will necessitate additional treatments, especially in the case of chronic conditions like osteoarthritis. It is not unusual for dogs to return to me from time to time over a period of years so that I can treat their myofascial pain as it creeps back into their muscles.

The Benefits of Myofascial Pain

Myofascial pain syndrome, although painful and at times infuriating, has one benefit to the practitioner trained in its detection and treatment: Trigger points are much more easily detected than most of the underlying conditions that cause the trigger points to form in the first place. This is because while dogs will not always react to an examination of their joints, even joints with a significant amount of pathology, it's the rare dog that can "grit his teeth" and pretend everything is okay when a trigger point is palpated. Even the most stoic of dogs will vocalize, attempt to get away, or even try to bite. This can alert the veterinarian to an underlying condition, such as arthritis. Furthermore, depending on the pattern of painful trigger points, the astute veterinarian often can get a good idea as to which limb or body part is affected by that condition. For your dog, this means an earlier path to diagnosis and treatment. The earlier a treatment is instituted, the slower the development of pathologies, like osteoarthritis, which leads to an overall improved quality of life for the dog.

Myofascial pain syndrome can have another significant benefit: Trigger points can often point to conditions other than the musculoskeletal problems. One of the most common conditions is an intestinal condition called irritable bowel syndrome. Dogs suffering from this disorder, which can be confused with occasional diarrhea from other causes, sometimes present themselves with a generalized pattern of trigger points. Careful history can link these two syndromes with each other.

In the past, finding a veterinarian who could understand and treat myofascial pain syndrome had been frustrating at best. Thankfully, times have changed. Today, with the recent increase in veterinary pain management, as well as a growth of interest in many of these pain syndromes, it has become much easier to find a veterinarian who possesses the necessary understanding and skills to treat this condition with the attention it deserves.

8

ITCHING
AND PAIN

THIS BOOK IS ABOUT PAIN, AND IN THIS CHAPTER WE will examine the pain that results from chronic and untreated itching. Most of us might not immediately think of an itch as a painful event . . . until we get an itch that we can't scratch. Recent research has shown that itch receptors use the same pathways as pain signals do. For this reason I am going to discuss the itching sensation and explain how unresolved causes of scratching by your dog can lead to serious and painful pathology. I will also discuss those medications most useful in controlling the itch sensation and thereby preventing some of the skin pathology that follows. Having areas of chronically inflamed and damaged skin is one more layer of pain that can cause a dog that already has other pain issues, such as osteoarthritis (OA), to be even more miserable.

Although itch and pain are not the same thing, they certainly have some similarities. On an anatomical level, they both have some overlap in the same neural pathways through something called the spinothalamic[30] tract. This overlap extends to the brain, involving both the itch centers and pain centers.[31] Another similarity is that both itch and pain have a protective function. In the case of itch, for example, if a flea is biting your dog, it causes an immediate itch. He reacts to that bite by scratching at it to dislodge the flea. In the case of pain, if he steps on a sharp object, he reacts to that sharp object by withdrawal of his foot to stop further damage. Both of these reflex actions are meant to keep him from harm.

There are some differences between itch and pain as well. One of the big differences between an itch and pain is your dog's reaction to it. In the case of an acute itch, the first thing he wants to do is scratch it. By contrast, in the case of acute pain, the last thing he wants to do is touch it.

In other words, his desire to interact with the itch and to avoid the pain tells us that there is something fundamentally different between itch and pain. Most obvious, one stimulus (itch) causes an interaction with the affected spot (scratch); whereas the other stimulus (pain) causes avoidance (withdrawal) of the affected spot. A curious difference is that if you have pain and itch in the same region, the pain can inhibit the itch, but itching does not inhibit pain. More curious still are the perplexing effects of opioids. An injection of morphine will dampen pain, but can actually cause a dog to itch.

Itch as the Source of Chronic Pain

I am not so interested in discussing itch as a reaction to a single itch-inducing episode, such as a fleabite. Itch as a result of something like a fleabite is short lived and poses no long-term consequence to your dog's health. Of greater concern is chronic itch, or something called atopy. Along with atopy, flea allergy dermatitis and food allergies are the most common cause of itch in dogs. Allergic reactions to pollen and mold are also causes of itching. In humans, allergies often result in typical "hay fever" signs such as sneezing, runny nose, and red, itchy eyes. In dogs, allergies most commonly result in something called pruritus, the medical term for itchy skin. As I mentioned previously, itch is not pain, but chronic itch can cause changes in the skin that lead to skin damage and inflammation. And inflammation is painful.

Atopy is widespread in dogs. As many as 10–15 percent of all dogs[32] suffer from atopy. This translates to more than 8 million dogs in the United States alone that suffer from itch secondary to allergy and receive medication for it. (This number does not include dogs that have not been seen or treated by a veterinarian.) Left unchecked, atopy can cause painful inflammation, painful cuts and abrasions to the skin from self-trauma, and painful secondary bacterial and yeast infections of the skin. I find the disease to be very frustrating to treat. Many of the treated dogs respond poorly to therapy, although with the advent of newer therapies, there are better options available for veterinarians to treat their itchy patients.

It is beyond the scope of this chapter to discuss the complex (and often costly) process that is necessary to make a diagnosis of the specific cause of atopy. Instead I will discuss treatments that are known to help the itchy patient.

Therapies Known to Help the Itchy Patient

Diagnosing atopy is an easy enough task. Diagnosing the cause of atopy is difficult and often expensive. If your dog is atopic, and it is a constant problem, it is certainly worth pursuing the cause of the atopy. If your dog is atopic and it only happens one or two months out of the year, then it becomes more of a personal choice: diagnose the cause or just treat the symptoms. In the case of short-term atopy, treating the symptoms with medication is preferred by many of my clients. I can't disagree with this decision.

The best way to treat atopy is to know what is causing it and either eliminate or avoid the offending substance. A small percentage of dogs with atopy are allergic to certain proteins found in their food. Discovering that your dog is allergic to something like beef or chicken allows you to remove that source of protein from their diet and feed them an alternative source of protein. However, if your dog is allergic to something like ragweed, then avoidance is impossible and it becomes necessary to treat your dog medically.

Pharmaceutical Interventions

For many caregivers, it makes more sense to treat the itch instead of discovering its source. Avoidance of an allergen is not always practical. As you will read later in this chapter, immunotherapy is expensive and not always successful. And very often, allergies are seasonal, making a pharmaceutical intervention less costly and more convenient. The following are a list of the most common medications used to treat dogs with an itch.

Antihistamines

There are many antihistamines on the market, and probably all of them have been used for the treatment of atopy in dogs. They work by doing what their name implies: stopping the release of histamines, one of several substances that cause itching in dogs. The advantage of antihistamines is that they are very safe and have few side effects, with drowsiness being the primary problem. The effectiveness of antihistamines in treating allergies seems to be hit-or-miss in many dogs. One mistake many veterinarians make is they only try them for a short period of time before giving up. It often takes several weeks of therapy of antihistamines before the level of histamines in your dog have been reduced. The other problem is that there are other substances besides histamines in your dog that may cause itching. As such, to help control itching it is common that antihistamines are given alongside other medications, such as corticosteroids. Dosing of antihistamines vary from type to type, but require at least daily dosing to be effective.

Apoquel

The drug oclacitinib, marketed by Zoetis under the brand name Apoquel, is the newest and probably the most effective drug on the market for the treatment of itch. It is the first drug of its kind, treating itch by the inhibition of something called the Janus kinase receptor. It is given once a day and successfully stops or slows the itch response in the vast majority of dogs that take it. It has no annoying side effects and can be given with most other medications, which is good because some itchy dogs require medications for other conditions. It is safe for chronic, long-term use in dogs. Since Apoquel was released for distribution in early 2014, it is the first pharmaceutical I reach for to treat dogs that itch.

Canine Atopic Dermatitis Immunotherapeutic

This is another product by Zoetis, which has obtained conditional licensing (which in this case means it is only being used by specialists at this point) and will probably be released to your general practitioner sometime in 2016. It is a first-of-its-kind antibody therapy that targets and neutralizes a key protein that is responsible for sending the itch signal to the brain. It is given as a once-monthly injection.

Capsaicin

As you might recall from Chapter 6, the topical application of capsaicin can help control pain. In the dog in which there might be localized areas of itch, capsaicin can be quite effective in controlling that itch.[33] Some dogs experience a worsening of the itch in the first week or so of therapy, but that is almost always followed by a decrease in the itch.

Corticosteroids

Corticosteroids, most commonly prednisone or prednisolone, have long been the mainstay for the treatment of atopy in dogs. Corticosteroids work by reducing the pain and inflammation associated with allergies. Until Apoquel came along, it was considered the first line of treatment against itch. Corticosteroids can be given by injection, orally, or as a topical application. Given topically, there are few side effects. Corticosteroids given by injection or orally come with some annoying side effects including increased thirst and appetite. It can also cause or exacerbate many conditions including liver, kidney, adrenal, and heart disease, meaning that corticosteroids always need to be used with caution. Regular blood monitoring is a must when corticosteroids are given by injection or orally.

Cyclosporine

Cyclosporine is marketed under the brand name Atopica and treats itching in dogs by suppressing immune cells, including those that play a role in allergies. It is initially given every day, but it has the advantage of a decreasing dosing regimen as the allergies get under control. When given to dogs, the side effects of Atopica are primarily gastrointestinal in nature, including vomiting, diarrhea, and loss of appetite. In some dogs, these side effects are temporary and decrease with adjustments in dose or sometimes just over time.

NMDA Antagonists

This class of drugs, described in Chapter 6, seems to have some effect on the chronic itch of atopy. The only drug from this class that has been looked at for its anti-itch properties is dextromethorphan. This drug is commonly used in cough medications, but it also has some NMDA activity as well. One study showed that twice-a-day dosing can help control the itch of atopy in dogs.[34]

Immunotherapy

Immunotherapy can be the best treatment for dogs with allergies. It is also the costliest treatment and generally is given for the life of the dog. Immunotherapy is what most people think of as "allergy shots" wherein a very dilute amount of the substances that cause an allergy are injected into the dog. There are several theories as to why injecting the very thing a dog is allergic to into that dog should work, but no one theory has been proven.

Before a dog can start immunotherapy, it must first be determined what he is allergic to. This starts with one of two allergy tests, either a skin test or a blood test. Positive results from that test determine what substances are going into the allergy injection. Obviously, not all possible allergens can be tested for, so some important allergens might be missed. Another problem can be that even if all of the allergens are discovered, some dogs just don't respond to the treatment. Side effects of this treatment are usually minimal and most commonly consist of an increase in the level of itching right after the injection. Reducing the amount of anti-gen in the next scheduled dose can minimize this side effect.

Other Therapies

Acupuncture has been shown to be useful in helping control a dog's itch. In my experience it seems to work best in acute flare-ups. I have treated outbreaks of hives in dogs (and in my own horse) using this method and have seen the hives disappear within minutes of treatment. In cases of chronic atopy, acupuncture usually does not work as a single stand-alone treatment. It is best to use it in addition to more conventional treatments.

Hardy kiwi is a vine that has been shown to reduce the itching associ-ated with atopy in dogs. It probably works by reducing the levels of both IgE and interleukin-4, substances that play a role in the itch response to allergens. In one trial, it showed a reduction in the itching score of 54 percent of the atopic dogs that took hardy kiwi.[35] Treatment with this plant appears to cause no side effects.

Oatmeal and aloe vera preparations are very commonly used in sham-poos to help relieve itching in dogs. Together, they have anti-inflammatory properties, and the aloe portion of the shampoo deposits a polysaccha-ride layer on the skin, which is both protective and soothing. Alone, these preparations are not considered sufficient to treat atopy in dogs. How-ever, they do provide an additional method of relief, and as they have no reported side effects or drug interactions, they can be used with any other therapy for itching. Probably the worst thing about these products is that in order to be effective, you would need to bathe your dog daily or every other day.

9

ACUPUNCTURE— WHAT'S THE POINT?

ACUPUNCTURE WAS ONCE OPEN TO RIDICULE, VIEWED as being on the fringe of medicine at best. In the past decade this changed, as the neurophysiology behind acupuncture became not only a subject for discussion but proven in medical studies. For example, there is emerging evidence that treatment of disk issues in the back using acupuncture on dogs instead of surgery has outcomes that are similar to surgical treatment. Similarly, when combined with rehabilitation for the treatment of a knee injury called a ruptured cruciate ligament, successful outcomes can be similar to surgical repair.[36] I have seen this outcome in my own practice.

Despite these truths, acupuncture is still a poorly understood treatment option among veterinarians, let alone dog owners. Here I will explain the acupuncture process, the science and realities behind it, and the reasons why it is very successful in the treatment of pain.

A Brief History of Acupuncture

When I talk about acupuncture, it conjures up images in many people's minds of an ancient Chinese art that remains the same today as it was when it first made its appearance some 3,000 years ago. It's worth noting that Western medicine had its origins several thousand years ago as well, yet no one thinks that it has remained unchanged. Just as most of us would not want to be treated by a physician from 3,000 years ago (or for that matter even 100 years ago), the same is true with acupuncture.

Originally started as a bloodletting technique, acupuncture has constantly evolved through the years. And it was not just the Chinese who developed acupuncture; many regions in Asia including Japan, Korea, Vietnam, and India have their own forms of acupuncture. However, as Chinese acupuncture, practiced in Traditional Chinese Medicine, is the most common form of Eastern acupuncture practiced in this country, its practice and concepts are what I will refer to in this chapter.

Unfortunately for acupuncture, in 1822, in an effort to "modernize" China and make it more like a powerful Western country, the Qing Dynasty emperor sent down an edict prohibiting the teaching of acupuncture at the Imperial Medical College. By the beginning of World War I acupuncture had reached a point of near cultural extinction. But with the advent of World War II, there was a disruption of society and the incidence of disease increased beyond the ability of China's physicians to treat everyone. To overcome the crisis, laypeople, mostly farmers, were trained by the government in rudimentary diagnostic skills that included tongue and pulse diagnoses. Observations of things like the color of the tongue and the character of the pulse was purported to give these laypeople, called barefoot doctors (because most of them were farmers who worked barefoot), a diagnosis so that they could then choose the proper acupuncture points and treat their patients.

After the war, as communist China pushed away many Western ideas, acupuncture was embraced even more tightly. Regrettably, this meant it often continued in the tradition of the barefoot doctors, with their limited medical skills and dubious diagnostic practices.

Modern Day Acupuncture

Western acupuncture had a rocky start. People unfamiliar with Eastern culture tried their best to adopt this foreign concept of medical treatment, learning what they could in a language in which they were not always fluent. In turn, one of the central concepts of Western acupuncture was based on a misinterpretation of something called *qi*. In Western acupuncture, *qi* is said to be an energy (but *qi* is actually the Chinese word meaning air or wind) that flows through imaginary channels in the body called meridians. Both *qi* and meridians are a central part of Traditional Chinese Medicine, to which Chinese acupuncture belongs, and both are considered by many veterinary practitioners and researchers to be mostly pseudoscience.[37]

Even worse is this belief system as it is applied to dogs. Although acupuncture in animals has evolved side-by-side with its developments in people, any science behind Traditional Chinese Medicine has been diluted even further as concepts developed for people have been transposed onto animals.

Although there is a lot of pseudoscience and folklore behind Chinese acupuncture, it remains popular among people who are not happy with Western medicine. With its colorful metaphors and diagnostic tests that seem almost mystical, I can see the attraction of this simplistic approach to health for those people who have had Western medicine fail them. And although many practitioners of Chinese acupuncture indeed practice this pseudoscience, there are nonetheless some fundamental truths about the power of an acupuncture needle placed in a living thing.

Medical Acupuncture

The development of medical acupuncture has come about from the efforts of individuals who have worked to explore the observed benefits of acupuncture from Traditional Chinese Medicine. Many of the proponents of medical acupuncture simply felt that the time had come to move beyond the ancient metaphors and elevate acupuncture into the realm of evidence-based modern medicine. This movement started on the human side but has spread to the veterinary side of acupuncture as well. The study of the neurophysiology behind acupuncture points has shed light on many of the physiological mechanisms that are involved in an acupuncture treatment and has brought acupuncture into the 21st century.

My ability to practice medical acupuncture absolutely depends on obtaining a Western diagnosis. Gait analysis, X-ray films, and even MRIs are all important in finding the exact cause of the problem. Without a diagnosis, I would only be able to guess at where the problem is and might miss it altogether. This sometimes becomes an issue for dog caretakers who come to me from a Traditional Chinese Medicine practitioner—they often don't understand why I can't just look at the dog's tongue and take a pulse.

With the advent of medical acupuncture, its importance as a therapy to use either alone or alongside conventional medicine has increased. It has risen from a position of ridicule to one of respect by those veterinarians who understand it. The American Animal Hospital Association in its 2015 pain guidelines has declared acupuncture an effective treatment for pain, stating that there is enough evidence to use as a stand-alone treatment if necessary.[38]

How Does Acupuncture Work?

I am asked this question by almost every caregiver when I bring up acupuncture as a possible treatment for their dog. Although I love acupuncture, I don't like this question because there is not enough time during a consultation for me to provide an adequate answer. A book, however, imposes no such limit. And so I will describe here, in as simple terms as possible, how acupuncture works.

What Are Acupuncture Points?

In Traditional Chinese Medicine, the objective of acupuncture is to affect the flow of *qi* through meridians. As I inferred earlier, no one has ever seen, measured, or put *qi* in a bottle. *Qi* doesn't exist. Meridians have never been dissected out of a body, nor have some of the mythical organs that they serve, such as one called the Triple Heater. And yet, manipulating most (but not all) of the points used in Traditional Chinese Acupuncture seems to deliver the desired effect. But why? Enter medical acupuncture, which has moved our understanding beyond *qi* and meridians in an effort to answer the questions of what constitutes an acupuncture point and why it works.

Very simply, acupuncture points are located in one or more of ten different types of locations that have specific physical characteristics. The one common element among all of the described points in each of these locations involves a nerve. What follows is a description of those locations. What truly amazes me is that most of these acupuncture points were discovered thousands of years ago by people who did not have the benefit of knowing neuroanatomy.

1. **Where nerves penetrate fascia.** There are sheets of connective tissue in our body called fascia. Fascia was long thought to have the sole function of acting like plastic food wrap: It kept things together and tight. More is being discovered about fascia, and it looks like it plays a role in other body functions as well, including roles in inflammation and neurology, which is why this is an important set of points. (I will discuss the interaction between acupuncture needles and the connective tissue of fascia a little later.)

2. **Where nerves are in close proximity to blood vessels.** Because acupuncture started as a bloodletting technique it was probably discovered at some point along the way that the desired effect happened with or without bleeding. The effects came about because these first acupuncturists were inadvertently treating the nerves that accompany blood vessels.

3. **Where nerves enter or exit a muscle.** These acupuncture points have an effect on both the nerve and the muscle itself.

4. **Nerve trunks.** These are the major nerves, such as the sciatic nerve, that serve large areas of anatomy.

5. **Superficial nerves.** This is where most acupuncture points are. Why? Because they are accessible from the surface of the skin by an acupuncture needle.

6. **Emergence of nerves through cranial foramina.** Your dog has many small holes in her skull; these openings transmit nerves from the brain to structures in the head. The nerves serve several functions, including sending sensations to the brain and motor impulses to muscles of the head, neck, and beyond.

7. **Mixed nerves.** Wherever there is a mixture of different types of nerve fibers, such as motor, sensory, and sympathetic (a nerve responsible for functions we don't have to think about, such as organ function). Acupuncture takes advantage of this rich collection of nerves that are all in one spot.

8. **Sites of nerve bifurcation.** This occurs, for example, in your dog's distal extremities where nerves "split" to run along his toes.

9. **Around joints.** These areas of dense connective tissue contain many nerves.

10. **Cranial sutures.** Cranial sutures are the area of your dog's skull where the different growth plates join together. If you ever have looked at a skull model, you will have undoubtedly noticed these suture lines. They make the skull look like it was actually stitched together. Cranial sutures appear to be quite solid, but despite the solid-looking appearance, nerves pass through them.

What happens when a needle is inserted into one of these ten acupuncture locations? Depending on the location of that particular needle, it can have an effect that includes part or all of the following outcomes.

1. **An interaction with connective tissue.** This is one of the most important effects an acupuncture needle has. When an acupuncture needle is properly placed, it isn't just stuck through the skin. Once it is in place, the needle is wound in circles until a slight grab by the tissue is felt. In Traditional Chinese Medicine this is called *da qi* and was thought to be the evidence for manipulating the body's energy with the needle. Medical acupuncture research has shown that what actually happens is that as the acupuncture needle is twirled, it starts to pick up and wind up collagen fibers that are within the connective tissue. (Think of putting a fork in a plate of spaghetti and twirling it.) Winding up these fibers on a microscopic level distorts the fibers and, as you might imagine, causes areas of "micro" trauma. This trauma causes the body to release inflammatory substances and to stimulate the nerves in the region. The body reacts by sending in anti-inflammatories, and the brain reacts by sending down signals that dampen pain in the area. In essence, an acupuncture needle directs your dog to heal herself. It does so by directing her body's attention, as it were, to an area that needs some healing.

2. **Neuromodulation.** The effect of acupuncture on the brain has been seen through the use of something called functional magnetic resonance imaging, or fMRI. An fMRI uses magnets to look at the function of internal organs in real time. It is more of a movie as compared to regular MRI, which is more like a photograph. The use of fMRI technology has been shown that the placement of acupuncture needles causes modulation in the pain centers of the brain.

3. **Effects on muscle tissue.** Muscles might be painful for a variety of reasons, be it trauma or referred pain from visceral organs or joints. Referred pain is a condition in which one

part of the body is actually the affected area, but through a complexity of nerve interactions, causes pain in other regions of the body. You may have known someone who has had gall-bladder pain, but feels pain in one of the muscles in the back. Or maybe you have heard of people having a heart attack but feeling a sharp pain in their left arms. Both are instances of referred pain. They can happen with any organ or joint. Treatment of muscles where nerves enter or exit them can treat this type of referred pain.

4. **Effects on the immune system.** Insertion of an acupuncture needle causes the release of inflammatory agents, as already described. These inflammatory agents in turn send signals through the sensory nerves to the brain. The brain sees this in part as an attack on the immune system and reacts by sending signals through the neuroimmune system to control the inflammation.

5. **Effects from the hypothalamic-pituitary-adrenal (HPA) axis.** This is probably one of the most complex reactions. It involves two brain structures (the hypothalamus and pituitary gland) and an abdominal organ (the adrenal gland). The HPA axis is stimulated by some of the mechanisms already described. It results in the modulation of pain signals by several different methods: the release of chemicals, modulation of several nerve pathways, and by sending down signals to inhibit the pain.

I warned you that this would be a complex answer to a simple question. As your dog's caretaker, you don't have to remember any of the specific answers to the question, How does acupuncture work? You merely need to understand that the practice of acupuncture is now known to bring about scientifically complex reactions that help treat your dog's pain.

Common Acupuncture Treatments

I use acupuncture in my medical practice to treat a range of conditions that include intestinal, cardiac, and reproductive issues. But for the purposes of this book I am going to focus on its use for the treatment of pain and neurological problems.

Osteoarthritis

When it comes to treating pain, osteoarthritis is my primary reason for turning to acupuncture. Nerves and connective tissue surround your dog's joints, and most of them are close to the surface of the body. Acupuncture treatments can take advantage of this location—needles can be placed in the vicinity of the problem joint. Any joint with osteoarthritis can benefit from acupuncture, but what follows is a description of the most commonly treated joints.

Osteoarthritis in the knees and hips are two of the more common regions that I treat. In the dog, these two joints probably suffer the most from genetic, traumatic, or developmental disease as compared to anywhere else in the body. Needle placement is relatively easy and well tolerated by most dogs, and this probably contributes to the high degree of success I get when treating these joints with acupuncture.

Osteoarthritis of the back, usually referred to as spondylosis, is another common area that needs treatment. Some veterinarians think of the implications of this type of spinal arthritis as more of a mobility issue than a pain issue (spondylosis "fuses" adjacent vertebrae and makes the spine more rigid). This is absolutely true. When I see a dog with a significant degree of spondylosis making a turn, it reminds me of a long bus trying to make a tight turn at a street corner. But the implications of spinal arthritis extend beyond mobility issues. The arthritis occurs at the point where nerves are emerging from the spinal column. The nerves, because of their close proximity to the osteoarthritis, get caught up in the inflammatory process and they themselves become inflamed. Thankfully, needle placement in these areas is also straightforward.

With the insistence by many dog breeders to have a dog's dewclaws removed, I see many issues of arthritis in the carpus or "wrist" of a dog. In both this area and in elbow arthritis, the acupuncture points are easy to find and needle placement is easily done. However, compared to putting needles along the back or in the rear legs, needle placement in the elbow and paw is in the line of a dog's vision. Their temptation to pull out the needles (and sometimes try to eat them) can be quite strong. It takes both the vigilance of the person sitting with your dog (and that might be you) and distractions in the form of treats to keep those needles in place.

Intervertebral Disk Disease (IVDD)

IVDD, sometimes called a slipped disk, is a condition wherein one of the intervertebral disks that serves as a cushioning pad between each of the vertebrae has ruptured. This rupture causes injury and inflammation to the spinal cord. This problem may occur as a result of trauma, but more often than not it results from a genetic disposition or is a secondary effect of the aging process. IVDD can cause pain that ranges from mild to severe, and neurological issues can range from barely noticeable to complete paralysis. In essence, the dog receives a double whammy of medical conditions in the form of both pain and nerve dysfunction.

The classic treatment for IVDD is some type of decompression surgery (the goal of this surgery is to relieve the pressure of the extruded disk material by making an opening that allows the disk material to go somewhere besides the spinal canal), followed by corticosteroids and cage rest. With the advent of medical acupuncture there is now another, less invasive, treatment option that has a similar chance at success. It is not uncommon for a dog to come to me with complete paralysis of the hind legs, start acupuncture, and be walking with assistance in one week or so. And we no longer cage rest these guys. The more they try to use the limb, the more quickly the nerve recovers.

Acupuncture works because it helps wake up these damaged nerves. Needles are placed in the region of the injury and also in points that are distal or "downstream" from the injury. These distal nerves are not damaged by the spinal trauma; they still receive input from their nerve endings but no longer receive descending input from the brain. In other words, the signals from both directions are unable to get past the site of injury. Stimulation of both the distal nerve and the nerves around the site of injury by acupuncture helps "remind" the nerves within the spinal cord that they have a job to do.

Not every acupuncture treatment works for every case. However, in the case of IVDD, as long as the owner has the time, money, and patience, only a rare patient needs to go to surgery because of unsuccessful acupuncture treatment.

Fibrocartilagenous Embolism (FCE)

FCE is another spinal issue, but in this case it is entirely neurological. An FCE usually accompanies some incident of trauma, often seemingly minor in nature. Rarely is there any more than the most transient of pain. It may hurt at that moment, but usually stops hurting shortly after. During an FCE event, an embolism is formed and blocks one of the blood vessels supplying a part of the spinal cord. This event means that areas of the spinal cord become anoxic, or deprived of oxygen. At the very least there is some damage and dysfunction, at its worst an area of the spinal cord dies off.

The signs are similar to that of IVDD, and based on signs alone making a diagnosis of FCE is somewhat of an educated guess. The lack of back pain usually makes me think "FCE," although without an MRI it is impossible to make an absolute diagnosis.

The treatment of FCE is similar to that of IVDD. Needles are placed in the region of the damage and at points distal to that. Recovery times can be similar to cases of IVDD, although severe cases may take longer.

Back Pain

Just like humans who suffer back pain, I see many dogs that have back pain but do not have any apparent OA or history of injury. Nonetheless, an injury or a muscle strain is probably at the root of this pain. These backs can be in quite a lot of pain when touched, and sometimes in almost too much pain for me to insert an acupuncture needle. If the dog is in enough pain, I will sometimes give an injection of a painkiller just to get in the first set of needles. Most of these dogs respond remarkably well to acupuncture treatment and seldom need that injection for the second treatment.

Tendon Injuries

Tendon injuries are not very common, but when they happen, they are often quite painful and recovery can take a very long time, if ever. Anyone who has tennis elbow can attest to the frustrating nature of this issue. Rest and pain medications help, almost to the point where it seems there has been a complete recovery. But using the limb can again cause an acute flare-up, setting you back to where you started. I see this happen in dogs as well, especially in injuries to the biceps tendon, which is located at the shoulder.

My treatment of tendon injuries with acupuncture relies on many of the processes by which acupuncture works. I place needles at the site of inflammation and at those areas of the spine that send and receive nerves from that tendon. Treatment often needs to be repeated off and on for the life of the dog.

How Often Does My Dog Need Acupuncture?

I remember hearing a veterinarian complain, "The problem with treating pain with acupuncture is that it has to go on forever." Of course he was discussing chronic pain conditions like osteoarthritis. I am not sure why occasional acupuncture sessions are seen as such a burden. And I certainly don't know of any cases of chronic pain, such as osteoarthritis, that is cured with a week or two of pills. When it comes to cost, although acupuncture can be costly up front with its more frequent treatments, in the long term it is much less costly than most medications and the laboratory testing necessary for monitoring those medications.

When I set up a schedule of appointments for acupuncture, it is based on both the condition and the severity of the condition I am trying to treat. If a dog comes to me paralyzed, then he is in serious condition and I may be performing acupuncture alongside other treatments. These treatments may happen as often as every one or two days and could go on for weeks or months. On the other end of the spectrum is a dog with hip dysplasia and some early osteoarthritis changes. I generally treat these dogs once a week until I see progress, usually within three weeks. And then depending on how well he is doing, I increase the interval of time between treatments. Most of these dogs can be treated once every month or two to control their pain.

The Case of the Mysterious Shifting Pain

Barney was a neutered middle-age dog that came to me after seeing about eight different veterinarians. He even had gone to a veterinary teaching hospital and had taken a trip to see a neurologist in private practice. He had been limping for almost a year on one of his back legs and also was having other vague signs of pain in his back end. My examination revealed a partial tear in one of his cruciate ligaments, a ligament in his knee. I also discovered the start of a painful and debilitating disease of the spinal cord called cauda equina syndrome. I did my first acupuncture treatment on Barney that day. When the owners returned the next week for the second treatment they told me, "In a half-hour of treatment, you were able to make our dog feel better than what a dozen other visits and thousands of dollars were able to." That is the power of acupuncture.

Of course, not all animals respond to acupuncture like Barney did, just as they might not respond to a particular medication or surgical procedure. And I rarely use acupuncture as the only treatment modality. Most of my acupuncture patients are also getting pain medications, perhaps some rehabilitation therapy, or maybe the addition of a joint-support diet.

Ruff and His Arthritis

Ruff was a Labrador Retriever that had been successfully treated with carprofen (Rimadyl) for several years to control the pain of the osteoarthritis in his knees. As he aged, Ruff slowly lost some kidney function, making it necessary to discontinue carprofen so as to avoid possible complications. I put Ruff on a variety of other pharmaceuticals in an effort to control his pain, but he continued to decline. At that time in my career I only recently had become certified in acupuncture, and so I offered acupuncture in addition to the medications we were already giving Ruff. Had Ruff come to me at this point in my career, acupuncture would have been part of my initial treatment plan. The caregiver consented to give it a try and after the second treatment called with the "complaint" that "Ruff was taking off out the back door like a rocket!" I continued to treat Ruff's arthritis successfully for another year until he succumbed to a different age-related illness.

Not all dogs respond to acupuncture treatment like Ruff did. Sometimes the treatment needs to be adjusted, adding other medications or rehab. And all dogs eventually reach a point where no amount of treatment makes them comfortable. But many dogs, like the two examples above, only make it to their advanced ages because acupuncture was a part of their therapy.

Acupuncture in Conjunction with Other Therapies

Acupuncture can control pain on many levels, from the origin of the pain all the way up to the brain. But the response to acupuncture is not always sufficient, especially in the more advanced pain states. In those cases in which I cannot adequately control the pain, I consider the addition of pharmaceuticals, rehabilitation therapy, and massage.

There is only one class of drugs with which acupuncture is incompatible: the local anesthetics. Acupuncture relies on the transmission of nerve signals, and any use of local anesthetics completely blocks their conduction. All of the other drugs noted in Chapter 5 are suitable adjuncts to acupuncture for the control of pain. It even works on dogs that are under general anesthesia.

Massage is another useful tool in managing pain, and it also reduces stress in your dog. There are several different massages that can be employed, which are discussed in Chapter 20.

Acupuncture in the Clinical Setting

I will tell you how I like to approach acupuncture and the reasons behind it. This doesn't mean that my methods are the only way, as there are many variations for how a practitioner approaches and uses acupuncture. But I can say that the following procedures have worked for the majority of my patients.

Insertion of acupuncture needles requires the cooperation of the dog receiving them. Palpating the location of the desired acupuncture points, inserting the needles, and getting them to stay in place can only happen if a patient is relatively quiet and willing to sit still for the 15 minutes or so that the needles are left in place. There are many behaviors that can interfere with this. Some dogs are needle phobic, some are scared and trembling, some want to jump up at every little noise or distraction, and some dogs just can't sit still for two minutes, let alone 15 minutes. One of my most difficult patient types are the enthusiastic tail waggers; by the time I have put in my last needle, I need to go back to my first needles and reset the ones that have started working their way out as a result of the vigorous back and forth of the tail. I have discovered several methods for managing all of the patient types.

The environment of the acupuncture room is one of the most important tools I have to compensate for many of the above-mentioned problems. In my practice, I have a dedicated quiet room in which I do most of my acupuncture treatments. This room has a rubber floor that is comfortable for the dog (and people) to sit on. There is low incandescent lighting available that makes the room less clinical feeling. It contains a stereo from which soft music plays, not only to help calm the patient but to help block out background noises from the rest of the clinic. And the room is scented with lavender, a calming scent for dogs. Within a few minutes of the dog entering this special room, I can often see the dog (and owner) relax.

Keeping the dog quiet during and after the insertion of the needles also can be a challenge. For some dogs, my only choice is a mild sedative that takes the edge off either their anxiety or their restless behavior. I even have the occasional patients where it is necessary to sedate them to the point of twilight sleep, in which they are only slightly aware of their surroundings. However, for the vast majority of my patients, reassurance by their caretaker and my staff is all that is needed to get in the needles. A treat of Frosty Paws or peanut butter keeps them occupied while they sit for the needles to do their job. The atmosphere is so relaxing that there have been times I have come back into the room at the end of the session only to find the dog, his caregiver, or both snoozing.

At the end of the first acupuncture session that a dog ever receives, I discuss with the caregiver some potential consequences that can follow the treatment. Most commonly, dogs go home and take one look at the couch and decide that is the best spot to be. These dogs find the acupuncture very relaxing. This should be no surprise because some physiological expressions of acupuncture can provide a sense of general well-being and relaxation. The next most common result of acupuncture is muscle pain. This is most prevalent when a dog has myofascial pain syndrome (see Chapter 7) but can happen in any dog that receives acupuncture. This pain usually resolves within 36 hours. The final result is uncommon but happens as a result of stimulation of the sympathetic nervous system: Affected dogs go home and have one or two bouts of diarrhea. This isn't really a problem and doesn't mean, alongside the other two potential consequences of acupuncture, that your dog should not receive further acupuncture. It is really just something that caregivers should be aware of and ready to deal with should it occur.

Successful Acupuncture

Acupuncture isn't successful in every dog that receives it. Some conditions are poorly responsive to acupuncture. And some dogs are poorly responsive to acupuncture as well. About 10 percent of all dogs are considered "poor responders" and experience little or no benefit from the treatment.

However, this means 90 percent of the dogs can show good to excellent improvements after receiving acupuncture. For these dogs, the success rate is even better when the underlying problem is managed with other appropriate treatments such as rehabilitation therapy, massage, or pharmaceuticals.

Probably the biggest factor in successful acupuncture treatments is you, the caregiver. Regular communications between you and your veterinarian are essential for success.

In my practice, I want to hear how my patient is doing; and I want to be told when a treatment isn't working. I do not see negative feedback as some indictment of that treatment, but an opportunity to change things around and make it work. I also need to know how long the benefits of each treatment last so that appropriate treatment intervals can be set up. In other words, if I am treating once a month, but a dog starts limping after three weeks, then waiting that extra week does not allow the dog to receive the full benefit of the acupuncture. And finally, as with all pain treatments, I need the caregiver to feel like we are partnering in managing their dog's health.

10

PROSTHETICS? BUT MY DOG HAS THREE GOOD LEGS TO WALK ON!

IF YOU EVER HAVE WATCHED A DOG WITH THREE LEGS walk, then you know how awkward and uncomfortable it can be for them. What you probably do not see is what I, as a veterinarian, see: The huge toll it takes on their other legs and the rest of their body.

Within months of a leg amputation, a breakdown begins in both soft and boney structures of the remaining limbs, which leads to pain and reduced mobility in otherwise normal limbs. This all can be prevented with the addition of a prosthetic device for the missing limb, or sometimes with an orthotic device (essentially a brace to provide stability) to protect the remaining limbs. Using this device can also prevent injury to the remaining limb. If a dog loses its entire front leg, for example, he might put added stress on the remaining front leg as he hops forward with each step. Doing so places his full weight on the remaining leg, typically causing an overextension of the carpus (wrist). An orthotic can prevent injuries, such as carpal hyperextension, and can be used to help heal injuries such as tears of the cranial cruciate ligament in the knee.

The use of an animal prosthetic was almost unheard of just a decade ago. The then-common solution for animals that lost limbs, or that were born without a part of a leg, was either to euthanize them or to take off the damaged legs as far up as possible so that they wouldn't try to walk on the remaining stumps. And that was the end of the story. This has changed in the past few years. Stories and videos abound on broadcast news, Facebook, and seemingly everywhere else on the Internet. And it just isn't dogs. A dolphin gets a new tail, a turtle gets a wheel to replace his missing foot, and the list goes on. However, I will limit the discussion to prosthetic and orthotic options for dogs.

Prosthetics

Dogs lose limbs for a variety of reasons. I have seen leg injuries that were beyond repair and mandated an amputation. I have seen dogs that are born without a portion of their limbs. I also have seen dogs lose their limbs to disease, such as cancer. Whatever the reason, if there is enough leg left, these dogs can be given a prosthetic limb.

Injuries Secondary to Having Only Three Legs

Dogs that lose a limb and are forced to walk on their three remaining legs do manage to get around. But there is a price to pay. The abnormal body mechanics of moving with three legs cause them to put stresses on the rest of their body that are atypical. Injuries are the result. Joint breakdown is probably the most commonly seen issue in dogs with three legs. As previously mentioned, the hopping motion in a dog missing one front leg often causes a hyperextension of the carpus or wrist of the remaining leg. Hyperextension describes the extreme upward angle that the wrist goes through as the paw makes contact with the ground and carries the full weight of the dog. Every time the dog lands on the remaining front leg, the ligaments of the wrist act as unwilling shock absorbers. This stretches and breaks down the ligament fibers, resulting in that joint moving farther and farther into extension. Eventually it will reach a point where the wrist is no longer capable of supporting the dog's own weight.

Myofascial pain syndrome (Chapter 7) almost always develops in not only the remaining limbs but also in the trunk and neck muscles as they try to compensate for and normalize the abnormal gait. Muscles are held in low-level contractions for extended periods of time, or they are braced repeatedly to take some of the impact of an atypical movement. Over a surprisingly short period of time, this causes the development of myofascial pain, which results in not only additional pain, but even more restricted movements of the remaining limbs.

Joint disease and osteoarthritis can result from only having one limb as well. The force from abnormal impact causes both ligament damage and joint damage. This is further exacerbated if myofascial pain is present; the contractions of the affected muscles compress the joint spaces, which in turn causes abnormal wear and decreased function of the joints. This all leads to inflammation and osteoarthritis.

As if all these complications weren't enough, dogs with only three limbs just don't exercise enough. This can contribute to obesity, which only hastens the cycle of decay and problems noted here.

All of these changes start to occur with the first step your dog takes after an amputation. Weight, age, and overall health and fitness of your dog impacts how quickly these changes occur, but these secondary problems will eventually catch up with all three-legged dogs. This underscores the importance of getting your dog a prosthetic limb as soon as possible.

What Type of Prosthetics Can Be Made?

Prosthetics in dogs can replace part of a missing limb, provided there is enough of the limb remaining to receive the prosthetic. In the front leg, prosthetics are made for amputations at the elbow or lower. In the rear leg, prosthetics are made for amputations at the knee or lower. Any amputation higher than these points is biomechanically unstable, meaning that dogs will have difficulty getting around using a prosthetic. It doesn't mean that something can't be done, but the results are not as good as those amputations done closer to the end of the limb.

Paw Prosthetics

Paw prosthetics can be made for just a few missing toes or an entire foot. In the case of the dog that is missing just a toe or two, depending on the toes that are missing, it can become very difficult for him to get around. Additionally, the remaining toes are prone to the injuries described above because they have to handle the additional stresses brought on by having to do the job of the missing toe(s) as well as their own. Another problem I sometimes see in single toe amputations are pressure-type sores that can affect the remaining toes or the area of amputation where the toe was removed. These paw prosthetics are not complicated, yet they add greatly to a dog's quality of life because they enable him to run, dig, and otherwise do the things that other dogs can.

Forelimb Prosthetics

Any time there is damage below the elbow, it is common to amputate everything beyond the elbow by disarticulation (literally meaning to take the joint apart). This provides a smooth surface of bone that easily can be covered with a skin flap to provide an appropriate surface for weight bearing from the end of the limb through the prosthetic and to the ground.

Another type of prosthetic device called an intraosseous trans-cutaneous amputation prosthesis (ITAP) also can be used, although the amputation approach is slightly different. Instead of the prosthetic being fitted on the end of the limb by a cup and straps (as in the case of a disarticulation), an ITAP is attached to an implant that is put into the bone itself. An ITAP can be used anywhere that a bony anchor can be utilized. If, for example, an injury was just above the wrist joint, but it required that the end of the radius and ulna (the two bones that make up the foreleg) be cut, then a procedure to accommodate an ITAP would be an alternative to removing the forelimb at the elbow.

Rear Leg Prosthetics

In the rear leg, for injuries above the ankle that require amputation, the amputation occurs at the knee (unless, of course, an ITAP is to be used). The skin is brought as a flap over the end of the femur (thigh bone) and a prosthetic device is attached, usually with straps, and a receiving cup is set over the end of the amputated limb.

Training for Prosthetics

A dog with an amputation doesn't just get a new prosthetic and then sent off to carry on as best as possible. In fact, some dogs get a series of prosthetics, starting with what is essentially a peg leg, and eventually moves on to a prosthetic with an articulating foot that allows her to ambulate in a more normal manner. Each step of the way requires training and exercises. Each dog brings her own set of issues to adapting to the new prosthetic. Some dogs understand immediately what the device is helping them to do, other dogs resent this fiberglass thing attached to the end of their stump. And of course, many dogs fall between these two extremes. This is why most veterinary prosthetic makers work only through a veterinarian and will not sell directly to the caregiver.

Getting a Prosthetic

The first step to obtaining a new prosthetic starts with a conversation between the veterinarian, the prosthetic maker, and the caregiver. Every dog is different and there is no such thing as an off-the-rack prosthetic with which you and your dog would be happy. The most obvious requirement is a good fit, and your veterinarian, working with the designer, is the key to this step being successful. Next, a discussion of both the dog and owner's lifestyle need to be considered. Simply, the design of the prosthetic must serve the functional need of the amputee. Finally, a plan to train the dog in the use of his new limb along with several adjustments of the fit are crucial to getting a satisfactory final result. Sometimes this even means sending the prosthetic back to the maker for adjustments.

Measurements for the new prosthetic can start as soon as the amputation site has healed and the sutures are out. It can take several weeks longer for a dog to be able to start working with his new prosthetic, but it also often takes several weeks to get the prosthetic, or maybe the training prosthetic, from the maker. This means early measurement is important. Every maker has its own guidelines, and there are slight procedural variations from one prosthetic maker to the next. Getting an exact fit involves some kind of impression of the stump and making careful measurements of both the affected leg and the remaining leg. Any impressions must be mailed back to the prosthetic maker, which adds to the time and cost of the prosthetic.

Whether in its first stage or its final form, the prosthetic then needs to be fitted to the dog and adjusted. If the straps that help hold it in place cannot be properly adjusted, then once again it must be shipped back to the prosthetic maker. This can occur several times until the prosthetic fits just right and is comfortable to wear. The goal is to ensure that there is no excessive tightness or play in it that might cause chafing and skin infections, which would necessitate that the dog goes without the prosthetic until the skin has healed.

This process can be costly and time consuming. The measurements and fitting fee charged by a veterinarian can be quite high. Even still, the fees he charges you might not cover his costs. Don't be surprised if the fitting fees you are charged approach 50 percent of the cost of the prosthetic.

Once the fit is finalized, it is time to start some rehabilitation training. In the case of a toe prosthetic, it might not be more than a few visits. In the case of a leg prosthetic, it could go on for several months. But now is not the time for caregivers to economize; it would be akin to buying a new car but never learning how to drive. In the end, the effort, time, and money will be worth it to you, and especially worth it to your dog.

I want to give one final warning on purchasing a prosthetic (or orthotic). Choose your manufacturer carefully. Find out up front what kinds of costs are involved with adjustments, what kind of warranties are available should it break, and what the reputation of the manufacturer is. Anyone can make a prosthetic—no one needs a license to do so. I have seen videos of people who have absolutely no rehabilitation training or veterinary experience make prosthetics using 3-D printers. They proudly post videos of their dogs running around. Some people see these as heartwarming stories, but I see dogs with body mechanics that are almost as bad as before they got their 3-D printed legs. I am sure these amateur prosthetic-makers are well intentioned, but they are doing these dogs a disservice because of their lack of knowledge of body biomechanics. Look in Appendix A to find manufacturers of prosthetics and orthotics that have worked with me and provided a good product.

Orthotics

Orthotics don't have the feel-good eye appeal of a prosthetic. But they are every bit as important as a prosthetic. Orthotics can be used both to heal and to prevent injuries. I will talk about a couple of the most common orthotics and their applications. If your dog has a problem other than the ones noted here, talk to a veterinary rehabilitation practitioner to find if there is an orthotic solution for your dog.

The Case of the Amputee with Cruciate Disease

Lucky first came to me because the owner had heard I had a great success rate with treating torn cruciate ligaments (the ligament that stabilizes the knee). I treat cruciate disease several ways: surgically, with braces, and with acupuncture. But no matter which treatment I use, my patients always get rehabilitation therapy.

Lucky's caregiver came to my clinic, wheeling her in using a carriage. It turned out that Lucky had previously had a complete amputation of her front leg, and with her recent cruciate injury she essentially lost the use of one of her back legs. The owner wanted the quickest return to function, and it was decided that for this particular case surgical repair would be the best way to reach that goal. I did the surgery, and Lucky was able to walk into my clinic two days later under her own power.

But the treatment didn't stop there. My examination of Lucky revealed that as a consequence of her "hopping" gait, she was already suffering from a breakdown of the ligaments in the carpus, or wrist, of her good leg. I knew that if that leg suffered a complete collapse, Lucky's options for treatment would be very limited.

My other concern was that Lucky had lost one cruciate, and since most cruciate ruptures are the result of a longstanding breakdown of the ligaments in the knee, the "good" knee might be getting ready to rupture as well.

Lucky's caregiver and myself both agreed that the best solution to protect her remaining legs would be to get both an orthotic designed to prevent hyperextension of the carpus of the front leg and to get an orthotic brace designed to reduce the stresses on the knee that can accompany the final breakdown of the cruciate ligament.

This story about Lucky reminds us that when a dog has an amputation, it puts an extra stress on the remaining limbs that, in turn, can result in a breakdown of joints. But it doesn't have to be this way. The stifle brace, or stifle orthotic, can be a lifesaver for those dogs that are unable to undergo surgery because of financial constraints, or because of other problems such as advanced age or disease that makes them poor candidates for surgery. In dogs like Lucky, they can be used to help prevent or delay the complete breakdown of the cruciate ligament.

Another common orthotic is designed to provide rigid support of the rear foot whenever a condition such as a fracture occurs. This orthotic can be used if any part of the foot is injured. These types of fractures can be treated surgically, but it is a complicated surgery, and the patient is prone to recovery problems. This type of orthotic gives the owner an alternative to surgery. Other applications include hyperextension of the front leg, tears of the gastrocnemius (a muscle that is important in moving the ankle joint), and correction of birth defects that can result in the foot pointing in or out instead of straight forward.

Leg-lengthening orthotics can be used when a dog is born with all limbs intact but one is shorter than the other. Walking with one short leg eventually leads to mechanical disturbances during movement that, in turn, can cause pain and breakdown in other parts of the body. This might look like a prosthetic to some people but it is not. It works more like the "lift" in an orthopedic shoe that fixes similar problems that occur in people.

Fitting an orthotic is slightly different than for a prosthetic. Since the leg is still there, a cast is made of the leg and sent to the orthotic maker so that an exact mold of the dog's leg can be made. Using this plaster image of the dog's leg, the maker can design the orthotic around it. Assuming everything went really well, the fitting should require few if any adjustments. Even better, little to no training is necessary for a dog to use an orthotic device. However, the same concerns for prosthetic makers apply to orthotic makers: reputation, skill and training, and warranty all matter here.

None of these possibilities will help unless intervention is early enough: Ask your surgeon to talk to a prosthetic maker, ask that as much leg as possible is left during an amputation, and ask your veterinarian if your dog's orthopedic issue can be helped with a brace or orthotic. Remember that early intervention is best, and if your veterinarian is unwilling to help, find a rehabilitation veterinarian who will. Consult Appendix A of this book if you need help finding one who is capable of helping you and your dog.

11

REHABILITATION THERAPY FOR YOUR DOG

PHYSICAL THERAPY FOR A DOG? ABOUT TWO DECADES ago there was an explosion of the use of physical therapy (PT) in the world of human medicine. For animals, physical therapy, or rehabilitation as it is known in the veterinary world, is also a rapidly growing field that has mirrored the rapid growth of PT in human medicine. As in human physical therapy, the basis of rehabilitation lies in trained individuals applying manual therapies to the dog. This is supplemented by modalities such as laser and therapeutic ultrasound, exercises, and conditioning programs.

In this chapter, I describe these helpful treatments but also warn you about useless or harmful treatments. For instance, many veterinarians (or people with no medical background) buy an underwater treadmill, put the dog in it for 15 or 20 minutes, and call it rehabilitation. Although the use of this treadmill can be a useful adjunct to manual therapy, used alone it would be wrong to call it rehabilitation. Another problem that occasionally is encountered is professionals who treat humans decide that they want to start treating animals instead of people. Someone with a degree in physical therapy no doubt has a lot of training in his or her field, and indeed some of that might even be applicable to dogs. However, without a complete understanding of the nuances of canine rehabilitation therapy, there is a real possibility of not helping a dog at all, or even worse, hurting him. I will provide you with the information necessary to find competent therapists so that you don't end up in a situation in which your dog is not getting treatment by a qualified individual.

Before I start talking about rehabilitation therapy, I want to share with you a story about my experience early in my rehab training. At that time I had been practicing veterinary medicine for approximately 25 years, and a big part of my practice always had involved orthopedic medicine. I really felt like I knew my stuff. I was taking the first of several rehabilitation courses in Florida at the Canine Rehabilitation Institute, and on the drive home after my third day of class I observed someone walking her beagle down the sidewalk. Suddenly, I was hit by a huge realization about my newfound diagnostic abilities: I noticed that by the dog's body set, his gait, and weight distribution that more than likely he had hip dysplasia with osteoarthritis. I diagnosed this dog from 60 feet away and at 25 miles per hour! I was both thrilled and mortified. I was thrilled because I had increased my diagnostic acumen for orthopedic issues many-fold after just a few days of instruction. And I was horrified to realize the years I had wasted by practicing without this diagnostic skill set.

The power of learning rehabilitation was one of the biggest game changers for my practice of pain medicine. Occasionally when a dog comes to me for a pain consultation after his primary veterinarian has had no success, I often have a strong hunch as to what his problem is just by reading the history or watching him walk to the exam room. But I always recall my humbling experience at the beginning of my rehab training, and I never pass judgment when someone else missed a diagnosis that is now obvious to me.

What Is Rehab?

First and foremost rehabilitation therapy, like its human counterpart of physical therapy, is about the hands-on treatment of musculoskeletal disorders. The use of all sorts of devices like underwater treadmills, laser, shock wave therapy, heat therapy, icing, electrical stimulation, and more might supplement the manual therapy. But it always returns to what we can do with our hands and the exercises through which we guide a dog. Although I keep stressing the importance of the manual aspect of rehab, I cannot stress enough that it "takes a village" to run a successful rehabilitation practice. From your veterinarian to a surgeon or neurologist, from the rehabilitation assistant to the kennel help, and from the dog to his family, everyone plays a role.

The primary care veterinarian for your pet does not have to be certified in rehabilitation. Your vet should, however, be familiar with what rehabilitation can do for your dog and know when a referral might be appropriate. If your veterinarian doesn't refer when appropriate, your dog will never reap the benefits of rehab. Your primary care veterinarian is also responsible for ensuring that your dog's overall health and cardiovascular health is in suitable condition for the sometimes-rigorous exercises he will be expected to perform.

The veterinary specialist, whether a surgeon, neurologist, or some other specialist, must also understand the essential role that rehabilitation plays in returning your dog to full function. It bothers me to see complex orthopedic surgeries performed on dogs that are then sent home with instructions of cage rest for a month, and sometimes even longer. During the first three days of cage rest, dogs experience a measurable decrease in muscle mass . . . at precisely the time when maintaining or even strengthening the affected muscles is paramount! The same goes for neurology cases that might result in partial or complete paralysis of a limb. If that limb is not kept in some sort of conditioning program, how can we expect the dog to ever use it when the neurological issue is resolved?

The certified veterinary therapist is the veterinarian who leads the rehabilitation team. This team usually includes a therapy assistant (a specially trained technician or veterinary nurse), who has almost as much rehabilitation training as a veterinarian. Together the veterinarian and the therapy assistant discuss the case and set up a program of treatment modalities appropriate for the case at hand. The veterinary therapist has the responsibility to oversee every aspect of a patient's treatment and recovery.

The therapy assistant is the person who does most of the work with the rehabilitation patient. A lot of this is hard physical work. She is also challenged to entice the dog into doing the required exercises. My assistant also makes progress reports for me. After I review them, it is then once again my turn to adjust exercises, medications, and other protocols.

The owner plays a critical role. Without owner participation none of the rehabilitation happens. Understanding the importance of what is being done is essential in cooperating with a therapy practice. The caregiver must take responsibility for much of the therapy's demands, and it is the caregiver who must make and keep appointments at appropriate intervals, medicate at home so their pet can deal with some of the rigors of the exercises, follow weight loss or other nutritional guidelines, and understand and carefully carry out necessary home exercises.

The patient is the most important participant of all. Thankfully, it is a rare patient that doesn't want to try. I pity our poor physical therapy cousins working with people who don't want to be there. In contrast, even the most debilitated dogs will usually approach rehabilitation with an enthusiasm that cheers my spirit even as it breaks my heart.

The Case of the Paralyzed Dog

Rusty's owners absolutely adored him. Rusty was a six-year-old Dachshund that had been diagnosed with intervertebral disk disease (slipped disk) and was paralyzed in his back end. Although his owners adored Rusty and wanted to do anything for him, they could not afford the hefty fee for back surgery that was required up-front at the time of the surgery. His owners found my practice and brought Rusty to me for help. Fortunately for both Rusty and his owners, using acupuncture and rehabilitation for the treatment of back issues is typically as successful as surgery. More important for them, there was not a huge up-front fee and they could pay session by session as time went along.

At the end of Rusty's first combined acupuncture and rehab session, he was able to wag his tail when the owners came to pick him up. The owners cried and we all got choked up. They knew they had made the right decision by seeking our help. Within six weeks Rusty was walking (albeit unsteadily) without assistance. He eventually made a full recovery.

Therapy for a condition like Rusty's is always expensive. But rehab, unlike surgery, is not an "all or none" commitment of time and money. And as more evidence is accumulated for the benefit of rehab, I suspect more and more dogs will be treated this way instead of the surgical route.

Modalities Used in Rehabilitation Therapy

Rehabilitation therapy encompasses so many different modalities—with the opportunity to approach cases from so many different angles—that it can be mind boggling. Certainly no one can call it boring. Added to this equation are the personalities of each patient and what they can be coaxed to do, the equipment available to the therapist, and how each dog responds to treatment. It truly can be said that no two cases are ever treated the same.

Keep this in mind as I discuss the most common of the modalities used in canine rehab. Sometimes a piece of equipment isn't available—

there just isn't enough room or budget in every rehab practice to provide every tool to a therapist. Sometimes that piece of equipment is there but won't be used because the therapist feels it isn't the best choice for a particular dog. And maybe the equipment is there but is collecting dust because the therapist has more confidence in other modalities.

Hands-On Therapy

The one tool every therapist has is her hands. They are the most essential part of every rehab case. These hands not only guide dogs through directed exercises, they also massage muscles, manipulate joints, treat painful trigger points, stretch fascia, and more. With the exception of some massage techniques that I cover in Chapter 20, you should attempt none of the following manual techniques at home unless you are directed and shown how to do them by your rehab practitioner. Some of the techniques may seem innocuous to the untrained eye, but when performed improperly can cause a lot of damage.

Massage

Because it is discussed elsewhere in this book, I am only going to briefly mention three basic massage techniques here. Effleurage is a very light massage that most often appears as a circling motion of the hand and usually is used at the beginning and/or end of most massage sessions. Petrissage is used to manipulate some of the deep muscles and often involves a lot of kneading and rolling of the skin. Tapotement is a percussive type of massage using one or more of several different techniques. Most often the percussion is done with the edge of the hands or by using a cupped hand. Tapotement is often used either to stimulate the nervous system or to help relieve the buildup of lymphatic fluid. There are many other massage techniques, but with a few exceptions, most of them are variations of these three techniques.

Joint Mobilizations

There are several types and intensities of joint mobilizations. This manual therapy most often is used post-surgically but can be done to almost any injured or diseased joint. Joint mobilizations help increase joint laxity. It also increases the flow of the joint fluid. Depending on the intensity of the mobilization, certain nerves called mechanoreceptors are also stimulated. The end result of these mobilizations can be a reduction in pain, an increase in the laxity of a stiff joint, and an awakening of the nerves necessary for proper joint function.

If you watch someone doing joint mobilizations, more often than not they are pulling on the distal part of the joint, similar to someone "cracking" their knuckles. This might be a steady pull, but it might also involve rapid movements called oscillations, which vary in the intensity of the pull and how quickly they are done. This looks very easy to do when you watch someone perform this manual therapy, but if done incorrectly it can cause pain or tissue damage.

Range-of-Motion Exercises

Performing range-of-motion exercises helps loosen stiff joints and helps with a dog's recovery after joint surgery. There are two range-of-motion exercises employed in canine rehab. The first is called passive range of motion (PROM), and the second is called an active range of motion (AROM). AROM has a different meaning in canine rehab than it does in human physical therapy. In PT, what we call AROM is called active assistive range of motion. Humans can perform AROM by themselves, but in animals we always assist them, as I will explain.

PROM is what it sounds like; the therapist flexes and extends a limb to get the most movement possible out of a joint, but without actually pushing it out of a neutral state and into one where there is tension as the joint reaches its natural limit of motion. In other words, the therapist is working a joint back and forth without any assistance from the patient. This might be done to help increase range of motion in an arthritic joint, but it is also used to increase or maintain range of motion in a joint that has undergone surgery.

AROM, as it is called in canine rehab, refers to an assisted and active range of motion. This exercise might be done by pushing the flexion or extension of a joint to the point where the dog pushes back with some resistance. It might also be done through the use of therapeutic bands that are placed on a dog's leg while she walks or uses the treadmill. In either case, the result is a strengthening of the target joint and muscles and is very important in either maintaining or building up muscles.

Both of these exercises can be taught to the caregiver and become part of a home exercise and rehabilitation program. But as in every manual therapy discussed here, your rehab person must teach you the proper methods first.

Trigger-Point Therapy

As noted in Chapter 7, the treatment of trigger points in dogs is best accomplished with a technique called dry needling. However, there are circumstances when trigger points can be "massaged" out by putting pressure on the trigger point until it is released. I find that although this manual technique almost always helps, the results are generally much shorter acting and do not provide the dramatic results that often are achieved by dry needling.

Myofascial Release

When a dog moves around, muscles and the sheets of connective tissue are meant to slide over one another, allowing smooth movement of both. As a result of aging, injury, and surgery this myofascial interface can become quite sticky. This causes a subsequent decrease in a dog's ability to move the affected muscles freely. Myofascial release is a type of deep manipulation of both the muscles and fascia, which helps break down adhesions and improve the mobility between these two tissues. Myofascial release can be quite painful, and although it doesn't usually require sedation it does require patience on the part of both the therapist and the dog. I have had myofascial release done on myself, and I can attest to how much it can hurt.

Tools and Toys

What follows is some of the modalities used in rehabilitation therapy that involve a tool of some kind. I called this section tools and toys, because most veterinarians I know really like the newest gadgets that come along and often buy them without a clear understanding of how they are going to make them work in their practice. At times, it seems like many of us are collecting toys. Like the tools of any trade, they only work as well as the person who knows how to use them.

Agility Tools

I have lumped together all of the special devices that are used to improve things like balance, strength, and agility. A strong component of manual therapy is required in order to make these things work. I will talk about a few of the most common of these devices and explain their basic use, but the actual number of items is limited only by the therapist's imagination.

Physioballs are those large round inflatable balls found in any regular gym, used to assist in exercise. In canine rehab the balls are usually quite a bit smaller and often a peanut-shape to accommodate the canine patient. Physioballs are used primarily as tools to help a dog with his balance and to strengthen his legs. A ball that is slightly higher than his hips or shoulders is used, and his midsection is draped over the narrow part of the peanut shape. The therapist then rocks the ball slightly back and forth, forcing the patient to balance himself and to use the muscles in those legs.

Therapy cones are specialized traffic cones that can be used one of several ways. They can be set up as an obstacle course, and the dog is encouraged to weave in and out of them. This exercise is designed to improve balance and to force the dog to use the weak side of his body as he weaves in and out of the cones. These cones also have holes in the side of them where PVC pipes can be inserted at various levels, depending on what the therapist wants to accomplish. They are used to work on coordination as the dog steps over them, work on strength as the dog high steps or jumps over them, or even work a different set of muscles if the therapist can get the dog to "army crawl" underneath them. Most of my patients find working with the cones and PVC pipes to be the most fun of the rehab exercises.

Wobble boards are a special set of boards that have a ball or a roller-bar on the underside. If a dog has a neurological problem that affects balance, the affected legs can be placed on the board and the therapist can move the board back and forth, stimulating nerve receptors and retraining balance. Small trampolines are sometimes employed to achieve the same results. The therapist bounces it gently while the dog stands on it.

Treadmills

Most rehab practices have an underwater treadmill (UWTM). A land treadmill, similar to a treadmill that runners use, may be present as well. UWTMs are used for strengthening in those animals that may not be able to support their body weight for any extended period of time. Dogs might not be able to support their weight as a result of injury, decreased muscle mass, surgery, or even neurological issues. The buoyancy provided by the water is used to lessen a dog's overall weight on his limbs. This buoyancy can be adjusted by adding more or less water; the higher the water, the less overall weight on the dog's legs. Depending on the problem and its severity, the water level might start out at mid-chest. But as the patient improves, the water level might be lowered and the speed of the treadmill increased to provide a more difficult workout.

A land treadmill for dogs, which is usually longer than a human treadmill so as to accommodate their longer strides, is used to condition those dogs that are able to bear weight on all four limbs. Some of these dogs start out in an UWTM and graduate to the land treadmill.

No matter which treadmill is used, it almost always requires a period of time to train your dog to use it. This might mean that the therapist puts on a wetsuit and hops in with your dog. Although some dogs just never like the treadmill, most of them do and actually look forward to their sessions. I need to give you a word of caution. Most therapists are already aware of this, but your dog must be in good cardiovascular health prior to starting any exercise program, but especially when using an UWTM. As anyone who has waded in water knows, especially if they have walked against a current, it is hard work!

Laser Therapy

The word *laser* is an acronym for **l**ight **a**mplification by **s**timulated **e**mission of **r**adiation. The light in a laser is a very concentrated and narrow beam of light. In veterinary medicine, the types of lasers used are generally either a class 3b or a class 4. For the sake of simplicity, the main difference between the two is their strength (class 3b must be 500 milliwatts or less) and safety (class 4 generates a lot of heat and easily can cause burns and tissue damage). In the end, it probably doesn't make a lot of difference as to which laser type is used, as long as the person using it has been properly trained.

The benefits of using a laser result from several things that happen to the tissue when laser light is applied at the proper strength and time. Probably the two most significant effects are an increase in blood flow and an increase in ATP (the basic energy unit in living things) by mitochondria in tissue cells. There are other possible mechanisms at work, including a reduction of inflammatory agents and an increase in endorphins and in the activity of different types of cells such as macrophages and fibroblasts.

The result of one or more of the actions above results in an overall improved health and function of the treated tissue. This means reduced inflammation, pain, and swelling, as well as an accelerated healing time of both soft tissue and bone. Although the effects of laser are significant, by itself a laser is not capable of treating pain. Lasers need to be a part of an overall rehab program. Some people have been known to buy a laser and call it rehab. Unfortunately for their patients, using only a laser is usually not enough to get good-quality results.

TENS and NMES Therapy

TENS stands for Transcutaneous Electrical Nerve Stimulation and it works by sending electric impulses through the skin to the underlying nerves. This is done to reduce the amount of pain a dog is feeling by two different methods. The first is something called the "Gate Theory," which says that the nerve "highway" only can handle so many nerve signals at once, whether they are pain or other sensory signals. The Gate

Theory is the reason rubbing a stubbed toe makes it feel better. The stimulation of "touch" nerves by rubbing your toe competes with the already stimulated pain nerves and only so many of those signals can get through the "gate." Stimulation of nerves around a painful area by electrical impulse is theorized to do the same thing, competing with the pain signals. The second method TENS is thought to work is by actually exhausting the nerves, including pain nerves that it stimulates. In any case, the effect is very short lived, but can reduce pain long enough to allow for the start of some exercises.

NMES stands for Neuromuscular Electrical Stimulation and it works similarly to a TENS, but its target is muscles. Anyone who has watched late-night television has probably seen the advertisements for these devices. They are purported to increase muscle tone and to strengthen your muscles while you sleep. Outrageous claims aside, these devices are used in rehab in an effort to maintain muscle tone in animals that are unable to do exercise because of the nature of their injury. This therapy helps, but it is certainly not a replacement for exercise. You can think of this tool as a bridge that helps patients recover enough so that they may begin exercise on their own.

Ultrasound Therapy

Ultrasound therapy has in recent years fallen out of favor, as many research projects have failed to show its benefit over placebo. The theory is that the sound waves, which are sent into the tissue, somehow speed healing and reduce inflammation. Many rehab practitioners swear by them; unfortunately, any evidence for their effectiveness is poor.

Pulsed Electromagnetic Field (PEMF)

Magnets of any type have been used for their purported healing powers for thousands of years. There is no evidence that a regular magnet has any effect on pain or healing. However, there is some evidence that PEMF-type magnets can be effective for alleviating pain. A PEMF exerts a magnetic field when electricity is passed through a coil. In veterinary medicine, these magnets are usually in the form of a wand or loop. They also can be placed inside dog beds or mats.

Blinded studies have shown that PEMF therapy has a minimal effect on alleviating pain, at least when the magnets are used by themselves. There might be some synergistic effect with other pain treatments, but it really remains for someone to do the proper research to find the evidence. One study in humans showed that there was a reduction in osteoarthritis pain if the PEMF therapy was at least six hours every day. This is impractical if you are holding a wand over a painful joint, but more practical if the PEMF is inside a dog bed.

Do I use them? I have on occasion but was never convinced of their effectiveness. It might be a matter of finding out the proper strength and duration of the electromagnetic field. This is one of those treatments that are completely safe, and the only harm in trying is on your pocketbook.

12

STICKING NEEDLES IN JOINTS

OVER THE PAST DECADE THERE HAS BEEN A DRAMATIC increase of medical treatments that involve injecting substances into arthritic joints, in both humans and dogs. The most common injections are corticosteroids. But stem cells, platelet-rich plasma, and other substances are now injected into these joints as well. I will explore the evidence and value behind the substances that merit a place in the list of possible pain treatments for your dog.

You might wonder, what is the advantage of injecting substances into one or more arthritic joints of a dog? Simply put, this treatment option delivers high concentrations of an antiarthritic substance directly where it is needed the most. Joints are their own little compartments that receive very little blood flow, the method by which most drugs are distributed. In addition to that, many of the drugs we want to get into the joint are large and complex molecules that simply can't pass through that compartmentalized joint barrier. Using a needle to physically get into the joint and to deliver a beneficial substance bypasses that hurdle.

Injecting joints is not without its risks. The most obvious risk is the needle itself and the placement of it. Some joints are easier to work with than others, and it can be difficult to know that the needle has been placed into the joint and not into some of the surrounding tissues. Also, the needle can inadvertently carry bacteria into the joint if strict antiseptic procedures are ignored, and sometimes even when they are followed. And finally, the needle has the potential for damaging the articular cartilage each time it is put into the joint.

Substances Put into Joints

This is not a complete list of all substances injected into joints. The following are, however, those things that have some basis in research to support their use.

Corticosteroids

Injection of corticosteroids into joints has long been known to have a strong anti-inflammatory effect. For some dogs, the result can seem almost miraculous. Unfortunately the effect is short lived, somewhere around one month. This would be fine if the injections were innocuous, but in addition to the risks of the injection procedure itself, continually bathing the joint in corticosteroids brings with it a deleterious effect on the cartilage itself, making matters worse in the long run. Even so, there are many reasons that I might inject a joint with corticosteroids. Sometimes I need to "calm" the inflammatory process enough to allow for what otherwise would be painful rehabilitation, exercise, and joint manipulation treatments. Working dogs sometimes need an immediate fix so that they can do their jobs of hunting or rescue work. And sometimes the inflammatory process in the joint is so severe that I inject it to drastically reduce the inflammation, which might then allow other drugs to maintain the now-lessened disease state. No matter what reason your dog might need corticosteroids in the joint, it is a commonly accepted practice to limit lifetime injections to three per joint to avoid the side effects of this potent drug.

Hyaluronic Acid

Hyaluronic acid (HA), a substance similar to joint fluid, is probably the second most common substance injected into joints. HA is a very viscous liquid that mimics the lubricating and cushioning effect of joint fluid. In addition, it is thought to have anti-inflammatory properties. There are no limits on the number of times HA can be injected into a joint. Unfortunately, the evidence for its effectiveness is not very strong. For the most part I have been unimpressed with the results of HA, especially when considering the costs of the drug, the risk of administering it, and the sedation that is usually required. On a positive note, when it does work, beneficial results can last for up to six months.

Platelet-Rich Plasma

Platelet-rich plasma (PRP) is a substance that is collected from your own dog and then injected back into him. Basically, blood is collected in a manner similar to that used for a blood donor. It is put into a special centrifuge to separate the different components, and then one of the layers that contain mostly platelets is drawn off and used in the pain treatment. This layer not only contains platelets but other biologically active components such as growth factor, a substance that promotes healing and reduces inflammation.

Platelet-rich plasma started out as a wildly popular treatment for joints, tendons, and ligaments in human medicine. Recent disappointing research and retrospective studies have taken some of the shine off this treatment. In dogs, evidence for its effectiveness is slowly accumulating. Unfortunately, the substances that should be in PRP, including the platelets themselves, vary from each of the systems designed to collect and prepare it. PRP also contains varying amounts of other blood components such as red and white blood cells, and plasma proteins like albumin. Some of these components might be helpful or harmful to the end product that is injected into the joint. More research is needed to completely understand what might make up the best combination of PRP components to optimize its affect on pain.

Interleukin-1 Receptor Antagonist Proteins

Interleukin-1 Receptor Antagonist Proteins (IRAP), like PRP, is collected from your dog and then injected back into the joint. There is an additional step in which the sample is incubated to increase the concentration of IRAP.

Interleukin-1 is one of the primary inflammatory substances responsible for the ongoing pain and progression of osteoarthritis. Introducing an antagonist in the form of IRAP can block the effect of its inflammation. There is even some evidence that IRAP might slow or halt the progression of osteoarthritis. Unfortunately, all of the evidence for its effectiveness is in horses and humans, not yet in dogs. The use of IRAP may become a major player in the treatment of osteoarthritis in dogs, provided that ongoing research supports its use.

Stem Cell Therapy

Stem cell therapy for the treatment of osteoarthritis uses adult (not fetal) stem cells. Stem cells are collected from your dog, concentrated, and then injected back into the affected joint(s). A stem cell is a cell that has the ability to turn into many different types of cells. Think of a tree with the stem cell as its trunk. From that trunk one branch may grow into skin cells, one into muscle, one into nerves, and so on. What if we can take those stem cells, inject them into a joint, and have them turn into new cartilage cells to replace the worn and damaged cartilage that is in an osteoarthritic joint? This is the concept behind using stem cells in joints.

Unfortunately, research has shown that, at least in dogs, this does not happen. But stem cells do affect the joint in other positive ways. It is thought that they carry with them things like cytokines and growth factors, which both decrease and modulate inflammation. This results in an improvement of your dog's pain, which may last as long as one year. I performed stem cell therapy on my own dog and although the results were short lived (about seven or eight months), it had a miraculous effect on her ability to move around, play, and jump up and down off furniture and into vehicles.

The decision to treat your dog with stem cells is a big commitment. It comes with a large price tag, around $3,000 depending on the system used and the cost of veterinary services where you live. It also means a surgical procedure to harvest the stem cells either through the collection of fat or bone marrow. This is followed by another visit where your dog needs to be sedated for the intra-articular injections.

One company, Aratana Therapeutics, is hoping to develop some off-the-shelf stem cells so that the procedure simply becomes one of sedation and injection, no surgery necessary. This would remove the cost of harvesting the stem cells and processing them. However, it may be some time before we see this happen because off-the-shelf stem cells would be subject to all of the trials, effectiveness, and safety studies that regular drugs have to undergo in order to be approved by the FDA. To follow the development of this product, go to www.aratana.com/therapeutics/pipeline/pain.

Botulinum Toxin

Botulinum toxin, commonly known by its brand name Botox, has been looked at for its anti-inflammatory effects. It is best known for its use in paralyzing muscles and thereby temporarily reducing wrinkles. It also inhibits the release of several inflammatory substances that are behind some of the pain of osteoarthritis. One early dog study in Finland using botulinum toxin to treat osteoarthritis pain showed some promise. As of this writing, it is not yet being used in a clinical setting.

Capsaicin

In short, capsaicin has the ability to temporarily deactivate the pain fibers that are most involved with the transmission of the signals of chronic pain. One U.S. pharmaceutical company, Centrexion, is currently supporting trials to see if intra-articular injections of capsaicin can help modulate joint pain. Early reports on capsaicin as a treatment for the pain of osteoarthritis are encouraging. For a more thorough explanation of the use of capsaicin and similar substances for the treatment of pain, please review Chapter 17.

13

DIETS AND NUTRACEUTICALS: WHAT CAN YOU BELIEVE?

DIETS AND FOODS WITH PURPORTED AND REAL EFFECTS on the treatment of medical problems are everywhere. Because nutritional items are considered food, not drugs, they do not have to undergo rigorous trials to prove to both the FDA and their customers that they actually deliver any suggested benefits. False claims can be made without repercussion because of the regulations and degree of scrutiny a food or "food supplement" receives in the United States. The bottom line is that these supplements do not need to go through rigorous testing for issues like safety and efficacy.

Wild claims abound as you walk down the diet and supplements aisle of any pet store. Even worse is visiting the "aisle" of the Internet. Some claims are true. Some claims are patently false. And then there are the claims that have enough truth to them to make the entire pitch seem reasonable. And to complicate matters further, lack of evidence does not necessarily mean a diet or supplement doesn't have some value—it is possible the research for that product hasn't been done.

Terms like "organic" and "natural" often appear on the packaging of dog food. That organic label is there to make us think that the food inside the bag must be the better choice for our dogs. But how often do you consider the makeup of that organic stuff? Too many caregivers don't make this consideration and, in the end, buy the premium priced organic because they think it is a superior product and want what is best for their dogs.

The truth is there has not been a single good study that has shown a significant difference in the outcomes of the health or longevity of our dogs (or us for that matter) by consuming organic over conventionally raised and grown products.

I do not have some personal complaint against organic products. I often buy organic products if the quality appears to be superior to the conventional products sold next to it. I bring up this point because I want to address the mindset that things are better or safer if they are organic or natural. If you have this mindset, you're not alone. Many companies that sell herbal/botanical products imply that their organic and natural products are "safe" or "better." Moreover, they do nothing to discourage the misconception that nothing bad could happen by taking one of their organic or natural products.

This chapter looks at some of the most common food items in use for osteoarthritis and categorizes them by the evidence of their effectiveness: strong, moderate, or poor. I am not out to expose fraudulent claims of any pet food or supplement manufacturer; I simply want to present a few facts about some common products. Use this information for guidance as you make your own choices.

Nutraceuticals

The word *nutraceutical* was coined to describe food supplements that have purported effects similar to that of a drug. (This term combines the words *nutritional* and *pharmaceutical*.) Some nutraceuticals are naturally occurring products and some of them are manufactured. It would be a Herculean task to discuss every single supplement on the market, so what follows cannot be an exhaustive list. Instead, I will discuss some of the more popular products that my clients ask me about and try to provide here the evidence (or lack of) for the worthiness of the products' use.

Aspirin

Aspirin is not a nutraceutical, but I feel that it fits into this part of the book because it often is found in the pain relief aisle alongside nutraceutical products, including those listed in this chapter. Aspirin is effective in the treatment of pain associated with arthritis in dogs; however, it is not safe. And even though it is not approved for use in dogs, there are several "dog aspirin" products on the market. Administration of even a few doses of aspirin has been shown to cause inflammation of the gastric mucosa or lining of the stomach.[38] If it is given along with an NSAID, the results can be even more disastrous, resulting in an ulcer that perforates the stomach,[39] which then leads to surgery or even death. Although the evidence for the effectiveness of aspirin in treating pain in dogs with osteoarthritis is strong, I do not recommend its use because of potential safety issues and adverse events.

Elk Velvet Antler

The ingredients of elk velvet antler include those that may help with the treatment of osteoarthritis pain in dogs. Those ingredients include collagen, glucosamine, and natural growth factors. It is taken from the antler of an elk that is in velvet (part of the growth cycle that their antlers go through). There was one double-blinded and placebo-controlled study[40] that showed improvement in the pain scores of dogs with osteoarthritis as early as 30 days after starting treatment. As with any nutritional supplement, the quality of the elk velvet antler is vital if you want to see good results for your dog. I rate the evidence for the effectiveness of elk velvet antler in treating dogs with osteoarthritis as moderate.

Essential Fatty Acids/Fish Oil/ Omega-3 Fatty Acids

Diets that are high in omega-3 fatty acid have several health benefits. The two most important fatty acids for your dog are called EPA and DHA. Although the benefit of eating these omega-3s extends beyond the treatment of pain, it is only their action on pain mechanisms that will be discussed here.

Fatty acids are one of the main culprits in your dog's production of prostaglandins. Prostaglandins are one of the perpetrators of pain and inflammation. The worst of these fatty acid malefactors in this prostaglandin pathway are omega-6 fatty acids. Omega-3 fatty acids directly compete with the omega-6 fatty acids in the production of prostaglandins, pushing the omega-6s out of the way with the end result of decreased production of pain-causing prostaglandins.

The second mechanism by which omega-3s can reduce pain is via the direct modulation or "down regulation" of the COX enzymes that are responsible for the pain of osteoarthritis.[41]

In one study in which dogs received a veterinary therapeutic diet for joints, it was noted by the owners that after six weeks of the therapeutic diet, their dogs could stand from a down position much easier; and as the trial progressed, they were able to see significant improvement in their dogs' ability to walk.[42] Researchers also were able to measure the improvement in a different blinded study that fed the joint diet to one set of dogs and a normal (placebo) diet to the other set of dogs. At the end of three months, dogs from both groups were physically evaluated and underwent something called a force plate test. A force plate is a special sensor that dogs walk on, and it measures the force or weight that the subject places on all limbs as he walks across it. Both the physical evaluation and the force plate analysis demonstrated a significant improvement in lameness for dogs in the joint diet group, but not in the placebo group.[43]

If you notice, both of these studies discussed diets high in omega-3 fatty acids, not just omega-3 fatty acid supplementation. It is my clinical impression that when omega-3s are part of a diet as compared to a supplement, they just work better. This might be in part due to damage that occurs to the fatty acids during the processing used to extract the oil. Another reason could be that many of these joint diets contain other antiarthritic/pain supplements in addition to the omega-3 fatty acids, resulting in a combined benefit. Or perhaps there is another factor we haven't considered. It is my recommendation that you talk to your veterinarian about prescription joint diets that contain omega-3 fatty acids and see if one is appropriate for your dog.

Many people often use flaxseed oil as a source of omega-3 fatty acids. Flax oil doesn't actually contain high levels of omega-3s. Instead, it is high in something called linoleic acid. Flax oil makes a good source of omega-3 fatty acids for humans because our bodies can convert the linoleic acid into omega-3 fatty acids. Dogs are very inefficient at doing this conversion. Always consider a fish-based source of omega-3 fatty acids.

I consider the evidence for omega-3 fatty acids as part of a diet to be strong, but when used as a supplement to be poor to moderate. Use caution when administering to dogs with poor platelet function (platelets are important for forming blood clots to stop bleeding), as high levels of omega-3 fatty acids have been known to interfere with clotting. Some dogs also develop diarrhea when they first start taking these fatty acids, and so I usually recommend starting at a low dose when given as a supplement. Gradually increase the fatty acids until the target dose is reached.

Green-Lipped Mussels (GLM)

Green-lipped mussels (*Perna canaliculus*) are shellfish that live in the waters off New Zealand and have been found to provide some anti-inflammatory benefits. It was discovered that GLMs are able to inhibit the 5-lipoxygenase pathways, a process that leads to the formation of leukotrienes. Leukotrienes are inflammatory substances responsible for part of the pain of osteoarthritis. There are several excellent studies that show when green-lipped mussels are given as a supplement or as part of a diet over several months that they help decrease the pain associated with osteoarthritis.[44] [45] I rate the evidence for green-lipped mussels as strong.

Oral Hyaluronic Acid

Hyaluronic acid (HA) in its most common form is used as an injection into an arthritic joint with the hope of reducing inflammation and providing additional lubricant to the diseased joint. HA occurs naturally in dog joints, which is the rationale for using it in dogs with osteoarthritis. In the past several years, oral HA supplements have shown up on the market for the treatment of OA. There is poor evidence at best for its effectiveness in treating the pain of osteoarthritis.

Joint Protectants

Adequan, an injectable joint protectant, is the only product in this class that is available by prescription only and must be administered or dispensed by a veterinarian. There is a mountain of evidence for its efficacy, and it has also received FDA approval for efficacy and safety (www .adequan.com). I use it all the time in my practice for the pain-reducing benefits it provides my patients. You can read more about Adequan in Chapter 5. I rate the evidence for this product as strong.

Glucosamine and chondroitin sulfate are probably the most studied dietary supplements for osteoarthritis (OA) on the face of the earth. Unfortunately these studies show both the effectiveness[46] [47] and the ineffectiveness[48] [49] of joint supplements in dogs. This is frustrating to both veterinarians and caregivers alike. Why are there studies showing such a diversity of results? Perhaps it works best on certain grades or locations of arthritis. Maybe there is an age, sex, or breed difference in its effect. Or maybe there is some other influencing factor yet to be discovered.

What we do know about these products is that the best form of the drug seems to be the low molecular weight chondroitin sulfate that, when combined with glucosamine, has the best absorption rate.[50] We also know that, when given with the NSAID carprofen, glucosamine/ chondroitin sulfate is more effective than given by itself and may provide even more joint protection than when given alone.[51] [52]

If you decide to use one of these supplements, I advise that you choose a product that contains a low molecular weight chondroitin sulfate, such as Cosequin or Dasuquin, and use it for at least 90 days. If you see an improvement, stay on it. However, sometimes it is hard to tell if things have improved, especially if it happened incrementally. If you are not sure, stop the supplement for a month. If your dog's condition seems to worsen, then chances are the supplement was helping. I rate the evidence for glucosamine and chondroitin sulfate as moderate.

Milk Protein Concentrates

Some veterinarians and the manufacturers of these milk protein concentrates have made claims that these proteins have anti-inflammatory effects. Concentrates of these proteins are available for oral administration with the intent of treating osteoarthritis. Although the claimed benefits for these products seem pretty spectacular, the actual evidence for their ability to reduce pain is very poor.

MSM

MSM is short for methylsulfonylmethane, which is a substance that has been shown to decrease pain and inflammation in animals with osteoarthritis. It is relatively safe to use; however, it should be used under the supervision of a veterinarian as high doses have been shown to cause atrophy in several organs including the liver and spleen. It is probably best used in combination with a glucosamine and chondroitin sulfate supplement, as it appears that their actions are synergistic. Many glucosamine/chondroitin supplements can be bought with or without MSM as an additional ingredient. The evidence for MSM is moderate.

SAMe

The exact mechanism of why SAMe (sometimes referred to as SAM-e or SAM) reduces the pain of osteoarthritis is not known. However, evidence suggests that it may reduce inflammation by an increased proteoglycan synthesis. Proteoglycans are substances that appear in many body tissues and have several different functions. For a dog that has OA, proteoglycans provide lubrication within the joint, helping to protect it. Besides this role as a lubricant, it has been proposed that SAMe may also have an analgesic effect, dampening the pain of OA.

There are several studies showing the effectiveness of SAMe in treating arthritis in people. One well-done study in dogs[53] showed that there might have been a slight decrease in pain scores, but it was not considered significant enough to consider its use as a stand-alone product in treating pain in dogs. These questionable results in its efficacy, along with the high cost, do not make SAMe an attractive alternative for treating osteoarthritis pain. The evidence for SAMe is poor.

Turmeric

Turmeric extracts are often recommended for arthritis pain because of their anti-inflammatory activities. Refer to Chapter 14, Botanical Medications for Treating Pain. There is moderate evidence for its use in treating pain in humans, though not in dogs.

UC-II

UC-II is a type of collagen that in its supplement form is derived from chicken cartilage. UC-II occurs naturally and makes up a significant portion of normal dog joint cartilage. It has been hypothesized that supplementing with UC-II orally reduces circulating levels of inflammatory substances, with the potential of decreasing both the incidence and the severity of arthritis. There are several studies that support the benefit of UC-II in dogs with arthritis when used alone[54] or alongside glucosamine and chondroitin sulfate.[55] UC-II is very safe with no known adverse events. It requires about 120 days of supplementation before the full benefit is seen. This benefit quickly disappears when supplementation is stopped. I rate the evidence for this product, with or without concurrent use of glucosamine and chondroitin sulfate, as strong.

Super Food Supplements

Several supplements for dogs are available that contain derivatives of what are called super foods—foods that are supposed to have positive effects on body health. I have not found any research proving any health benefits, including the treatment of pain, of these products. One product I looked at listed its main ingredient as flaxseed, which has very little benefit because a dog cannot effectively convert linoleic acid into omega-3 fatty acids. I rate the evidence for their use as poor.

Diets

There are many diets on the market that claim to help dogs suffering from osteoarthritis. Some of these diets are by prescription only, and some can be found in pet stores or grocery stores. Whether over-the-counter or by prescription only, dog food diets designed to help dogs with osteoarthritis should contain several key ingredients, which are noted in the next section of this chapter.

Although some of the over-the-counter foods might be helpful in treating osteoarthritis pain, many over-the-counter brands have a tendency to change their ingredients rapidly based on whatever the current fad is—grain free, corn free, gluten free, and so forth. These changes may or may not affect the usefulness of the products, so I am reluctant to discuss any one of them in particular because the product I describe today may be totally different tomorrow.

Prescription diets, sold through or on the order of a veterinarian, are less subject to the types of changes of over-the-counter foods. There is much more research and thought put into the ingredients that comprise a prescription diet. I am going to discuss those prescription diets that are used the most. This is not meant to be a comprehensive list of every prescription diet that has a claim for the treatment of osteoarthritis.

Before examining the prescription diets, it is important to briefly discuss raw food diets. Raw food diets are usually homemade and contain uncooked sources of protein: meat, poultry, or fish. Many people who lovingly devote the time to make these diets have made claims that the raw food diets have solved a myriad of their dog's health problems. Maybe some of these results are real and maybe they are imagined. As our dog's caregiver we want the best for our dog. And when we go to the effort to do what we think is best, we sometimes become blind when it comes to evaluating the outcome. This is called the caretaker placebo effect—we want something to happen so badly that we imagine it is real, and even our dogs may start to react in a positive way to these hopes and encouragements. Only a properly created trial can find the truth of the matter.

Unfortunately, feeding your dog a raw food diet comes with risks, mostly to you and your family.[56] Isolates of pathogenic bacteria can be found in most dogs that eat raw food diets.[57] These include harmful bacteria such as Salmonella and E. coli. Even though your dog may show no signs of illness from harboring these bacteria, they can cause severe illness, even death, in people.[58] It is the advice of the American Veterinary Medical Association[59] and the U.S. Food and Drug Administration[60] that people do not feed their dog a raw food diet. The Centers for Disease Control and Prevention (CDC) made the statement, "Raw diets, especially raw meat diets, are not recommended because of the risk for Salmonellosis and other infections that can affect pets and their owners."[61]

I understand that many people prefer to feed their dog raw food diets, and it is not my intention to tell anyone that they shouldn't. I merely want you to understand that there is no evidence for the benefit of treating osteoarthritis with a raw food diet, and that feeding a raw food diet comes with some inherent risks.

One last word on "joint" diets: although these products can be useful in treating the pain of osteoarthritis, the results may be less than what you desire if you use them alone. They work best by supplementing many of the other treatments described in this book, especially in cases of moderate to severe osteoarthritis. And for some dogs in pain, adding a joint diet is often that extra little something that makes a difference in your dog's ability to move around. Like many nutritional supplements, feeding a joint diet may take three or four months before the full benefit is realized. Which diet should you choose? Sometimes it comes down to picking one based on your dog's willingness to eat the food, and less on the diet you want him to eat.

What Should a Prescription Mobility Diet Contain?

Just as in the human field of nutrition, veterinarians and other nutritional experts can't agree on everything. But there are many things that most agree on and I have listed them below.

Omega-3 Fatty Acids

The one thing that all joint diets should have in common is food sources that are high in omega-3 fatty acids. As already mentioned, it seems that when omega-3 fatty acids are part of a foodstuff, the benefit to the dog is much more obvious. Look for fish to be one of these ingredients. Fish oil or omega-3 fatty acids as a supplement added to the food are okay, but are only second best to food made with ingredients that have naturally high levels of omega-3 fatty acids.

Glucosamine and Chondroitin Sulfate

Glucosamine and chondroitin sulfate are effective as either part of a diet or as a supplement. However, when it is part of a diet then there is one less pill to give. Being part of the diet almost always realizes an economic savings as well. It is not unusual for the cost of one month's worth of a glucosamine and chondroitin sulfate supplement to cost as much as one month of a prescription dog food. In other words, it is almost like getting the glucosamine and chondroitin sulfate for free when you buy most prescription joint diets.

Green-Lipped Mussels (GLM)

There is an ever-increasing amount of evidence that GLMs can significantly help the pain of osteoarthritis. Having this included in your dog's diet can improve his mobility. And as in the case of glucosamine and chondroitin sulfate, if it is already in the diet it does not need to be given as a supplement, which saves the cost of buying an additional supplement.

Botanicals

At this point in time, none of the prescription diets I am familiar with use botanicals in their diets. Botanicals could prove to be a benefit, and hopefully this possibility will receive more attention in the future.

Reduced Calories

Almost all dogs with osteoarthritis have a decreased caloric need due to the disease's impact on mobility and the decreased amount of energy they use. Overweight dogs with osteoarthritis can achieve a good level of pain control by losing 10 percent of their body weight. That percentage change is the equivalent to the pain control seen by giving an NSAID. This is a really powerful and motivating reason to maintain a lean body mass in your dog.

Royal Canin Mobility Support

Mobility Support is one of the diets I often prescribe in my practice to treat the pain of osteoarthritis. It has several of the ingredients discussed earlier in this chapter: green-lipped mussels, omega-3 fatty acids, and glucosamine and chondroitin sulfate. Additionally, it has a moderate calorie level to promote healthy weights in dogs that might be less active because of their osteoarthritis. It does not have fish as the source of omega-3 fatty acids, but lists fish oil instead. When Mobility Support is compared to similar diets that do not contain green-lipped mussels, there is a clear benefit to feeding your dog the Royal Canin diet.[62]

Purina JM Joint Mobility

Purina JM Joint Mobility is different from the Royal Canin joint diet in that it does not contain green-lipped mussels. It does list trout and salmon along with fish oil in its ingredients. Purina JM features a moderate calorie content and contains glucosamine and antioxidants to help stop arthritis pain. I have seen improvements in animals that eat Purina JM; however, my concern is that chondroitin sulfate is not listed in the ingredients (glucosamine is not well absorbed in the absence of chondroitin sulfate).

Hill's Prescription Diet J/D

J/D contains omega-3 fatty acids and glucosamine and chondroitin sulfate. It does not have a fish source as the protein, but uses fish oil instead. It also has a moderate calorie content to help maintain a healthy body weight. Like the Purina JM diet, it does not contain green-lipped mussels.

Iams Veterinary Formula Joint Plus

Joint Plus is another prescription diet for managing osteoarthritis. The ingredients list both fishmeal and fish oil. It contains glucosamine and chondroitin sulfate, omega-3 fatty acids, and antioxidants but does not have green-lipped mussels. It also has a claim that it supports fat metabolism to promote lean body weight.

14

BOTANICAL MEDICATIONS FOR TREATING PAIN

MANY CAREGIVERS ASSUME THAT JUST BECAUSE something is herbal (or natural, or organic) it must be safe. The fact is that some herbal supplements and botanicals used to manage pain, most commonly for osteoarthritis, can and do act like drugs. Each has its own potential contraindications and side effects—some of them lethal. It is my aim to give you guidance on how to find reputable herbal supply companies and how to avoid bad ones. I also will provide you with a list of herbal remedies that have at least moderate evidence for relieving pain, along with their side effects and contraindications.

Let us remember that manufacturers don't have to reveal anything: The Food and Drug Administration (FDA) consider their products to be food additives or supplements even though manufacturers can insinuate that their products can be thought of as drugs or drug substitutes. In other words, this food category doesn't require warnings. In the same way a bag of sugar doesn't have to carry a warning about potential adverse events of consuming it, such as diabetes, weight gain, and hyperactivity.

Another issue with botanical supplements is that FDA requirements do not compel manufacturers to show that their products even work. Read the labels: "this product promotes . . ." or "clinical studies show . . ." or "use this product for. . . ." These phrases do not establish a level playing field for trying to compare the claims made by botanical companies against the indications, contraindications, warnings, and so forth. Contrast this to the terminology that a pharmaceutical company must display when describing a given product.

In doing the research for this book, I read more than 200 research papers on the use of botanicals as medications. About half of these studies were well conducted and showed the potential good that certain botanicals might hold for the treatment of a variety of medical conditions. However, almost none of these papers mentioned side effects, adverse events, or drug interactions that could potentially occur with their use.

What's more, botanicals do not have to go through the same purity testing as pharmaceuticals do. When independent labs test botanicals, it is common to find impurities such as heavy metals and other adulterations that are not on the label—even parts of endangered animals are sometimes found. This is especially true of traditional Chinese herbal supplements that are proprietary. These proprietary blends are formulations that have exotic sounding names but no list of ingredients. Furthermore, the majority of randomly tested botanical supplements do not even contain the botanicals listed on the label, but instead contain things like rice and wheat powder. Even as I write this section of the book, the state of New York is investigating several prominent retailers for selling products with well-known label brands that have false labeling claims.

Yet there is no reason that product testing cannot be done (and some companies do). The technology is both simple and inexpensive. High-performance thin layer chromatography for quality control of multicomponent herbal drugs is a reliable and reasonably priced test that is within the reach of most labs. And it is certainly within the reach of the manufacturer's ability to pay for testing.

By now you are probably thinking that I am not going to recommend any botanicals! That is not the case. But I do want to warn you of the many problems that can accompany these outwardly safe-appearing treatments. I will guide you through this maze so that you can make important and well-informed decisions for the care of your dog.

How Do I Know a Botanical Is Safe and Effective?

What do I mean by safe? My definition of safe is this: The product must have only the ingredients that are stated on the label, in the concentrations that are stated on the label, and must be free of harmful levels of pesticides and heavy metals. What do I mean by effective? A botanical can meet all of the criteria above for safety, yet still not work because your dog's body cannot absorb it. As a reminder, botanical production is not covered by the same rules as pharmaceuticals, and all testing is voluntary. But some manufacturers do submit their products for testing, which can confirm that it is safe and effective.

There are two labs that do independent testing of botanicals, among other products. Both the U.S. Pharmacopeial Convention (USP) and NSF International test dietary supplements, including botanicals, to verify the concerns already stated. You may even have seen the USP or NSF seal on vitamins or other products you have bought in the past without realizing what it really meant.

Both the USP and NSF test for pesticides, heavy metals, microbes, and other contaminants before they put their seal of approval on a product. Additionally, they test products for their ability to be absorbed by the body by making sure they conform to federally recognized dissolution standards. And last, they make sure these products have been made according to FDA current Good Manufacturing Practices using sanitary and well-controlled procedures. Products meeting these standards have been made using safe, sanitary, well-controlled, and well-documented manufacturing and monitoring processes. This, in turn, helps consumers know that the botanical will be manufactured with consistent quality from batch to batch. You can visit the website of both organizations to review lists of those products that have undergone testing.

Botanicals for Osteoarthritis

Not all botanicals are suitable for treating the pain of osteoarthritis. Complicating this issue is that the purported effects of botanicals are often transposed onto dogs from human specifications. The following list was compiled after an extensive literature search in which botanicals were looked at and found to have a positive impact on arthritis pain.

Proprietary Blends

I just finished telling you that I am uncomfortable with recommending proprietary blends, but there is one exception that I really like. It is distributed by the drug company Bayer and goes under the brand name Alenza. The word *proprietary* means that the product is a unique blend of ingredients that otherwise have no patent on them. In order to protect the formulation from competitors, makers of proprietary supplements often do not disclose what is actually in their product. This, however, prevents us from knowing what we are giving to our dogs. Alenza is different. Not only does a reputable pharmaceutical company make it, but Bayer also is willing to tell us exactly what is in it.

Alenza is a blend of several ingredients; the two most important are Boswellia serrata and Bayer's own special blend of bioflavonoids called Vexadol. A bioflavonoid is a polyphenol substance that comes from a plant, which in this case is used for its medicinal activity. There are many different bioflavonoids, and not all of them have drug-like activities. Alenza contains a patented combination of two bioflavonoids called baicalins and catechins. The other ingredient, Boswellia serrata, will be discussed separately in this chapter.

Alenza has the ability to reduce the inflammation associated with osteoarthritis. It also increases the levels of omega-3 fatty acids by an unknown mechanism. It is considered extremely safe and can be taken by all dogs with osteoarthritis unless they have a known sensitivity to one of the ingredients. Alenza is not going to fix an osteoarthritis issue, especially an advanced one, all by itself. However, it is a great addition to any multimodal therapy and may even allow other drugs and therapies to be used with less frequency.

Ashwagandha

Sometimes known as Withania somnifera, ashwagandha is a plant that originally was found in the Asian subcontinent, primarily India. It has been used in traditional medicine for a variety of reasons, including arthritis pain. It is thought to help arthritis pain through its anti-inflammatory properties. There are no known adverse events in dogs taking this botanical, although there have been a few reports in the human-related literature, including thyrotoxicosis and inflammation of the mucous membranes.

Boswellia Serrata

Boswellia serrata is a tree found in India that is tapped for its sap, much as a maple tree is tapped to make syrup. Instead of syrup, something called an oleoresin is collected that is then purified to use as a botanical preparation. That purification results in isolating the active constituents, which are called boswellic acids. Several studies have shown that boswellic acids act as anti-inflammatories by inhibiting pro-inflammatory mediators by way of 5-lipoxygenase inhibition.[63] In other words, they act very much like the pharmaceutical NSAIDs but without any known side effects or drug interactions.

Corydalis

Sometimes known as Chinese poppy, corydalis is a plant that has been used to treat a variety of illnesses, including osteoarthritis. The active ingredient in corydalis is probably a chemical called tetrahydropalmatine (THP). One of the other uses of corydalis is for sedation, which may lead to an unwanted side effect in your dog. There are no known adverse events or drug interactions known in dogs, but it probably should be used with caution if your dog is already on a medication that is intended for sedation.

Devil's Claw

Devil's claw is the common name of the plant *Harpagophytum pro-cumbens*. It is used for its analgesic effect in dogs with osteoarthritis. The active ingredient is probably something called a glycoside, which has COX inhibition. Devil's claw also can cause an increase in stomach secretions, so it should be used with caution in any dog that is prone to gastrointestinal upsets. There are no known drug or food interactions with the use of devil's claw in dogs; however, it should be used with caution in the presence of NSAIDs because of its COX inhibition.

Hemp

Hemp contains cannabinoids, terpenoids, and flavonoids, all of which may have positive benefits in the treatment of osteoarthritis in dogs. Unlike medical marijuana, hemp does not contain significant amounts of THC, the substance that causes the "high." More research is needed to explore these benefits.

Ginger

Ginger contains volatile oils, which are probably responsible for its medicinal effects. In addition to its well-known ability to reduce nausea, it can also reduce the inflammation associated with osteoarthritis. There are no known drug or food interactions with the use of ginger in dogs.

Marijuana

There are no adequate studies that have shown the benefit of treating osteoarthritis pain in dogs with medical marijuana. I would not be surprised to see such studies published in the near future. The only reason I have listed marijuana in the botanical section is as a warning to you about the potential side effects and cost of treatments. It is rare that a dog does not survive an overdose of medical marijuana; however, they often need to be hospitalized and given costly supportive care as part of the treatment. Until such time as there is a proven benefit with a known safe dose, I do not recommend the use of medical marijuana for the treatment of osteoarthritis pain.

Meadowsweet

Meadowsweet is the common name for the plant *Filipendula ulmaria*. Meadowsweet works because it contains several salicylates, similar to aspirin. Like aspirin, it reduces pain and inflammation, including that from osteoarthritis. Meadowsweet can cause stomach irritation and ulcers in dogs, although this is uncommon. There are no known food interactions; however, it should not be used alongside any medication that also contains salicylates, including aspirin. It should not be used in dogs taking nonsteroidal anti-inflammatory drugs (NSAIDs) because of possible interactions.

Prickly Ash

Prickly ash is the name of the bark and sometimes the fruit of two American ash trees, *Zanthoxylum americanum* and *Zanthoxylum clava-herculis*. The ash bark contains alkaloids and a volatile oil. The fruit of the ash also contains the volatile oil. It is these oils that are thought to reduce the inflammation associated with osteoarthritis. There are no known interactions between prickly ash and foods or medications.

Sarsaparilla

You may have heard of sarsaparilla. It was once a common flavoring ingredient used in root beer. Besides tasting good, it contains anti-inflammatory substances called phytosterols that are useful in treating osteoarthritis. There are reports of interactions with salicylates in human medicine, so do not use them if your pet is on any medication with salicylates. There is also a possible interaction with the heart medication digoxin. Digoxin mostly has been replaced by newer heart medications, but if your dog is taking any medication for his heart, talk to your veterinarian before starting any treatment with sarsaparilla.

St. John's Wort

St. John's wort is commonly used in people to treat depression. St. John's wort most likely exerts its antidepressant actions by inhibiting the reuptake of the neurotransmitters serotonin and norepinephrine. These two neurotransmitters also play a key role in how the body perceives pain. There are similar medications used for osteoarthritis, such as tricyclic antidepressants and tramadol, which your dog already may be taking. There are also several other products (some parasite controls, for example) that also may inhibit these neurotransmitters. The use of St. John's wort in the presence of one of these medications can cause severe side effects, even death, from a condition called serotonin syndrome. Never give St. John's wort without a discussion with your veterinarian about possible interactions with other products.

Turmeric

Turmeric is a spice with which you may be familiar. It often has been touted as a potent botanical for the treatment of osteoarthritis pain. As of this writing there have been no studies showing the benefit of turmeric in the treatment of osteoarthritis pain in dogs. In fact, there have been several that have shown that it was no better than placebo at treating pain. This is not true on the human side. In fact, in one study, turmeric was comparable to ibuprofen in the treatment of knee osteoarthritis.[64] So does it work in dogs? I don't know the answer. However, it has no side effects, and as long as it is not being used as the sole source of pain relief for a dog in pain, it can't hurt anything and it might actually help.

15

SHOCK WAVE THERAPY

SHOCK WAVE THERAPY, ALSO KNOWN AS EXTRA- corporeal shock wave therapy (ESWT), utilizes certain frequencies of high-energy sound waves to break up kidney stones (lithotripsy). Although it first came into being as a method for treating people with kidney stones, its most common use today is to treat pain in humans and horses. There has, however, been a steady increase of its use to treat pain in dogs.

Although shock wave therapy holds the promise to treat certain painful conditions such as joint or muscle pain, it cannot be used for everything. Not all shock wave machines used in veterinary medicine are the same. I will discuss those conditions for which shock wave therapy is best suited. I also will discuss the different type of shock wave units and the advantages that some have over the others. And finally, I will tell you what to expect should you elect to have your dog treated with ESWT.

The How, Why, and What of ESWT

Shock wave therapy has nothing to do with an electrical shock going into your dog. All ESWT units utilize electricity to produce the shock wave; however, the "shock" wave itself is more akin to the sound (and pressure) produced by an explosion. Ultrasound machines for diagnostic imaging—used, for example, during a pregnancy exam—also use sound waves but at a lesser intensity. The shock wave unit by contrast uses significantly higher energy in order to reduce pain and inflammation.

No one is exactly sure why shock wave therapy even works. Several theories have been explored, and evidence points to some kind of biological response to the shock wave. Similar to acupuncture, shock wave therapy causes inflammation, taking a chronic inflammatory condition and adding acute inflammation to it. In many cases, a dog that is experiencing chronic inflammation has quit responding to it on a biological level. By adding some acute inflammation, the body's natural responses can kick in. The damaged tissues bring in anti-inflammatory agents, and these anti-inflammatory agents then dampen down all of the pain, both the new acute pain and the old chronic pain.

Other research shows that the shock wave therapy releases growth factors. This results in soft tissue regeneration and subsequent healing. Shock wave therapy also causes the release of trigger points in dogs with myofascial pain syndrome (see Chapter 7). In the end it doesn't matter to your dog how the treatment works so long as it makes him feel better!

The Different Types of Shock Wave Units

An intense sound wave or shock wave can be produced by a number of means. Three different units for producing shock waves have been utilized for medical treatment: piezoelectric, electromagnetic, and electrohydraulic.

Piezoelectric shock waves are created as the result of rapidly vibrating crystals. This type of shock wave is often used in veterinary dentistry to create a vibrating probe that breaks up the tartar on a dog's teeth during cleaning. The probe used for treating pain is much larger and the intensity is much stronger. This particular type of piezoelectric shock wave unit is popular because the probe has a long life. It can create hundreds of thousands of shocks. However, the intensity of the shock waves are less than what I like to see for some pain treatments and the probe is therefore limited in its use.

Electromagnetic shock wave units work very similarly to a stereo loudspeaker. However, this "loudspeaker" focuses the intense sound energy into a small focal area, enabling it to penetrate tissue and reach the target area. Although it produces a stronger shock wave than the piezoelectric unit, it is still not strong enough to treat all painful conditions.

The electrohydraulic unit is my favorite of the three. This unit works by sending electricity through water, producing sound waves much in the way they are produced during an electrical storm. I think of this as the "thunder and lightning" shock wave. It has the advantage of delivering high-intensity shock waves to depths and areas that are most suitable for treating osteoarthritis. One of the disadvantages of this unit is that the probe only holds approximately 20,000 pulses or shocks in it. After that limit is reached, the probe must be replenished. Because some joints need up to 1,000 shocks per treatment, this unit is one of the most expensive to operate. But in the long term it is probably the most effective of the three.

Is There Research to Support Shock Wave as a Pain Treatment?

Shock wave therapy is fairly new to small animal medicine. As such, not a lot of studies have been done that specifically look at shock waves for the treatment of pain in dogs. Of the studies that have been done most are retrospective in nature, meaning that they look at a population of treated dogs over time and compare patient outcomes as evaluated by both the owner and the veterinarian. There are, however, many clinical reports on the benefits of shock wave therapy.

One study[65] was on the effect ESWT had on inflammatory conditions of the shoulder in fifteen dogs for which conventional conservative therapy such as rehabilitation and NSAID therapy failed. The dogs in this study were treated every three or four weeks using a VersaTron shock wave device (the stronger electrohydraulic unit) for a total of three treatments. Of the nine dogs that returned for evaluation at the end of the three treatments, six showed improvement and the other three were no longer lame. In the long term (months to several years), eleven dogs were evaluated by phone interviews with the caretakers and 64 percent of those dogs were reported as still showing an improvement in the lameness scores.

What does this tell us? The potential for response to treatment is excellent, and the long-term outcome is good. You should keep in mind that most of these dogs also had undergone more traditional and conservative therapy prior to the ESWT, and the decision to use shock wave therapy was made after that traditional therapy proved to be inadequate. This doesn't mean that shock wave therapy couldn't be the first treatment of choice, but it is entirely possible that pretreating these dogs with NSAIDs, acupuncture, or rehab set the stage for a successful shock wave treatment.

What Pain Conditions Can Be Treated by ESWT?

I recommend the use of shock wave therapy most often for those conditions that effect joints and the function of joints. Osteoarthritis, hip dysplasia, and elbow dysplasia are probably the three problems most treated at my clinic with shock wave therapy. Lumbosacral disease (cauda equina syndrome) is also very high on my list for treatment using ESWT.

Shock wave therapy also has uses for healing soft tissue, particularly ligament and tendon injuries, inflammation, and wounds. It also can be used to treat non-union and delayed-union fractures of bones, that is, when the bones are not knitting together as quickly as expected after a fracture repair.

What Should I Expect the Day of Treatment?

No matter which type of shock wave unit your veterinarian utilizes, your dog will need to have his hair clipped over the site of treatment. Hair can trap air around it, and air reduces or even prevents the sound wave from entering your dog's tissue. Ultrasound gel is spread on the skin to help eliminate the probe-air-skin interface and to create a clean probe-skin contact area. Even small amounts of hair will trap the air, ultrasound gel or not, so only those dogs with very short and thin hair coats might avoid being shaved. Without shaving you run the risk of the sound wave not reaching the target and the subsequent failure of the treatment. There is no way the person operating the shock wave unit can tell if the wave is penetrating past any trapped air and going into the tissue. In my opinion, skipping the haircut can put the treatment and your money at risk.

If a piezoelectric or electromagnetic shock wave unit is being used, the intensity of the shock wave and the noise that the unit makes are usually tolerable by the patient. Remember, these are the two units that do not have the same high intensity as the electrohydraulic unit. If your veterinarian is using an electrohydraulic unit like I have in my practice, an analgesic sedative needs to be used.

Even without touching the shock wave unit to the skin, the noise produced by an electrohydraulic unit is very loud and almost always disturbing to the dog. Additionally, the sound wave itself can cause discomfort to normal tissue, and might be even more uncomfortable when being applied to painful tissue or joints. Despite my patients being sedated and given a painkiller like morphine, some of them still react to the treatment, both to the noise it makes and the pain it causes.

How Many Treatments Should My Dog Receive and How Much Will It Cost?

Most research points to three treatments at two- to three-week intervals as being optimal. Most treatments cost $200 to $300 per joint, per visit. When multiple joints are involved, as they are in most dogs, the treatment cost can add up.

What Should I Expect After Treatment?

If your dog was sedated, she naturally will have some aftereffect from the sedative that can take up to 24 hours to wear off, depending on the sedative and pain medication used and, to an extent, on your dog's reaction to these substances. Your veterinarian should warn you of the most common things you might see after you get her home.

Starting the day of treatment, and for up to 48 hours, one of two things might happen. Some dogs seem much worse after treatment.

This is not surprising when you consider the fact that the veterinarian was targeting shock wave energy at some very painful areas. Interestingly, this same treatment can have the opposite effect and produce a temporary analgesic effect, allowing a dog to move around better than she was prior to the first treatment. If this should happen, it is almost always short lived and will not last more than the first two days.

Actual benefits from the treatment can be seen in as little as one week after the first treatment. Most dogs, however, will realize an improvement within the first week or two. As encouraging as this might be, you should follow the schedule your veterinarian sets up for you and finish all of the treatments to get the full benefit. The full beneficial effect might take as long as six months after the last treatment.

No treatment lasts forever and sooner or later your dog might need to go through an additional course of treatments. But as the aforementioned studies noted, some dogs can experience the benefits of ESWT months to years after finishing the three treatments.

As you might expect, there has been a lot of excitement in the pain "community" about ESWT. But as I say again and again throughout this book, no single treatment is going to fix the pain. Expect that your dog may need additional therapies to supplement the ESWT.

16

PAIN RELIEF THERAPIES BEST AVOIDED

ON THE SURFACE, MANY OF THE PAIN THERAPIES available today might seem plausible. But upon closer study the effectiveness of these pain therapies is questionable, even suspect.

Chiropractic, for example, has a lot of good research behind several of its applications—for humans. There are other therapies, such as homeopathy and Reiki, for which there is absolutely no evidence that they are effective for the treatment of pain. And depending on these particular modalities to treat pain, when used to the exclusion of proven pain treatments, these so-called therapies are essentially tantamount to withholding pain treatment.

I understand that the contents of this chapter may upset many people, especially when I discuss some of the treatments that they really believe in but for which there is little or poor evidence to support the claimed benefits. Know that I even find myself conflicted when I look at a treatment from the approach of, "Is there the evidence to support its use?" As a pain practitioner, if I were to take away from my armamentarium every modality, drug, and exercise for which there was not strong evidence, I would be left with very little with which to work. Nonetheless, in this chapter I discuss treatments that might have potential benefits for treating pain but have not been adequately studied; and I also examine treatments that are the modern-day version of snake oil.

An Ineffective Pain Treatment Is the Same as No Pain Treatment

With the exception of two therapies, it is not my intention to talk you out of engaging in these treatments. Instead, I would like you to understand some of the risks of the treatments and the known benefits for which we have evidence, so that you can make an informed decision when providing pain care for your dog.

Chiropractic

It is hard for me to discuss chiropractic for dogs. It is one of those modalities I have benefited from as a human, and I would like to see our dogs enjoy the same benefit as well. When I speak with veterinarians who have undergone chiropractic training, they unanimously claim the benefit of chiropractic for their patients. But where is the evidence? For dogs all of the evidence is anecdotal, mostly in the form of success stories by both veterinarians and their dogs' caregivers. There are, of course, some horrifying stories as well. As for research and studies, I have not been able to find a single result proving the benefit of chiropractic in dogs.

So what is the problem? Chiropractors learn about chiropractic over the course of years. And during those years they learn how to diagnose and treat problems in humans. Some programs offer a brief course in animal chiropractic but these are almost always post-graduate courses. A chiropractor learns almost nothing about the unique neuroanatomy and physiology of a dog, especially when compared to the training a veterinarian receives.

What about veterinarians who learn chiropractic? Again, this is a medical professional who is going to take four weeks or so of training, hoping to learn in a month everything that a chiropractor learns over many years.

And no matter if the professional is a chiropractor or veterinarian, both learn a skill that has been transposed from human chiropractic to animals. In essence, the science behind animal chiropractic is scanty at best with no proven benefit to the canine patient.

If practicing chiropractic were totally benign at its worst, then this would not be an issue. But things can and do go wrong at an alarming frequency: strokes, paralysis, even death can result from chiropractic manipulation. And this happens in humans for whom professionals are trained and licensed to practice on. There are no statistics kept for problems arising from dogs that undergo chiropractic, so we really don't know how many have been helped or hurt.

In the American Animal Hospital Association's 2015 AAHA/AAFP Pain Management Guidelines for Dogs and Cats,[66] their pain task force states, "This Task Force has not found sufficient, reliable, noncontradictory evidence for the use of chiropractic care for pain management in veterinary medicine at this time. That said, chiropractic care has many well-defined applications in human medicine that have been supported through reliable research." In other words, the evidence does not support its use for the treatment of pain in animals.

If you decide that you still want to try chiropractic, I can recommend the following three bits of advice. First, never see a human chiropractor who does not work with a veterinarian. In fact, in most states it is illegal for chiropractors to practice without the consent and consultation of a veterinarian on a case-by-case basis. Second, never have a "disk" case treated by chiropractic manipulations, as the procedures will probably worsen the problem. And finally, insist that the chiropractor does not perform high-impact manipulations (think of getting your neck "cracked"). There is little room in human chiropractic for this kind of treatment and no room in veterinary medicine.

Homeopathy

I am somewhat conflicted about telling you to never have chiropractic done to your dog. There is no such conflict when it comes to homeopathy. There has not been a single reliable study done for homeopathy in dogs that has shown any benefit for the treatment of pain. In the American Animal Hospital Association pain guidelines, it is stated, "Incontrovertible evidence that homeopathy is effective in either human or veterinary medicine for the treatment of pain is lacking. Sole reliance on homeopathy to treat a painful condition is in essence withholding pain treatment. Thus, the guidelines' Task Force discourages the use of homeopathy for the treatment of pain."[67] The key idea here is that relying on homeopathy to treat pain is the same as withholding treatment.

Naturopathy

Naturopathy is a field of medicine based on the belief of the existence of a vital energy, the manipulation of which guides bodily processes and allows it to heal. This vital energy has never been seen nor measured. There are no studies looking at naturopathy in animals. Naturopathy should not be considered for the treatment of pain in dogs.

Prolotherapy

Prolotherapy, sometimes called proliferative therapy, involves the injection of a substance near damaged ligaments or tendons with the desire to hasten healing. The substance injected is most commonly some form of dextrose (sugar) solution. However, anything can be injected in prolotherapy, with the intended effect of causing some kind of irritation at the site of the injury.

The theory of how prolotherapy might work has some merit. The logic is this: The body often "gives up" on trying to heal chronic diseases (such as tendonitis); thus, injecting an irritant in or near an area of disease can turn a chronic problem into an acute condition that the body might try to heal. As discussed in the chapter on acupuncture, this is one of several mechanisms by which acupuncture works. Rotating the acupuncture needle causes connective tissue disruption, which releases inflammatory agents, and the body responds by sending in anti-inflammatories.

Unfortunately, there have not been any good studies proving the benefit of prolotherapy. Some practitioners inject corticosteroids into the affected area and claim a result. Unfortunately, this outcome is not the work of prolotherapy; rather, it is the corticosteroids that are providing anti-inflammatory relief. Indeed, substances like corticosteroids are the opposite of what a prolotherapy substance should be.

Although I don't think that prolotherapy will ever be a major player in treating pain in dogs, there probably will be some advancement in it as time goes on. I cannot recommend prolotherapy as a first line of treatment in cases of tendon and ligament pain; however, I don't have a problem with it if it is used as a treatment of last resort.

Reiki

Reiki is perhaps the most well-known therapy from a group of therapies variously known as healing touch, hands-on-healing, or palm healing. The theory behind this practice is that the practitioner is transferring through his or her palms to the patient some kind of universal energy that allows for self-healing. There can be and sometimes is a real psychological effect on the person receiving Reiki in the form of a feeling of peace or equilibrium as a result of both the desire to get better and the attention the patient is receiving. However, Reiki has been found to have no known medical benefit to treating any disease in humans or dogs.[68] Reiki should certainly not play a role in treating your dog's pain. If you want to give your dog some attention to make him feel peaceful, and provide him with an actual medical benefit, consider massage instead. Please see Chapter 20 for more about massage.

Traditional Chinese Veterinary Medicine

Some of my colleagues, whom I hold in high esteem, practice Traditional Chinese Veterinary Medicine (TCVM). I like to kid them that someday I will bring them over from the "dark side" and show them the true path. It is not so much that they never get results, often they do. But the evidence for many of the diagnostic methods and treatments using TCVM are, more often than not, sorely lacking.

TCVM is separate from Chinese acupuncture. In other words, it is possible to learn and be a practitioner of Chinese acupuncture without ever learning any of the other aspects of Traditional Chinese Veterinary

Medicine, and *vice versa*. It is a common, but mistaken, assumption that because they are both Chinese and both have something to do with veterinary medicine, that they must go hand-in-hand. And sometimes they do, but not always. The other branches of TCVM involve herbal therapy, diet, and Tui Na.

A few ancillary aspects of TCVM can have some value in treating pain in dogs. Instead of discussing TCVM as a whole, I will discuss each of these three branches individually. For a discussion of Chinese acupuncture, please see Chapter 9.

Herbal Therapy

I briefly discuss Chinese herbal therapy in Chapter 14 in my discussion of botanical therapies. Most Chinese herbal therapies rely on the use of proprietary, and therefore secret, ingredients. These proprietary mixtures are not regulated by any government agency, and any adverse event reporting is entirely voluntary and more often than not, never done. Some of these mixtures contain powerful botanicals that can cause serious side effects on their own merit and can interact with other medications with disastrous results.

As if there isn't enough concern about efficacy and safety of the ingredients that these mixtures *should* contain, there are concerns for contamination with heavy metals such as arsenic and lead, and adulteration with non-medicinal plants and materials such as weeds, rice, and wheat powder. These ingredients are used in an effort to make the final product cheaper to produce.

The use of Chinese herbal therapy might hold some ethical concerns as well. Many animal parts, including those animals that are on endangered species lists, are sometimes put into these products. Risk of side effects, contamination, adulteration, and ethical concerns makes the use of unregulated Chinese herbal therapy a poor choice for the treatment of pain.

Chinese Dietary Therapy

Dietary therapy is a huge part of modern veterinary medicine. Some dogs need more of one thing or less of another, whether it is calories, fiber, trace elements, essential fatty acids, and so forth. Chinese dietary therapy is designed to manipulate organ function and the movement of *qi* (discussed in Chapter 9 in the section on Chinese acupuncture).

There are known medicinal benefits to many foods. For example, many people use ginger, often in the form of ginger ale, in order to calm an upset stomach. Chinese dietary therapy often involves foods that have similarly modest benefits, but this therapy also can make claims about the benefits of certain foods for which there is no known evidence. This mixture of both fact and fiction makes it impossible for the uninformed caregiver to make a good decision for their dog. The evidence for Chinese dietary therapy is poor. If you want to feed your dog nutritional supplements in a diet that is beneficial in the treatment of pain, then I recommend you review the recommendations that are given in Chapter 13.

Tui Na

Tui Na is a form of Chinese manipulative therapy. Tui means "to push" and Na means "to lift and squeeze." This is done in an effort to move energy, or *qi*, around the body and to restore proper balance. Tui Na is often misunderstood in that it is sometimes thought to be a type of massage for the sake of the benefits of massage. But this is not the case: Tui Na is about manipulating "energy." While there may be some benefit from the physical manipulation that results from "pushing and squeezing," and indeed there are real benefits from massage therapy when done properly, there are no studies proving the benefit of Tui Na in the treatment of pain. In fact, one human study showed that when Tui Na was combined with a type of yoga called "relaxing yoga" in the treatment of fibromyalgia in humans there was an actual decrease in the long-term, pain-relieving benefits of yoga.[69] Ultimately, there is no good research proving the benefit of Tui Na for the relief of pain in dogs.

17

FUTURE PAIN TREATMENTS

NEW PAIN TREATMENTS FOR BOTH ACUTE AND CHRONIC pain are on the horizon, some of which promise to be revolutionary. I will discuss those treatments that, in my estimation, have the most promise and will hopefully get approval by the FDA.

All of these "future" treatments must first go through the strict and vigorous trials mandated by the FDA in order to prove that they not only do what they are supposed to do, but that they are also reasonably safe for the condition and patients that they are intended to treat. Licensing for new treatments often takes many years, and may not even happen in time to treat your dog's pain. However, it doesn't hurt to ask your veterinarian from time to time if there are any new pain treatments on the market. Who knows, your dog may be one of the first to benefit from one of these new treatments.

"Vaccinations" for Pain: Anti-Nerve Growth Factor Antibodies

Wouldn't it be wonderful to take your dog in for his annual vaccinations to protect him not only against communicable diseases but against the pain of osteoarthritis as well? This is a possibility. Such an injection, however, would not be a vaccine in the true sense of the word, but would more likely be an injection of antibodies. Vaccines against infectious diseases encourage dogs to make their own antibodies, which is why the protective value of these vaccines can last for many years. Injections of antibodies would probably only last a few months, but the value of this pain treatment could be tremendous nonetheless.

Pain, especially chronic pain, is invariably caused by a variety of mechanisms all working at once. At the same time, not every single mechanism behind the pain needs to be treated in order to reduce the level of pain to a tolerable point. That being said, in most cases the more pain pathways that are treated, the better the results. A pain vaccine probably will be no different in that it probably only will address one mechanism of pain, not all of them. But for some dogs that might be enough to improve their quality of life, and for other dogs it might be the extra treatment necessary to achieve that same goal. The National Institute of Health has many research papers in its library looking exactly at this idea of antibodies to treat pain. There are several different approaches that seem to hold promise.

One such mechanism is to give antibodies against a substance called nerve growth factor (NGF). NGF is a protein secreted by various tissues, and its primary role is described by its name, stimulation of the growth of nerves. However, under certain conditions, including mechanical stress on cartilage, there is an increase in the production of NGF. These higher levels of NGF produce pain and inflammation in joints.

There have been several studies done that show a benefit in targeting NGF to reduce pain in animal models of arthritis. One study showed the benefit of treating osteoarthritis in rats with a single injection of anti-NGF antibodies.[70] Another study in dogs showed reduction in pain for approximately four weeks after a single injection.[71] However, NGF in small amounts is necessary for proper function of many tissues including joints, and adverse events have been described, including the destruction of cartilage in people who received anti-NGF antibody injections.[72] In other words, this treatment caused cartilage destruction in the very joints the antibodies were meant to help. As with any pharmaceutical, safety studies and research need to be done in order to determine if anti-NGF antibodies can be safely administered and under what circumstances and with what potential but acceptable consequences.

The Piprant Antagonist Drug Grapiprant

The piprant class of drugs inhibits the production of prostaglandins by a mechanism different from NSAIDs. NSAIDs target an entire cyclo-oxygenase (COX) pathway. As you might recall, this COX pathway is responsible not only for pain-inducing prostaglandins, but it has protective functions as well that may be interfered with, causing most of the adverse events associated with NSAIDs.

The pharmaceutical company Aratana Therapeutics will soon release Galliprant (grapiprant tablets) from this class of drugs. Galliprant holds great promise for the relief of pain in those dogs who are unable to tolerate the NSAID class of drugs. Galliprant will not require the costly monitoring necessary with NSAID use because of its apparently higher safety profile.

Resiniferatoxin

Resiniferatoxin is a natural substance that is related to capsaicin, the chemical that makes chili peppers hot. The Scoville scale is often used to measure the "hotness" of peppers. For example, a jalapeño pepper has a score of approximately 5,000 whereas a habanero pepper has a score of roughly 100,000. Compare this to pure capsaicin that has a score of nearly 16 million. Resiniferatoxin has the highest score of them all at 16 billion Scoville units. If you recall from Chapter 6, the action of all of these substances is not only to stimulate pain through C fibers, the fibers responsible for most chronic pain, but also to cause a die-off of C fibers, thus eliminating that particular source of pain.

Clinical studies have been performed to treat the pain of bone cancer, one of the most painful conditions that dogs suffer from, with intrathecal (spinal cord) injections of resiniferatoxin.[74] The resinifer-atoxin killed off only those neurons in the spinal cord responsible for transmitting signals from the C fibers, leaving other neurons and their functions intact. These studies were very successful when compared with the regular standard of care used to treat bone cancer pain in dogs. Some dogs walked as though there was no pain, even when the cancer caused pathological fractures through the destruction of the bone.

Although a treatment of this kind is very complex and unlikely to be performed at most veterinary hospitals, it holds promise for the treat-ment of osteosarcoma pain at specialty centers and in university set-tings, should this treatment become FDA approved.

Substance P-Saporin

Substance P-saporin is a combination of two chemicals that are neuro-toxins. They can be injected in a manner that is similar to resiniferatoxin when used to target and destroy pain receptors in the dorsal horn of the spinal cord of dogs suffering from the pain of bone cancer. Although the results of the studies did not produce pain relief as quickly as the resiniferatoxin study, most dogs had satisfactory pain relief starting at two weeks after injection.[75]

Gene Therapy

Can you imagine using a virus for good instead of harm? This is the stuff that sounds like science fiction, but it has already been tested for several applications. The relevant application of genetic modification for the control of pain will be discussed here very briefly.

One of the problems encountered in the control of pain in our dogs is that we often need to flood their entire system with a pain-controlling drug when in reality we only want it at one specific site. With gene therapy to modify viruses, there is a real possibility of targeting particular tissues.

We have been scientifically modifying viruses to serve our purposes for more than 100 years, changing them so that they can provide immunity through vaccinations without causing disease. It is possible to change them further by modifying them to release pain medications such as opioids or other pain-modifying substances, and then "infecting" the spinal cord to stop the pain before it reaches the brain. Research into this type of treatment for severe types of pain such as bone cancer has shown promise.[76] It is even possible to give these viruses chemical "on and off" switches so that they can be activated or deactivated as needed. There are no products currently on the market, but this modality has real potential for the treatment of chronic pain.

18

THE PAIN "MAKEOVER" FOR YOUR HOME AND DOG

IF YOUR DOG SUFFERS FROM CHRONIC PAIN, YOU CAN do many things to help him more easily move around the home. Most of these changes are simple and inexpensive and take only a moderate amount of time and effort to put in place, but will offer significant relief to your dog. For example, you can spray rosin on the bottoms of your dog's feet so that he can better navigate wood floors, or you can add a ramp out the back door to help him negotiate those two or three steps. Both of these accommodations can make a world of difference to your dog. After all, even though a dog is in pain, exercise and social interactions are essential to maintaining a good quality of life. In other words, if your dog is unable to move around freely, his life is diminished.

Things You Can Do with Your Dog

Walking on slippery surfaces is sometimes difficult even for dogs with no pain issues. It is almost always an issue for dogs with osteoarthritis. A dog's ability to walk on slippery surfaces usually worsens as the osteoarthritis advances and muscle strength decreases. What to do?

Nonskid Socks

My favorite approach for these dogs is to put nonslip socks on their feet. There are several brands that are made for dogs, and they are similar in design to the hospital socks that are often given to human patients so that they do not slip on the hospital floors. The socks are generally made of cotton, and the nonskid portion is either a fabric paint or rubberized material that is applied in various patterns. It is best to get a style in which the nonskid pattern extends up the sides of the socks so that if they twist about on your dog's foot, the nonskid surface still remains in contact with the floor.

Sizing is very important. The common mistake everyone makes is to get too large a sock that will not stay on. Carefully follow the manufacturer's recommendations for sizing your dog's foot. Look for a retailer that provides sample sizes so that you can check your dog for fit prior to making a purchase.

Rosin

Not all dogs will keep their socks on. My own dog loves her socks as long as she is moving around. If she decides to sit for even a short time she also decides it is time that they come off, and one by one she gently pulls them off her feet. She doesn't consider the fact that she might be walking on the wood floor in the next little while. And no matter how many times I explain it to her, she won't listen!

An alternative to socks is a rosin spray often used by tennis players and acrobats. The rosin is derived from wood, and in the quantities sprayed on your dog's feet, it is harmless if licked. The spray itself has a slightly objectionable odor and is flammable, so always follow the manufacturer's warnings.

In a well-ventilated area, spray the bottoms of your dog's footpads with the rosin spray. Then wait a few seconds before allowing him to walk. The results are not as good as wearing the socks, and you will need to reapply it throughout the day depending on how much your dog walks around. You will have to experiment with how much spray to put on and how often you need to reapply it to your dog's feet.

Grooming

Certain breeds have a lot of hair in between their toes, which if long enough will cover part of the entire pad. This of course makes it even harder for these dogs to walk on slippery surfaces. Even if excess hair isn't an issue, some dogs extend their nails as much as possible when they encounter a slippery surface. Their instinct is to grip the surface, but of course they can't. And because the smooth, hard nail interfaces with the smooth, hard floor, these dogs slip. It is akin to putting on ice skates. Before using either nonskid socks or rosin to help your dog, make sure that the hair on his feet is cut short and that his nails are trimmed back so that neither contributes to the problem in any significant way.

Boots

All of the previous solutions are great for indoors, but you need to take measures for taking your dog outdoors too. This is especially true if you live in a northern climate where winter weather conditions are an issue for a large part of the year. The best solution comes in the form of boots. Primarily used by canine athletes, these boots are designed to help protect dogs' feet from ice and snow. They are made in a huge variety of styles, so when you choose one, try to get one that can be put on easily and isn't too heavy or bulky.

Balloon Socks

An alternative to boots, socks, and rosin is something called balloon socks. They actually look like a balloon and feature a large opening to slip over your dog's foot. These stay on very well and provide great traction indoors and some traction outdoors. I am not a fan of using them indoors because the only sweat glands your dog has are in his feet. The resulting high humidity inside these waterproof balloon socks can cause skin issues, including infections, if they are worn for too long of a period of time.

Harnesses with Handles

Sometimes your dog needs a little extra lift when getting into a car, climbing or descending a few stairs, or walking across slippery or uneven surfaces. A harness that has a handle on it means you can provide just that lift. This harness is something that can be worn all of the time, that most dogs cannot get off, and that really can benefit your dog. A dog with osteoarthritis often gets around during 98 percent of his day just fine, but needs help in just a few circumstances. I like these harnesses with handles on them because they are always ready to use (simply put it on your dog in the morning and take it off at night), and they help protect your own back from lift strains and injuries.

There are two types to consider. The one that will serve most dogs' needs is styled to look like a classic harness but simply has a handle on the top. The other harness style extends down your dog's back and features a handle at the shoulders and another handle over the pelvic area. This style is useful for dogs that have difficulties rising from a down position. For these dogs the single, front-handle harness just isn't enough. The two-handle harness is more expensive, more difficult to fit, and takes into consideration whether your dog is male or female. It is my recommendation if you are going to invest in either one of these harnesses, that you purchase it through a canine rehabilitation center.

Emergency Harness

It is possible that your dog only needs a harness on rare circumstances. Although a harness that is designed for assisted lifting is best because it provides less chance of injury to yourself or your dog, it is possible to make a temporary harness out of a leash. The leash needs to be long enough in relationship to the size of your dog in order for this to work. With the clip end of the leash attached to the collar in a normal fashion, take the handle end of the leash and pass it under the abdomen and secure it just in front of the rear legs. This can give you a temporary handle to help lift your dog's hind end.

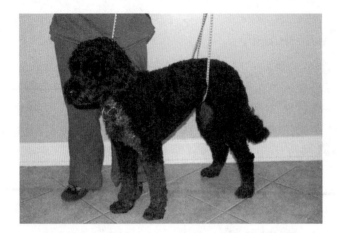

Emergency harness made with a leash.

Things You Can Do with Your Home

You have many opportunities to make your home a friendlier place for your arthritic dog. These solutions are simple and inexpensive, yet can greatly increase your dog's comfort and her ability to move around.

Food and Water Bowls

Elevating food and water bowls is a simple thing that you can do to make it a lot easier for your dog to get the nutrition he needs. Some 20 years ago, I remember searching high and low for an adjustable water-and-food bowl contraption to help my aging dog with some of her osteoarthritis pain. It was a long search and an expensive purchase. These days, elevated bowls are commonly available and are much cheaper to buy. It is best to get one with adjustable legs so that you can experiment with the height to find what is most comfortable for your dog.

Orthopedic Bedding

Orthopedic bedding for dogs is available at almost every pet store. Manufacturers you might recognize as having made your own mattress make many of these beds. There is a confusing array of features and styles, and I will describe what I feel are the best ones.

Soil resistance is important. And by soil resistance I mean two separate things. The cover should be removable and machine washable; even if your dog never has an accident, who among us would want to sleep on the same bedding for weeks on end without it being washed? The second thing is that the main part of the bed should have a cover or lining that is impervious to liquids. Old dogs have accidents, and you do not want to throw away your investment should an accident occur. While shopping, don't be afraid to unzip the lining to see what is underneath and to make sure that portion of the bed meets this requirement. Check to see if the manufacturer or pet store backs its product with some kind of guarantee or warranty.

Does your dog like to sleep with her head elevated? If so, buy her a bed with a bolster on it. But the bolster should only extend on one or two of the sides of the bed. If she has osteoarthritis, the effort to step over the bolster might be too much and she will not even try to use the bed.

Just as not having a bolster on all sides is important, the bed itself should not be too thick or come with a frame that elevates it off the floor. This is the voice of experience. The first orthopedic bed I bought for my dog came with a fancy steel-wrought frame that made it look very nice but also added 6 inches or so to the height of the bed. This made it too difficult for my dog to get in and out of the bed. In fact, she never used the comfy mattress until I got rid of the wrought-iron frame.

How firm should the mattress be? Unfortunately this varies with your dog's own preference. Just like in people, mattress preferences vary by individual. Try to recall what types of surfaces your dog seeks out naturally and go with that type of padding to start. If you can get your pet store to agree to a one-week trial, all the better for you and your dog and your wallet. The one body type I do have a recommendation for is the skinny, old dog that has knobby-looking joints. These dogs often do best on beds with memory foam. Memory foam can be difficult to walk on, so don't get a mattress with too thick a layer of the memory foam.

Stairs

The easiest stairways to deal with are usually the ones associated with the outside doors of your house. Not every set of stairs needs to be adapted, but you should choose the stairs that your dog uses the most.

Some dogs only need nonskid strips to be put on the stairsteps, and these can be purchased on the Internet and most home-improvement stores. Other dogs must be accommodated with an actual ramp.

If your dog needs a ramp for two or three steps, I would recommend that you invest in a custom-built, semi-permanent ramp. Temporary ramps are often wobbly and many dogs refuse to use them. Temporary ramps can also slide out from either you or your dog and cause injury. A quick search of the Internet can give you plans on how to build a ramp. If you are not handy as a carpenter, you might want to contact a company that specializes in adapting homes for human accessibility and tell them what you are looking for.

If the stairs your dog is having trouble with are those going to different levels of your multistory house, the solution is going to be more difficult. No matter what you do, depending on the condition your dog has, the stairs may be too hard or treacherous for your dog. I have had several cases of injuries over the years, sometimes involving fractures, when a dog takes a spill. There are three possible solutions: carpet, nonskid stair treads, and a handled harness. Of course if your dog is small enough, then simply carrying her up or down is a good choice. Carpet and nonskid stair treads can provide firm enough footing for a dog that has the strength to use the stairs but is unsteady on them. Adding a handled harness as described earlier and always assisting your dog up and down the steps is probably the safest choice.

If none of these solutions is either feasible or practical to your dog's condition, then consider adjusting your living habits at home so that you can spend as much time as possible on the same floor level as your dog. Doing this will increase the amount of social interaction you have with your dog and vastly improve her attitude and quality of life. I have had many clients tell me they have even taken turns sleeping on the couch so that their dog could have someone nearby at night.

I have one last word of caution. If you cannot make it safe for your dog to maneuver on the stairs by herself, you should get a baby-gate to put at both the top and bottom of the stairs. Some dogs will not attempt the stairs for months or years, and then suddenly find some compelling reason for using them, with disastrous results. I have had a few of my clients over the years come home to find their dogs seriously injured at the bottom of a stairway.

Slippery Floors

Although this was already covered from the perspective of what you can do for your dog, let's look at it from the perspective of what you can do to your house. For short distances, such as from a front door over a tiled floor to carpet, you can place a nonskid rug. There are many inexpensive nonskid rugs, and they come in all manner of shapes, sizes, and designs. By contrast, buying a 20-foot or longer carpet runner can cost many hundreds of dollars. There is an easy solution: yoga mats. Yoga mats can be purchased in rolls of 30 feet or more for a very reasonable price. They even come in a variety of colors to help you blend them in with the room's color scheme. Buy the thinnest mats available and cut it to length for a custom, nonskid pathway for your dog. Although they take a considerable amount of time to dry, yoga mats can be washed and rinsed in a washer if small enough, or washed by hand or with a garden hose if longer. I did this for my own dog, and it was wonderful to see her move from room to room with us instead of hanging back in the hope we would return to her.

Things You Can Do with Your Vehicle

If your dog is like mine, she loves to go for rides. A day without a ride in my car or truck is a bad day in her mind. But as she has aged, her hip dysplasia and subsequent osteoarthritis has made it harder and harder for her to get into and out of the vehicle on her own. And at some point, I decided I did not want her to try and make the jump unassisted due to the real risk that she might hurt herself while doing so. Now I help her to get in and out of a vehicle in a way that is safe for her and me.

Getting In and Out of a Vehicle

Car ramps always seem like a good idea. But because ramps are not firmly fixed to the car, and shift slightly while a dog uses them, many dogs refuse to use them. I see a lot of people pull up to my clinic, hook a ramp to the edge of the door, and watch their dog take one step onto the ramp and then jump off it onto the ground. The same is true while getting into the vehicle; most caregivers practically have to drag their dog up the ramp with his leash. If you are going to buy a car ramp for your dog, and he was not a former agility or obedience dog that had previous experience with climbing and ramps, expect that you are going to have to spend a fair amount of time teaching him how to use the ramp in a safe manner.

An alternative is giving your dog assistance to get into the vehicle. I actually like this approach because your dog still has to do some of the work, and that helps maintain muscle strength. If your dog's front legs are reasonably strong, you can teach him to approach the open door, put first one foot then the other on the threshold of the car door, and wait. Then all you have to do is simply reach under his bottom and give him a boost, which encourages him to pull himself in with his front legs.

When it comes time to get out of the vehicle, you can assist him with a jump by putting your arm around his body and supporting the bottom of his chest so that he does not come down with all of his weight on his legs. A handled harness can help with this as well.

Many vehicles now have second-row seats that easily can be folded up or even removed. Providing a wide and clear path for your dog to get in or out of the vehicle can boost her confidence.

Riding in a Vehicle

Every dog riding in a vehicle should wear a seatbelt harness that is designed for dogs and sold at most pet stores or on the Internet. This is true for young dogs but especially important for older dogs with declining balance and muscle strength. It protects them not only in the case of an accident, but also during sharp turns or abrupt braking. These seatbelt harnesses for dogs usually have additional chest padding to help protect the dog in case of a sudden stop. There are a variety of buckle types available to accommodate the different manufacturer styles of seatbelts. Simply buckle the correct tab into the seatbelt and snug the strap tight enough that he won't go flying like a yo-yo on the end of a string, but not so tight that he can't sit comfortably on the car seat.

It is also helpful to make sure that your dog is riding on a car seat that provides some traction for her. Fabric upholstery itself often provides enough traction. In the case of leather or vinyl seats, fitted cloth seat covers are a good choice.

19

HOME EXERCISES

THIS CHAPTER CONTAINS MORE THAN A DOZEN EXERCISES designed to increase agility, mobility, strength, and balance in dogs with painful conditions. Not all exercises are appropriate for every condition, so it is important that your dog receives an accurate diagnosis prior to starting any of these rehabilitation exercises. It is equally important to make sure that your veterinarian gives the okay for your dog to start these exercises. Some are vigorous in nature and not compatible with certain medical conditions such as, for example, congestive heart failure.

Treatment of certain conditions, especially serious ones, through exercise and physical manipulation should only be carried out by a physical therapist who has received additional training for dogs or by a rehabilitation therapist who has either completed a rehabilitation certification course or is board certified in rehabilitation. But there are many exercises that you, as your dog's caregiver, can do at home to lower your dog's pain and to improve his quality of life. Most of these exercises are aimed at stretching, general core and limb strengthening, and balance. Doing these home exercises can be both fun and rewarding for you and your dog. But before we start on the specific exercises, you need to understand the "why" of rehabilitation and understand some basic precautions.

All dogs in every stage of life need to maintain their strength. Even dogs with physical limitations brought on by surgery, pain, or old age require exercise for health, strength, and maintenance of normal body functions. To carry out a successful exercise program you, as the caregiver, must be committed to finding the time and patience to work with your dog. In addition, the caregiver must take the time to understand the precautions that go with the individual exercises and the start-up of any strengthening and conditioning program.

Following are some guidelines for keeping things safe:

1. **Prior to starting any increase in physical activity it is important to make sure that your dog does not have any medical condition that might make it dangerous to do so.** Have a discussion with your veterinarian before starting your dog on any exercise program and get the okay before proceeding. If your dog is already being treated for a chronic painful condition and recently has been examined, this might only require a phone call to your veterinarian.

2. **Always show your veterinarian the specific exercises you have in mind for your dog, whether you picked them from this book or got them elsewhere, to make sure they are not contraindicated by any existing medical condition.** For example, one strengthening exercise I will show you is called "sit to stand" and could be an unsafe practice for a dog with intervertebral disk disease.

3. **Always begin with stretching.** This both readies the muscles for exercise and lets your dog know that something is about to occur. Stretching is an important part of starting a physical activity for dogs that have experienced a loss of function and muscle mass. The act of stretching fires off nerve endings in the muscles, preparing them for the coming activities. Stretching also helps warm up the muscles, possi-

bly averting damage from the exercises that follow. Finally, stretching tender limbs and joints on your dog, if done properly, can build trust between you and your dog as you prepare to do some of the harder (and from your dog's point of view possibly scarier) strengthening and balance exercises.

4. **If it seems like it hurts, stop.** Review the instructions on how you are supposed to perform a specific exercise. If you are doing it correctly, and it still hurts, strike that stretch or exercise off the list until you next see your veterinarian and get his opinion.

5. **Strengthening exercises should come after stretching exercises.** Improvement of muscle strength helps a dog to maintain proper posture and proper distribution of weight to all four legs. A leg weakened by nonuse because of pain may never be used again even if the original cause of the pain is long gone. The muscles, which were underutilized during treatment and recovery, may no longer have the strength for the tasks they were designed to do. Even short injuries and recovery times can cause muscle weakness. One study demonstrated significant muscle atrophy after only three days of strict cage rest.[77]

6. **Balancing exercises should come after strengthening exercises.** Working to maintain good balance is important in the treatment of many painful diseases, especially those that involve nerve dysfunction. Improving balance not only helps prevent serious falls, but the exercise itself can actually restore lost nerve function through retraining of the dysfunctional nerve.

7. **Follow the schedule recommended by this book or by your veterinarian if she says to do it otherwise.** She knows your dog and I do not. She might know of some med-

ical issue that is not covered here but that could impact the safety of the exercise for your dog.

Don't forget, you are trying to rehabilitate your painful dog, not put her through boot camp. It is okay to take water breaks and rests as needed throughout the entire session. Start by choosing an appropriate stretching exercise and do it once or twice, followed by two to three of the approved strengthening exercises. Just like we might do for our own workout, do these strengthening exercises as "sets." In other words, do each of the chosen exercises sequentially for the suggested number of repetitions, never doing more than two to three sets at one sitting. Finish up with a balance exercise if needed. Make it fun and reward your dog with praise and the occasional treat. Don't make it boring by doing the same exercises day in and day out. Vary them, and if your dog seems to like one over the other, save it for the last exercise of the set or maybe when she is appearing tired so that you can end on a good note. You want her to finish with the memory of rehabilitation as being a fun thing.

The following sections are divided by type of exercise. At the end of the chapter there is a table with a few sample rehabilitation regimens for several painful conditions.

Stretching Exercises

So-called cookie stretches are used to help increase flexibility and range of motion. These stretches are useful for both the canine athlete and the pain patient. None of the stretches listed here put undue stress on any part of the body because the dog himself (with the aid of a cookie under his nose for encouragement) decides on the degree of stretch. I recommend doing all the cookie stretches, not just the ones that seem to focus on a particular body part. Remember how the old song goes, "The hip bone is connected to the thigh bone, the thigh bone is connected to the knee bone . . ." No matter where an injury is in his body, your dog will compensate by twisting, leaning, weight shifting, and so forth so that even the "good" limbs start to experience excessive wear and tear. This means that all areas, not just the problem areas, can benefit from stretching exercises.

Cookie Stretches

When doing the cookie stretches, the treat doesn't have to be a cookie. Use any food that your dog finds irresistible. A small piece of cheese, bit of lunchmeat, or chunk of hot dog will work great. Just remember, it is not the size of the treat, but the smell of it hidden in your hand that will make your dog stretch. You can often get three or four stretches out of a single treat before rewarding. Dogs actually try harder if you don't reward after every desired stretch—they think they are doing it wrong and try even harder on the next one. Some dogs need to have types of treats alternated in order to keep their interest.

If your dog isn't the type to take treats out-of-hand, a good trick is to put a dab of peanut butter or canned cheese on a part of his body that you would like him to stretch toward. Most dogs will sit down and work to clean it off, although you too might have a little bit of cleanup to do yourself when he is finished. The dog thinks he is getting a treat, but the work he must do to reach the treat is really just a stretch. Start with one

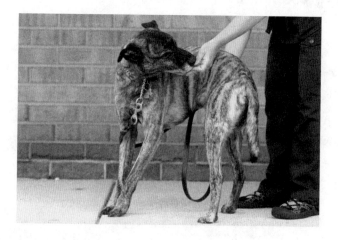

Cookie stretch to hip.

Cookie stretch to hocks.

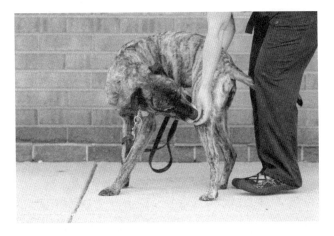

Cookie stretch to shoulders.

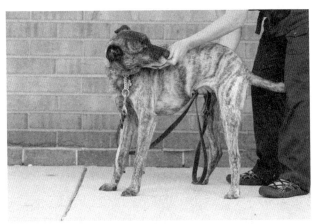

Cookie stretch to elbows.

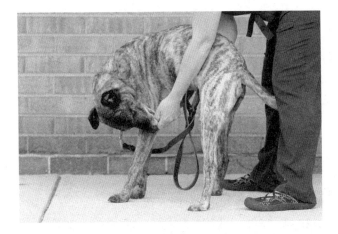

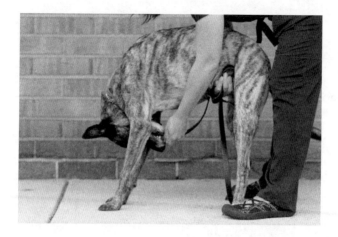

Cookie stretch to floor.

rear foot then repeat with the other foot. Next put some on the elbow and when the first one is cleaned up, repeat with the other elbow.

Physioball Stretches

Several other "self-directed" stretches are generally safe because, like the cookie stretches, the intensity is directed by the dog. The first of these

involves a physioball, preferably one that is a peanut-shape. The ball should be no higher than the dog at his shoulders. This stretch gets front legs, trunk, and especially hips all in one long stretch. Again, you might have to coax your dog up onto the ball with a treat at first. But most dogs will eventually understand what you are asking and this coaxing will become easier and easier to do. Keep a hand on him and the ball

Physioball stretch.

at all times so that he does not slide off or have the ball roll out from underneath him, which might cause him to be fearful or worsen the problem you are trying to treat.

PROM Stretches

The next set of stretches can be a little bit riskier and you should consult your veterinarian before attempting them. They fall into the category of passive range of motion (PROM) exercises, and they are exactly as they sound. They are usually done with the dog lying on her side as you move the limbs passively without resistance from your pet. These motions are meant to provide gentle stretching to the muscles while you work each joint through its normal range of motion. This improves mobility, stimulates muscles and joint receptors, and redistributes joint fluid through-

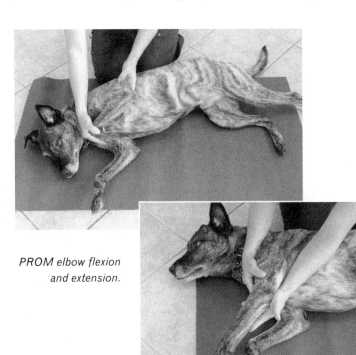

PROM elbow flexion and extension.

out the joint being moved. You should never push any harder when you feel that a limb is flexed or extended to its normal limit. You should stop if the slightest sign of discomfort is seen in your dog. Each of these

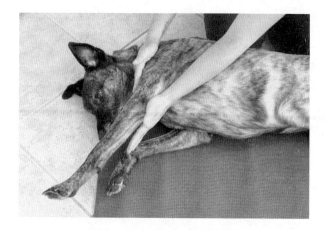

PROM of upper arm.

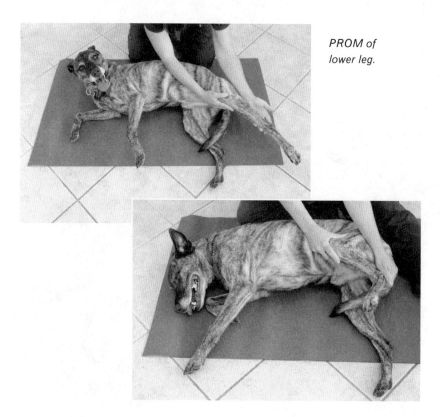

PROM of lower leg.

PROM of lower leg.

PROM of hip away from body.

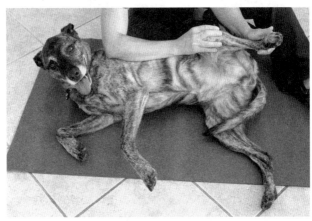

PROM of hip toward body.

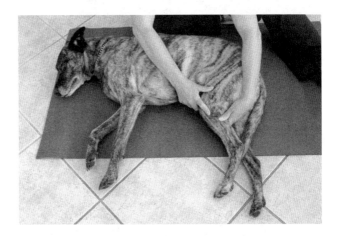

stretches should be done about six times before moving on to the next joint. Unlike the self-directed stretches that work all of the limbs, these PROMs are generally confined to the affected limbs.

Tail Pulls

I know your parents probably told you to never pull the dog's tail, but there are certain conditions, such as a disease called cauda equina syndrome, where gentle tail pulls can loosen spinal adhesions and bring pain relief and a return to more normal function. The tail should be gently pulled straight out from the body in line with the dog's head and back. Never pull the tail at an angle and never pull the tail of a dog with a corkscrew-shape tail, such as a bulldog.

Tail pull.

Strengthening Exercises

Strengthening exercises are an extremely important part of any patient's rehabilitation. There is a huge variety of exercises that have been devised for use in veterinary medicine that can help rehabilitate a large number of conditions. Many of these exercises should only be done under the direction of a trained professional. Many of them also can be done by the caregiver, but not without one-on-one training with a certified rehabilitation expert. The ones that I detail here are, in general, safe to perform at home. My only caveat is what I have already suggested: Talk with your veterinarian prior to starting any exercise to make sure that it is safe for your dog.

These exercises can be fun for both you and your dog. Many are a challenge to start, but we have seen many dogs that suddenly "get it" and turn an exercise into a game. If you find that your dog hates doing one specific exercise, drop it. Just like people, dogs find some exercises more or less tolerable than others. Perhaps the hated exercise is just not fun, but maybe it is too painful. Listen to your dog and work together with her on this project.

Begging

One of the most useful exercises is one that your dog might already know how to do: begging. A dog doing a few begs is the exercise equivalent of a human doing a couple of "crunches." You can increase the difficulty of the begging exercises by increasing its complexity. Teach your dog to stand from a begging position, and suddenly balance alongside increased pelvic and leg muscle use comes into play.

If you haven't done a "crunch" in a while, if you are able you might want to get on the floor and pump out a few to remind yourself of how hard they really are. Keep this in mind as you work with your dog. Take it slow and easy to start. Most begging exercises are safe for most dogs; however, the more difficult ones involve standing upright. I generally do not like to see these exercises done with any dog that has a back condition. Standing upright for extended periods of time for people is normal, but standing upright for a dog is not and it can put undo strains on the vertebral column.

The begging part is easy and usually involves a treat. Chances are you already have taught your dog how to beg. A healthy dog can beg

Sit to beg.

while standing on almost any surface, but your dog may not find a slippery surface amenable to begging. If you are outdoors, choose a firm and stable surface such as concrete. If you are indoors, choose a carpeted surface or use a yoga mat. Using a treat, entice your dog to sit up onto his haunches in a typical begging position. Have him hold this position for 10 to 20 seconds, give him his treat, and let him sit and rest for a minute prior to repeating this two or three times.

When your dog has mastered the beg and you want to increase the intensity of the exercise, take it to the next level and get your dog to stand. This is hard to accomplish and hard to teach. This exercise also carries additional risk to dogs recovering from an injury and should be avoided in those dogs. Just as

Sit to stand.

you enticed your dog to sit up on his haunches with a treat, continue the motion by moving the treat to an even higher position, encouraging your dog to move through the beg position to a standing position. Most people hold the treat out too far in front of their dog and the dog tips forward because their weight is not properly distributed. Hold the treat almost directly above the dog's head and slowly lift it up so the dog stands on his hind legs to get it. Do not ask your dog to hold this position; simply getting him to stand is enough effort. Limit the number of "stands" to two or three total.

Down to Stand

Another good exercise to strengthen your dog's core is one he does all the time: standing up from a lying position. To get an understanding of what your dog must do, sit in a chair where your hips are just slightly lower than your knees. Now try to stand up without using your arms. Imagine if you were to sit down and do this over again, for a total of 12 times. Not only would your legs get a workout, but your core also would get some exercise. What is true for you in this case is also true for your dog.

This exercise should be done on a surface with good footing: carpeted floors in the house, or grass or cement outdoors. If

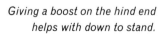

Giving a boost on the hind end helps with down to stand.

your dog already knows the command to sit, then the first step is easy. Otherwise tell her to sit while applying firm and steady pressure over his hind end, being careful with any painful areas. It might help to have a leash on her if she doesn't understand the sit command so as to prevent her from going into a down position. It is more likely that your dog does not have a command for standing up. Teach her to do so while saying "stand" and pulling forward slightly on the leash and/or lifting her hind end with your hand under her fanny. Standing up from a lying position can be a challenge for dogs that have hip dysplasia or rear leg issues, and they will want to drag themselves up from the down position by using as much of their front legs as possible. If need be, do a little bit of a fanny boost as your dog starts to stand, and he will respond by putting more effort into the rear legs.

Figure 8

Walking your dog in a figure 8 can accomplish muscle strengthening in the core muscles as well as those muscles on the inside and outside of the legs. You should use a leash to encourage your dog to follow you as you make the figure 8. Some dogs are extremely treat motivated and will heel at your side for the figure 8 pattern if you are carrying one. You want to start with large figure 8s of whatever size is comfortable for your dog. As your dog becomes better at these, you can make the figure 8 smaller and smaller.

Ladder Walking

Ladder walking is another great home exercise using equipment you might already have. Simply place a ladder on the ground and have your dog walk through the rungs. This forces him to step just a little bit higher than normal, and the exaggerated movement strengthens the muscles used for walking. A larger dog might need a brick under each corner of the ladder in order to elevate it properly. Of course, most dogs

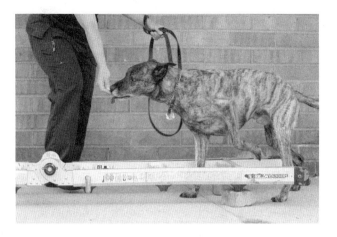

Ladder walking.

will try to avoid the ladder and walk next to it, so it is best to place the ladder against a wall, put your dog on a leash, and then walk her through the rungs. As the dog progresses, you should walk beside the ladder to keep your dog from cheating.

Diagonal Leg Lifts

A great exercise that helps both with balance and strength is the diagonal leg lift. Most dogs will cooperate once they understand what you are trying to achieve, but the first time or two might require the help of someone who can keep your dog from walking away by using a leash.

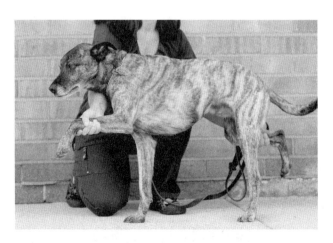

Diagonal leg lifts.

Pick up first the front left leg and then the back right leg and hold the legs in a raised position for a count of ten. Then repeat with the opposite legs. If the legs on the floor start to tremble, you have done it long enough, maybe even a bit too long. This particular exercise might be too strenuous for geriatric dogs or dogs with profound muscle weakness.

Uphill, Downhill

Uphill and downhill walking can strengthen a dog's back end and front end, respectively. Find a mildly steep hill with few or no obstructions such as trees or bushes, and an even terrain. To strengthen the rear legs and pelvic muscles, walk your dog directly up the hill. When you walk down, do so at an angle as most dogs with rear limb issues already have a strong set of muscles up front due to trying to carry more weight up front. Do the opposite for front leg strengthening: Walk up at an angle and then straight down.

Loving on the Stairs

If your dog is too weak in the back end for hill walking, or if you are like me and live in an area with almost no hills, you can do an alternative

Loving on the stairs.

exercise called "loving on the stairs." Sit toward the bottom of the stairs on either the first step or higher, depending on how long your dog is. Encourage your dog to put her front feet in your lap so that she is bearing weight almost entirely on the rear limbs. Give her hugs and kisses and praise while she balances on those hind legs. Whoever knew loving could be so good for both you and your dog?

Balance Exercises

Balancing exercises can be important for dogs with either neurological disease or arthritis. Good equilibrium means a lower likelihood of falling down a stairway, slipping on a slick surface, or experiencing an accidental fall that could result in injury. If your dog has a severe balance problem, then it probably would be wise to buy a harness that is designed for assisting your dog in walking. These harnesses have a handle on the back of them that you can easily hold on to and give your dog maximum support without hurting yourself while doing so. Bending over while pulling up on a weight and then walking for any length of time can put undo strains on your own back.

Three-Legged Stands

Some of the strengthening exercises also double as balance exercise. Diagonal leg lifts and ladder walking are two of them. Additionally, you can do three-legged stands, where you simply hold up the "strong" leg and force your dog to balance using the "bad" leg.

Pick-Up Sticks

This is another fun exercise that improves balance and increases conscious proprioception (discussed earlier) but seems like a game to most dogs. Buy several sections of 1-inch PVC pipe that has been cut in

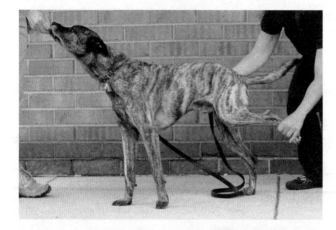

Three-legged stand.

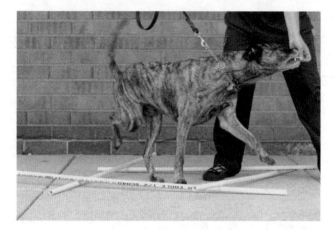

Pick-up sticks.

6-foot lengths. Pile them on the floor in a random pattern like a game of "pick-up sticks." Then place treats on the floor in various locations so that your dog has to walk though the sticks to get at the treats. Occasionally a dog will ignore the pipes and just plow right through them. If this is the case, you can get some aluminum beverage cans, bend them a bit in the middle, and place some of the pipe ends on the cans. Now if your dog tries to plow through the pipes, he will make a lot of noise and many dogs so dislike this noise that they will do their best to avoid knocking them over.

Rhythmic Stabilization

For another good balance exercise, put your hands on either side of your dog, usually at the level of the hips, and gently push him first to one side, then the other, varying the rhythm and the force of the push so that he cannot anticipate the strength he needs to counter each push. When you first start this one you may have to have an assistant hold your dog in place so that she doesn't try to get away from your hands.

Rhythmic stabilization.

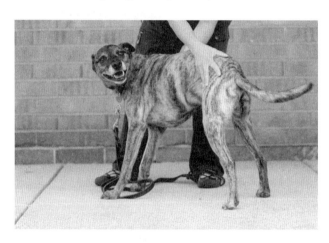

Air mattress.

Air Mattress

Walking on cushions or a partly deflated air mattress is a great way to reinforce balance. The air mattress is preferred because it is a single piece. Cushions set end-to-end can work too, but they have the disadvantage of being separate pieces—dogs can step into the cracks between them. Simply blow up an air mattress with just enough air so that your dog wobbles when stepping on it as you walk him back and forth on the end of a leash. You might have to put the air mattress up against a wall to keep him from taking a shortcut and stepping sideways off the mattress.

A FEW SUGGESTED EXERCISES

Problem	Exercise	Repetition
Hip dysplasia or arthritis	Cookie stretches. Uphill walking, sit to beg, sit to stand, diagonal leg lifts, down to stand. Eventually start all begging exercises as progress is made.	Cookie stretches, 1 of each. Start with three repetitions of each and work up to 10.
Knee arthritis or surgery	Cookie stretches, ladder walking, pick-up sticks, rhythmic stabilizations.	Cookie stretches, 1 of each. Others, start with 3 and work up to 10. Start rhythmic stabilizations when others are mastered.
Neurological issues	Ladder walking, diagonal leg lifts, three-legged stand, pick-up sticks, rhythmic stabilizations, air mattress.	It is important to get approval from your veterinarian and to set up a schedule for these exercises.
Front leg surgery or pain	Cookie stretches, all begging exercises, figure 8, ladder walking. As progress is made, include downhill walking, three-legged stand, and air mattress.	Cookie stretches, 1 of each. Others, start with 3 and work up to 10.

20

MASSAGE

MASSAGE CAN ALLEVIATE PAIN ACROSS A BROAD array of painful conditions. For example, muscles become painful secondary to issues such as surgery or osteoarthritis. Limb extremities can become edematous following certain surgeries as well as inactivity secondary to immobility. Massage can help increase circulation. Massage can have other benefits as well. It reduces stress in dogs, especially those burdened by pain and disease, and increases the bond between the dog and caregiver. In this chapter I discuss the benefits of massage for your dog and illustrate some simple, common massage techniques that you can perform.

Most massage techniques for dogs have been transposed from human massage, and if you know human massage techniques you are already a few steps ahead. There is one important caution about moving human massage experience to dogs: The amount of pressure used during dog massage must be considerably less than that applied to people. The size of the dog should also be taken into account with special care being given to smaller dogs.

Don't worry too much about your technique; I cannot train anyone to be a massage therapist in one very short chapter. If your approach is gentle and your dog visibly relaxes during the course of the massage, then you are doing great! If on the other hand, he keeps trying to get away, or tries to guard an area of his body, or just really tries to convince you to do something other than massage him, then you might want to stop and determine why. Is your massage causing pain because of the way you are doing it or is there something wrong with the massaged area(s) of your dog that is making it too sensitive?

Finally, I want to give a few tips that apply to all of the different massage techniques noted in this chapter.

1. **Never concentrate on one area for too long.** What starts out feeling good, but receives too much attention, can start to feel annoying and eventually will become uncomfortable.

2. **Listen to your dog.** If he acts uncomfortable in any way, you might want to try another area, use less pressure, and try slower movements. If he is still resistant, then it could be something as simple as he doesn't feel like getting a massage that day. But if his resistance persists, have your veterinarian check it out.

3. **Protect yourself.** Massage takes time and if you are massaging your dog while in a stooped-over position, you might be heading to a massage therapist yourself. Find what is comfortable for you. Anything that elevates the dog from the floor, such as a dog bed or a low piece of furniture, can make your task easier.

In her book *Canine Medical Massage*, Dr. Narda Robinson recommends that all massage sessions start with what she calls passive touch. This is simply laying your hands on your dog's body and resting quietly together. This helps set a calming mood and lets your dog know that something nice is about to happen. Remain in this position until you and your dog feel calm and connected with one another. At this point you can move into the massage itself.

Massage Procedures

I would like to tell you about three different massage procedures. The first two are borrowed from Swedish-style massage, and the last is designed to help eliminate edema (swelling secondary to lymph fluid accumulation) from the limbs.

Effleurage

Whenever you pet your dog, you are already performing effleurage! Effleurage is a steady flowing movement using an open hand or fingertips with light to moderate pressure. Simply stroke your dog in the direction of the hair coat, with one exception (noted later). With each stroke, try to move steadily from one end of your dog's body or limb to the other. Some people like to time the length of each stroke so that it corresponds to the length of time it takes them to inhale and exhale once. Try to cover your dog's entire body, using a half-dozen or so strokes to each area, before moving on to the next area.

If certain areas of your dog have been neurologically compromised, it is beneficial to perform effleurage with a faster stroke. However, if this neurological issue is secondary to some painful disorder like a ruptured disk, you should ask your veterinarian if it is okay to massage that particular area and to what degree of pressure. Geriatric dogs often benefit from a faster-paced stroke. According to *Canine Medical Massage,* this helps stimulate different body systems in older dogs.

There is one reason why you might want to perform effleurage against the hair coat. Some dogs may have swelling or edema of their limbs. This is often due to decreased venous or lymphatic return that results in a build-up of fluid in the legs. In this case effleurage of the legs—pushing in the direction of the heart—can increase venous and lymphatic flow, thereby reducing painful swelling in the affected limbs.

Petrissage

Petrissage is a more forceful massage technique than effleurage. Petrissage is more like kneading the tissue, gently picking up the skin and underlying tissue, and then rolling forward with it. As most dogs have very loose skin and underlying tissue, this is fairly easy to do, especially along the upper limbs. This should never be done over the site of a recent surgery, wound, or infection—there is a real possibility that you could make matters worse. You should also exercise caution when doing petrissage over your dog's trunk. Geriatric dogs especially may have a decrease in muscling in that area, which could make this type of massage feel painful, even with a light touch.

Compression

Compression is a technique I like to use when there is swelling or edema of one or more limbs. I already mentioned how effleurage toward the heart can reduce edema. Compression can help as well.

Start at the distal or farthest end of the limb you want to massage, near the toes. If the limb is small in circumference, as it probably is toward the toes, you can sometimes encircle the limb with one hand and squeeze it, using firm and well-distributed pressure. As you move up the leg, you probably will have to use two hands and compress from both sides of the leg. Keep moving up the leg, past any areas of edema if possible. Just like effleurage can push the fluid in the right direction, compression can squeeze the fluid out of the limb and toward the heart. As in the precautions of effleurage, be careful and ask permission from your veterinarian if you see edema around a surgical site or if the area you are compressing is hot, red, or painful, as these are indications of a possible infection.

Thoughts on Massage

I want to leave you with some final thoughts on massage. Not all dog personalities are equipped to accept massage, even from their own caregiver. On top of that, you as the masseuse must have a great deal of patience if your dog seems resistant. Remember, you don't have to massage every square inch of your dog's body, not on the first day and not with every massage session. Start with those areas he is already used to having touched, such as along his back when you pet him. Work on building up his confidence and get him to relax as you slowly start to incorporate those areas he might be more sensitive to, such as his feet. And if he is never comfortable with one area, leave it out. Even a partial body massage can go a long way for relieving pain and making your dog feel loved.

21

I HAVE BEEN THINKING ABOUT ANOTHER PET

IT IS A DIFFICULT DECISION FOR MANY PET OWNERS to bring a new dog into the home where a dog in pain lives, yet I'm asked advice on this subject all the time. There are several common reasons for taking this step. Many caregivers see the slow demise of their dog and fear the void that will be left when the dog is finally gone. Others hope that a new companion may bring a renewed interest in life to their aging dog in pain. For some, the motive may lie in the hope that the old dog will teach the new dog the common routines of his daily life, thereby leaving his imprint even after he has passed on. For whatever reason you might be considering a new dog, I want to explore with you the pros and cons of introducing a new dog in an effort to help you decide if this is the best course of action for both you and your dog.

I often look at my own aging dog, Joy, who at best has another three years, probably less. I get an ache in my heart every time I think of her advancing years. I hesitate every time I accept a chance to give a lecture at some distant place or plan a vacation that cannot possibly include her. "What if something happens?" I ask myself. I know many of my clients experience the same feelings.

My wife and I had spoken often about getting Joy a companion. At the end of every conversation, we always put off any kind of decision and plan to discuss it again at some future date. We put it off partly because of the practicality of buying and training a new puppy, but mostly because of the emotional issues that these conversations bring up. What would Joy think of a small puppy following her around and nipping at her heels? Would another dog encourage Joy to move around or would it be too much for her? Would it make Joy happy or would it make her give up? Are we somehow betraying our relationship with her, and would she see this new dog as a replacement?

The decision to get Joy a companion was almost taken out of our hands. I had just returned from teaching a pain class in Finland. When I went into work the next day I found an urgent message from one of the local rescue groups. There was a six-month-old Portuguese Water Dog, the same breed as Joy, that desperately needed a home because her owner had just passed away. Almost without considering all the concerns we had discussed so many times before, we said *yes*. The new addition to our family arrived later that day.

To this day, I jokingly blame jet lag on my decision to take Kiki in. But the reality of her adoption is that we had thoroughly thought out and accepted all the ins and outs of getting a new dog, and the suddenness of her appearance and the decision to bring her into our family was like standing at the edge of a pool: You know the water is cold, you know you are going to jump in, you are just trying to get up the nerve when someone walks by and gives you a nudge to do what you already were going to do anyway.

Although we hoped that bringing Kiki into our family was the right decision for us, we knew it might not work out. Within weeks, we saw confirmations that we had made the right decision. The transition was not without its problems, most of them revolving around the interactions between these two dogs. But Kiki turned out to be a quick learner and soon understood how important it was to be "polite" around her older sister.

Is There an Empty Place Needing to Be Filled?

Few of us think of our dogs as being our property first and foremost. If you feel like many of my clients, your dog is part of your family. Because we feel this way, we need to make sure that another dog not only fills our needs, but that we can be good caregivers to our dog and fill her needs as well. I suggest to everyone that they sit down and make a list of answers to the following questions.

1. **Do I have the time for both dogs?** A dog's life starts as a puppy and with that comes the demand for a huge amount of interaction including training, housebreaking, social interaction, and play. These needs change and diminish after the first year or so and remain in a steady state until illness or age-related disease starts to appear wherein they demand a lot of attention once again. If your older dog has reached this final stage where she is taking a lot of your time, it could mean that the puppy might not get the attention she needs.

2. **What is the breed of your dog and what breed of dog are you considering?** I can't list the personality of every breed here, but do your research and decide if the breeds are compatible. If you have an aging Papillon and you are considering any of the larger breeds with more aggressive personalities, trouble might ensue as the puppy grows. Research your breed, and do so not by asking a breeder or a breed-specific dog club. They all love their breed and more often than not overlook their faults. The American Kennel Club is a good source of unbiased information.

3. **Should you consider another species altogether, such as a cat?** Cats are wonderful companions for aging dogs.

They give each other company and any games they devise between the two of them will often be less rambunctious than games invented between two dogs. Additionally, kittens are usually much less effort to raise as compared to puppies.

4. **Should you consider an older puppy?** When we adopted Kiki she came to us already house trained. She also already understood many rudimentary social skills and "doggy things" like walking on a leash. There was still a lot of work to do to make her the member of our family that we wanted to have, but not nearly as much as a younger puppy would have. The time she took from our older dog Joy was minimal and didn't much interfere with her daily routines.

5. **Should you consider an older dog?** You already are taking care of a dog in pain with special needs. Adding a second aging dog with similar needs means that you might not have to make any additional changes to either your routines or the dog's surroundings. Older dogs surrendered to shelters are rarely adopted out and often spend their last months or years in a cage or get shifted from foster home to foster home.

6. **Consider the personality of your aging dog.** It seems that some dogs are meant to be the only dog in the family. My first dog got along with almost every dog she met. My second dog thought she was a human and completely disdained and ignored other dogs. Joy falls somewhere in the middle. She ignores dogs at first but eventually finds a common ground with them, although it might take a day or two. If your dog is like my second dog, the intrusion of a canine companion might be too hard for her to take.

In the end, it is your decision. As long as you think through the decision and talk about it with all members of your family or any other involved people, and as long as you honestly consider the questions and concerns noted here, your chances of smoothly introducing another pet into your family should be good.

22

OUR ANIMALS, OUR OBLIGATIONS

I HAVE OWNED MANY PETS OVER THE COURSE OF MY lifetime, and I want to clarify for you precisely my views on animal care. I don't expect everyone to share the exact same views, but for certain needs of our pets I feel that some adherence to minimum standards is necessary. When I take an animal into my care as a veterinarian, I take on certain obligations—as I think most people would agree that I should—to feed and shelter the animal, care for its injuries, and give it respect and love. What has surprised me, as a veterinarian, is that for some animal caretakers these obligations do not extend to treatment for pain and discomfort. I'd like to see that change.

I adhere to a set of carefully thought-out guidelines for the treatment of our pets developed by the British Farm Animal Welfare Council. They are called the Five Freedoms and outline the humane treatment of farm animals. It is clear to me that these principles should apply to all animals under our care, not just those that live on a farm. I believe *we have the moral obligation to apply these same concepts to our dogs*. The Five Freedoms are:

1. **Freedom from Hunger and Thirst**—by ready access to fresh water and a diet to maintain full health and vigor.

2. **Freedom from Discomfort**—by providing an appropriate environment, including shelter and a comfortable resting area.

3. **Freedom from Pain, Injury, or Disease**—by prevention or rapid diagnosis and treatment.

4. **Freedom to Express Normal Behavior**—by providing sufficient space, proper facilities, and company of the animal's own kind.

5. **Freedom from Fear and Distress**—by ensuring conditions and treatment that avoid mental suffering.

Every one of these five freedoms is important, and I don't want to minimize the significance of any of them, because they all have a role in the health and happiness of our pets. However, as this book focuses on pain, my concern here is the third freedom: "Freedom from Pain, Injury, or Disease—by prevention or rapid diagnosis and treatment."[77]

Freedom from Pain, Injury, or Disease— by *Prevention*

Consider the word *prevention* in this freedom. Freedom from pain requires us to be proactive in *our* pet's health. Obviously we should provide a safe environment for our dog. We also have the obligation to be aware of when our pet is in pain so that we can get appropriate help. Likewise, we must consider the less evident need to anticipate the development of any painful disorders. Awareness of the potential for the development of painful conditions also means the chance for earlier intervention. Prompt treatment of pain results in less overall pain for your dog, reduced intervention and costs when such conditions are treated at an early stage, and a lesser probability of existing pain leading to more advanced pain states.

Foreseeing potential pain might seem like a tricky problem to address, but it is actually simpler than you might think. The first step is to become informed about your dog's breeding. Should you have a purebred dog, you need only get the facts on that breed; in the case of a simple mix of breeds, you must consider the breed of both the mother and father. Breeds and genetics play a huge role in problems that may develop in purebred dogs. You might anticipate back issues if you own a dachshund, hip dysplasia in German shepherds, stress on joints due to conformational issues in English bulldogs, and so on. A brief discussion with your veterinarian when your dog is still a puppy, or when you first acquire him or her, can help you make a list of potential key issues to watch for as your dog ages. Other good sources of information on this subject include numerous breed-specific books.

You can be even more proactive by seeking medical help to screen for any genetic issues by way of X-ray films and regular examinations. Radiographs can be instrumental in finding genetic issues like hip dysplasia, but they also can detect problems like osteoarthritis, sometimes even before you or your veterinarian can see the signs of it in your dog. Knowledge is power, and comprehension of a disease means early intervention, more treatment options, and in most cases, less money spent on your pet's healthcare in the long run.

A decade ago, the mindset of most veterinarians, at least when it came to pain, was reactive rather than proactive—in other words, treating the pain only when it could no longer be ignored. This mindset has dramatically changed in the intervening years, especially through the efforts of the American Animal Hospital Association, which has been the driving force behind the inclusion of pain evaluations in every examination.[78] They refer to pain as "the fourth vital sign" to be evaluated and recorded alongside the classic vital signs of temperature, pulse, and respiration. Every veterinarian in practice should be examining every dog for signs of pain, not only by taking a careful history but also through observation and palpation. Doing so is now considered the gold standard for any veterinary examination.

What if your dog has a "job"? Obedience and agility dogs often acquire repetitive strain injuries, which are exactly what they sound like: repetition of the same task or motion over and over again, leading, for example, to a breakdown of a joint or ligament. Compare this scenario to that of a person who develops carpal tunnel syndrome secondary to a repetitive work condition. Working dogs can also be prone to certain types of injuries, depending on the type of job they perform. Anticipation of some of these injuries might be self-evident, but unless your veterinarian is certified in rehabilitation, she might not be aware of all of the potential injury issues. Talk to people in the agility community and ask what kinds of problems they have experienced. Also speak to a rehabilitation veterinarian and get recommendations from her. In every case, there is usually something you can do to minimize or avoid potential injury. For dogs with jobs, prevention might take the form of warm-up exercises and stretches, or perhaps icing stressed joints and massaging overused muscles.

When it comes to pain issues, the old adage, "An ounce of prevention is worth a pound of cure" cannot be truer. Anticipation leading to early diagnosis and early treatment of pain is not only humane, it also will prevent untold future suffering. By taking these steps, you actually alter the course of the disease, and hence the pain itself.

Freedom from Pain, Injury, or Disease — by *Rapid Diagnosis*

Next, consider the phrase "rapid diagnosis." Unfortunately, I find that people commonly postpone bringing their pet to the veterinarian for a number of reasons. They may believe in one or more of the pain myths I outline in Chapter 1. Or it may be because, although the animal's leg might appear painful, it seems to "get by." Too often I see people bring in a dog after weeks or months of ignoring an obvious pain issue. Of course there are times when you might wait a day or two, hoping the problem is minor and will resolve of its own accord. But if the issue—seemingly minor or not—doesn't go away after a couple days, it's essential to seek veterinary attention.

Of course, if the animal has, for example, blood or pus emerging from an ear or the skin, then it's obvious that problem will not resolve on its own, at least not without health risks and accompanying pain. In such instances, it becomes even more important to seek immediate attention. Sadly, I often see problems like this go unattended.

I want to emphasize that putting off your pet's appointment not only makes your pet wait in pain, but the resulting delays in diagnosis and treatment often can lead to irrevocable harm. The following example is a case in point.

The Case of Buddy's Limp

Buddy was a seven-year-old neutered male dog that came in limping one evening after a half-hour spent out in the backyard. Not only was he limping, he would barely touch his right hind leg to the ground. His owner searched the pad for thorns and cuts, and manipulated his leg with no reaction. Not seeing any life-threatening issue, his owner confined Buddy to a small area of the house to rest the leg while he was at work; then when it was time to let him outside, he put Buddy on a leash so as to minimize stress on the leg. After several days, the owner noticed a gradual improvement, which seemed to continue every few days until the two-week mark when to the owner's untrained eye, Buddy seemed normal. About six weeks after the original injury, Buddy began to limp again. This time it started out slowly and got progressively worse, to the point where he held up the leg most of the time.

Buddy's owner finally brought him in to me for an examination. Through a physical exam and confirmatory radiographs, I quickly ascertained that Buddy had ruptured the cranial cruciate ligament of his right knee. What is more, after the initial pain of the rupture abated several weeks prior, he had started using his now-unstable knee and slowly but surely caused severe damage to the meniscus, cartilage pad in the knee. This meant that even though I could treat the ruptured ligament and meniscus, and give him back a functional knee, the inflammatory response was such that Buddy was destined to a lifetime of osteoarthritis in that knee, mandating chronic pain treatments and reduced function of that limb.

Had the owner brought Buddy in at the three-to-four-day mark, when it was obvious the problem wasn't going to abate with a little rest, all of this collateral damage could have been avoided. In the end, the owner saved no money; to the contrary, he spent much more treating Buddy's condition. No time was saved either; Buddy would now have to visit me much more frequently than he would have otherwise. And finally, Buddy would have to suffer his osteoarthritis for life—because he certainly couldn't have called my office to make an earlier appointment himself.

Freedom from Pain, Injury, or Disease— by *Treatment*

This seems like an obvious and reasonable premise. Why wouldn't we want to treat our pet's pain? Treatment options abound, as described throughout this book. It can be frightening for caregivers to walk through their veterinarian's door, contemplating what proper treatment may cost. But this shouldn't be the case—it is the rare pain condition that doesn't offer several options for treating pain, some relatively inexpensive for those caregivers who are willing to devote some time to their dog's care. A long list of possible treatments can seem daunting, but this shouldn't discourage you. Your veterinarian is an expert in these matters and should always take the time to explain the benefits as well as the downsides of each presented treatment in terms you can understand. As a caregiver you must overcome any fears or other concerns that may otherwise prevent you from visiting your veterinarian—for unless you do, your pet has no chance of getting help.

It distresses me to no end when an owner brings his dog to me with some clearly treatable issue, yet is reluctant to spend the necessary time or money for the proper treatment. We have to remember that if we choose to take an animal into our care, that care does not stop with food, water, and a place to sleep. It is our moral responsibility to provide for all aspects of our pet's needs. I only wish that every dog came with a warning label: "Requires food, love, and veterinary care. May get sick, the treatment of which necessitates money and devotion. Will grow old all too quickly and will depend on you for care and comfort in old age."

23

I CAN'T AFFORD
TO TREAT MY PET.
NOW WHAT?

THERE ARE PAIN TREATMENTS FOR EVERY BUDGET.
For a simple comparison, consider your options when buying a watch:
A Timex and a Rolex both tell time and get the job done. The more
expensive watch might offer you additional features for certain situations,
such as swimming underwater. Or maybe it just costs more. The same
applies to pain treatments: A more affordable treatment may not provide
all the benefits of an expensive treatment, but maybe it does while being
perfectly adequate for a caregiver's needs. I will explore with you how
to take care of your dog on a tight budget and help you assess whether
these choices adequately address the pain your dog is experiencing.

Some diseases, such as osteosarcoma (bone cancer), are very painful. Even intensive treatments for these diseases poorly control the pain.
And unfortunately, there are no inexpensive alternatives. There are
other conditions almost as painful, such as intervertebral disk disease.
This condition has classically been treated with surgical intervention,
but now it can be treated much less expensively with an NSAID, acupuncture, and rehabilitation exercises.

In the case of the disk disease, the biggest difference in treatments,
besides the amount of money spent, is time. Both the time to recovery
and the amount of time you need to put in to make your dog better

are at work here. Surgical intervention can often (but not always) give instant relief to a dog with disk disease. The alternative therapies can bring about an equal amount of pain relief, but it may require a few weeks to deliver satisfactory results. At the same time, properly treating this condition requires a large commitment of your time as you care for a partly or completely paralyzed dog and all that entails, performing home exercises and massage, and engaging in other related tasks.

Pharmaceuticals

The cost of pharmaceuticals is always changing. Inexpensive drugs sometimes become unaffordable. Conversely, when some drugs go off patent, inexpensive generics often appear.

Generics often seem like a good deal. They certainly give me an opportunity to provide medications at a lower cost to my clients. But time and time again I have been disappointed by both the quality of the generics and the lack of support by their producers. Generic versions of brand-name drugs are not held to the same high production and performance standards as the original drug. I don't really understand why this is the case. But in my own experience with generics, with a few exceptions, I find many of the generic formulations to be unreliable. Moreover, if I suspect that a patient is experiencing a problem secondary to the generic drug, there is usually no one I can call for expert advice. My experience is quite different with brand-name drugs. If I call the maker of a brand-name drug, then I get to talk to a veterinarian who is an expert on the product. This expert can make suggestions for the problem and often offers financial support to my client, sometimes by reimbursing for out-of-pocket expenses or offering to pay for diagnostic testing.

The good news is that many drug companies provide some kind of help when you buy their brand-name pain drugs. This often comes in the form of a rebate or sometimes as a credit toward future drug purchases. For example, many of my clients who use Rimadyl for their dogs often pursue cost-reducing offers put out by its manufacturer, Zoetis.

Another way to save money with some pharmaceuticals is to download one of several apps available for smartphones. These apps can help you search for the least expensive local drugstore that is selling your dog's prescription drug. My clients often find medications for less money than I can buy them for wholesale! I am always happy to see my clients buy the products they need elsewhere if doing so saves them money—money that can be used for the physical treatments their dog needs.

The reality is that, in the case of chronic pain, a dog's issues didn't start the morning of the veterinary appointment. Although your goal should be to get rid of as much pain as possible, if you are on a limited budget I recommend that you start with one drug at a time and add or switch medications depending on your dog's response to it. When money is not a big issue, then start with a multimodal approach. For such circumstances in my own practice, I start my patients on several medications at once to get the most benefit the fastest.

Rehabilitation

Canine rehabilitation is an all-encompassing term that includes many different treatment modalities. The most important part of any rehabilitation program for your dog is the directed exercises and hands-on manipulations performed by the therapist. Other treatments, like an underwater treadmill, laser, and shock wave, provide additional levels of therapy and in many instances can help speed the healing process. But there was a time not so long ago where these "extras" were not even in existence. Back then all we had was our hands and exercises.

I bring up this point because at some rehabilitation clinics there is an incrementally increasing pricing structure for the use of these very expensive additional equipment pieces. Your dog doesn't *have* to use them to get better. If you forego the use of such equipment, you might be able to provide a less expensive, albeit possibly lengthier, recovery for your dog.

Regardless, be open and honest with your rehabilitation therapist and ask what you might be able to do at home to supplement the entire healing process. Look at the exercises in Chapter 19 and ask your veterinarian if any of these, or others she might suggest, would be appropriate for you to do at home. I always give my patient's caregivers some home exercises. If they are willing to learn some of the safer yet more complex exercises, I will spend some time teaching them the proper techniques. Of course it takes time to learn how to do these exercises, and you should expect there to be some kind of charge for the therapist's time to teach these exercises to you. But it is the difference between buying a fish dinner and buying a fishing pole to make your own fish dinners. Just remember, do-it-yourself can only go so far. Regular rechecks and adjustments in treatments are an absolute must.

Veterinary Clinic Programs

It is common for many veterinarians to offer discounts when a "package" treatment is purchased. This makes it necessary for you to pay up-front before the treatments start, but it can result in substantial overall savings. Veterinarians who provide some kind of hands-on treatment options—massage, acupuncture, and rehabilitation, for example—most commonly offer these packages. Treatment packages are most commonly presented in two forms.

The first package, and probably what most veterinarians offer, is a discount when you buy a set number of treatments up-front. For example, if you commit to a package of ten acupuncture or massage sessions, you only pay for eight or nine sessions, as compared to purchasing them individually. As veterinarians, we always want to help make things affordable. At the same time, we want to help your pet heal. In essence, we give away one or two sessions in order to get something in return: commitment from the caregiver. Many people experience appointment burnout for chronic medical issues. At some point they start to feel that their dog isn't quite where they wanted her to be, but it is good enough. And so they stop the appointments too soon. This is less likely to happen if a caregiver has already paid for an entire, nonrefundable treatment package.

The second package most commonly involves rehabilitation. Use of the more expensive equipment pieces, like an underwater treadmill, is often charged separately from the main rehabilitation charge. Some rehabilitation clinics offer a rehab package that not only gives a discount for paying up-front but also includes the more expensive treatments like an underwater treadmill, to be used (or not) at the therapist's discretion. If your rehab clinic offers a discount deal like this, take it if you can afford it. Not only will you get a discount but doing so greatly increases the chance that the more expensive modalities will be used to help your dog. Rehabilitation therapists *all* want to see a success story, and they will do whatever is necessary to help your dog attain it.

If the pain practice you go to doesn't offer one of these packages, ask them to consider it. They may have been thinking about it for a while but just have been kicking the can down the road, putting off making a decision. You might be the catalyst that makes it happen for your dog and others. If your care provider won't provide a discount package, and you can't afford the regular prices, then consider looking around for a practice that might be able to offer more flexibility in this regard.

Weight Loss

I cannot stress enough how important weight loss is for the treatment of painful conditions. To encourage weight loss, you can buy diet dog foods that might be slightly more expensive than the food you normally provide to your dog, or you can just feed your dog less of her regular food.

I have treated many dogs in my practice that are both in pain and overweight. And every week it seems I work with a client who complains that they feed their dog nothing and yet the dog is not losing weight—or even worse, is putting on the pounds. This of course goes against the laws of nature and is completely impossible. Someone is either not being honest with himself or herself, or the dog is getting a source of food from somewhere or someone else.

The truth is that many caregivers can't get beyond the look of reproach in their dog's eyes when the food bowl is empty, or they can't walk past the dog-treat jar without pulling one out. But these caregivers must overcome the reproaches and refrain from giving excess treats. Numerous studies have shown that a very modest 10 percent weight loss *has the same pain-reducing benefit as giving a dog an NSAID!*

And there is another incentive for weight loss: As your dog loses weight, he experiences less pain. And less pain means that he can move around better and, now that he is moving, can lose even more weight by burning calories. The result is a no-cost win-win.

Financial Help

As most of my clients have experienced, when they go to large institutional humane societies to seek financial aid for the medical care of their dog, they discover that none is available. Nevertheless, it may be worth a phone call to see if they have a veterinarian on staff who can help you with your dog's pain issues at a reduced cost.

A better course might be to locate local privately run, volunteer-staffed rescue groups in your area. Many of these organizations have funds set aside to help special needs cases. Even if they don't, they may be able to help you find the necessary funds through donors or fund-raising events. If they can help you, then know that it represents a huge commitment on their resources, and it would be only fair for you to return this charity by both volunteering your time and repaying the money should your future circumstances permit it.

Outcome Measures

Early in the book I mentioned the importance of frequent evaluation in order to know if a treatment is working. This is true in any case, but maybe even more important to do if you are providing a lot of your dog's care at home.

When money is tight, outcome measures are vitally important. There might come a time when the pain treatments your dog is receiving have not made things perfect, but have possibly made things good enough so that your dog can do all the things she likes and needs in order to get through her day.

Of course it is my goal to make a dog as pain free as possible, but even a pain expert like myself needs to be reminded now and again when an outcome is "good enough." As Voltaire said, "Perfect is the enemy of good." You can use this observation in reference to the "80/20" rule, which says that it takes 20 percent of your effort to complete 80 percent of a task, but the remaining 80 percent of your effort to finish the remaining 20 percent of your task. Of course I am talking in generalizations here, and it is your beloved dog in particular we are discussing. But it is absolutely true that sometimes the first things we do for pain management often accomplishes about 80 percent of what we hope to achieve.

Being unable to afford the best care possible is more common than you probably think. Barely a day goes by when at least one of my clients needs to make a choice, some hard and some not so hard, about the financial realities of their dog's medical care. Be honest with your veterinarian. She cannot know why you might decline a needed treatment, and she might even put the blame on herself for not explaining it to you properly. We veterinarians want to help, and most of us will work with you to find a treatment that works for your dog and your budget.

24

WHEN CHRONIC PAIN TREATMENTS MEET QUALITY-OF-LIFE ISSUES

WHAT HAPPENS WHEN AN ANIMAL'S PAIN CANNOT BE relieved? In most of these cases, in which a caretaker does not wish to say goodbye, I recommend that they look into the relatively new movement of animal hospice.

Hospice fills the much-needed gap between aggressive treatment and death. In this chapter I show you how to find a hospice veterinarian and what you should expect when you put your dog in hospice care. I also discuss the ethics of euthanasia along with some rational guidelines for the caregiver who is considering this route.

A common desire for the caretakers of animals that are living with chronic health issues is that their pet will die peacefully in his sleep. In other words, these caregivers are hoping that their pets will take any end-of-life decisions out of their hands. Sadly, in my professional experience, this is seldom the case. Instead of a sudden decline in which a dog might die with little to no warning, many dogs experience a slow decline in their health that, in some cases, can last years. Any chronic health issues, especially if those issues are painful, can take a path that will often involve many difficult decisions, some of them heart-rending. These difficult decisions may involve diagnostic tests and procedures, treatment options for medical problems and pain control, and constant veterinary reevaluations. Alongside the many choices to be made when considering the large assortment of treatments, the costs of emotion, time, and finances must be part of the decision-making process.

Considering the Ethics of Euthanasia

When is it time to consider euthanasia? Many of us think we will know it when we see it. That notion is, in truth, an attitude that is embedded in well-meaning naivety about how straightforward the decision will be. When faced with the reality of the complexities of the situation, that certainty often melts away. Many times I have seen old dogs come into my practice that act confused, have trouble walking, experienced extreme weight loss, and overall look like a dog that might be moments away from death. But when I asked the caretaker how their dog is doing, I might be told, "She is happy to see us come home every day, still likes going for a short walk, eats reasonably well, and even initiates play with us." Her obvious age-related issues may have a solid hold on her physicality, but from an emotional and mental point of view it's evident to the caregiver that the dog still has a strong will to live. The decision becomes even harder when outsiders, sometimes even family members who don't live in the same household as the dog, make the caretakers uncomfortable with their decision not to elect for euthanasia.

A Case of Unwanted Advice

Tyson was a five-year-old pit bull that was suffering from both severe allergic skin issues and an advanced case of osteoarthritis. He was being treated by a dermatologist at a specialty center but had come to me for help with treating his painful joints. Tyson was one of the most lovable dogs ever to come into my practice. Despite

(continued)

his pain, he was like an 80-pound love bomb that sometimes literally crashed into me in his exuberance to be friendly and to get attention in return. His skin was hard to look at. Much of his fur was gone, and his red and thickened skin was oily to the touch. He sometimes was broken out in hives as well. Despite his skin issues, he never went without hugs and pets from my staff and me . . . Tyson's personality outshined his diseased skin.

Tyson's caretaker told me of an incident where she was at the specialty center waiting her turn with Tyson to see the dermatologist when a middle-age woman came in with her own dog, took one look at Tyson, and started haranguing the caretaker. "Your dog is diseased and disgusting; you shouldn't be here having him treated and exposing all the other dogs to what he has, you should have him put to sleep!" Thankfully, at this point, someone from the dermatologist's office came out and informed this shrew of a woman that if she was made uncomfortable by Tyson, then she was the one who had to leave.

This true story represents what many pet owners with terminally ill or just plain aged dogs have to endure. This woman was obviously ignorant of what Tyson's issues were (they were not contagious) and made no considerations as to why Tyson might have been visiting the specialty clinic. Her comments were not only wrong, they were uninvited and inappropriate. This would likely have been much more hurtful had those comments come from a neighbor or friend. When people see an old and arthritic dog taking 20 minutes to walk the length of a block and back, they only get that single snapshot of this dog's life. They have no knowledge of his daily interactions with his family. Their comments may be well intentioned, but they really have no idea what the rest of that dog's life is like.

I like to put situations like this into perspective by taking examples from our own lives. A person may have had something they really liked to do in their youth that evolved over time. For example, someone might have really liked the water and anything to do with it. This could have started in youth with a vigorous activity like snorkeling and ended in old age with sitting on a dock and fishing. Both activities involve water, and even though they are worlds apart, they still are enjoyed at both ends of the life spectrum by the very same person. No one would suggest euthanizing Grandpa because he can't snorkel anymore!

But When Is Enough, Enough?

Too often I have seen an animal treated for an illness, one for which there never will be a cure or resolution, go on beyond what seems sensible. This might happen for several reasons that involve both the caretaker and the animal's veterinarian.

Caregiver Issues

Of course, our dogs aren't going to live forever. And for some, their final living days on Earth can be downright miserable, to the point where there is not enough daily reward to warrant carrying on. It might be hard for you to consider any really good days and not interpret them as some kind of upward trend in your dog's overall condition. It might be equally as hard to look back over several weeks and recognize that your dog's last days are, more often than not, following a path of steady decline. A slow decline toward death by old age or cancer or pain offers reprieves now and then, whether intentionally through treatment or just through the normal waxing and waning of any disease process.

So how do we know when it is time?

Herein lies the importance of monitoring your dog on a regular basis. By *monitoring*, I mean really taking a look at her routines in as dispassionate a way as possible and making the most honest assessment that you are able. I will discuss some monitoring tools a little later in this chapter. When I say that this needs to be done on a *regular basis*, I mean at intervals that are sufficiently long enough to make comparisons that are more likely to have meaning. You should not try to discern differences on a one-day-to-the-next basis. This interval will probably get shorter as time goes on, because health issues have a tendency to snowball toward the very end of life. But I feel that a good rule-of-thumb is a two-week interval. This is a good time frame to look for change. I use this two-week rule in my practice when I am initiating a pain treatment, and it seems to be a period of time that allows all involved to most accurately assess change. Too-frequent evaluations should be compared to the axiom, "A watched pot never boils," wherein the moment-to-moment changes are too minor to be significant. Even with this in mind, it can be difficult to decide when that threshold is crossed because a caregiver's visualization of what the end point might look like often changes; it is impossible to anticipate every change in body function and ability as the end draws near. It is common for caregivers to make the decision for euthanasia telling me that they probably waited a few weeks too long.

Veterinary Issues

Veterinarians choose their profession for a variety of reasons. But one of the most common threads that bind veterinarians in that choice is the desire to help. It is anathema for us to stand by and do nothing. Lacerations need to be sutured, infections need to be treated with antibiotics, and tumors need to be removed. But in the murky waters of pain management, where measurements of progress are not precise and where it sometimes seems that there is yet one more treatment, it is easy to get lost in the miasma of treatments, focusing only on the disease and not the patient.

And what veterinarian can look a caregiver in the eyes and not want to offer hope? It is easy to become complicit with the owner's desire to keep the dog around as long as possible, ignoring the price the patient must pay. Veterinarians are subject to the same traps as the caregivers—reading too much into a few good days and not looking at the bigger picture of steadily declining health. It would be a good idea, as hard as it might be, to have a discussion with your veterinarian about the end point fairly early in the process of discussing end-of-life issues. Just as in the case of setting forth some outcome measures when you are expecting your dog to recover, you should discuss some measures that will trigger a decision to consider euthanasia. As with the outcome measures, these are not set in stone. Even if you change these measures as they are approached, at least it will prompt a discussion between you and your veterinarian, and continuing past that point will be a conscious decision, not something that just slips by.

Hospice Care

For too long, euthanasia was the only option available for treating a gravely ill animal (besides aggressively treating a disease, of course). Attitudes have slowly changed over the last decade, and hospice care is now available for our animal companions. Still, too many people don't realize that hospice for their dog is even an option.

Hospice care treats the patient and not the disease. In other words, in hospice no effort is made to change or forestall the course of a disease. Instead, all of the effort is put into maintaining the patient in a comfortable state. Hospice can be a good choice for a few key reasons. The disease might not have a cure. Or a cure might not be the most desirable outcome: prognosis, cost of treatment, and inability to provide adequate home care are among the many factors that can make hospice care the best choice.

In human medicine, hospice care may involve a hospice facility as well as hospice homecare. Animal hospice is not a place where you take your dog. Rather, it is a philosophy based on the relief of pain and suffering, the decision not to extend an animal's life, and a nurturing of the human-animal bond.

Hospice care should be done through many different modalities that include but are not limited to medication, massage, and acupuncture. Hospice care should also involve many different team members. The International Association of Animal Hospice and Palliative Care lists many potential people on this team that include veterinarians and their staff; mental health professionals; religious support personnel, such as chaplains; pet sitters; and community volunteers.

Palliative care is often confused with hospice, but it is not the same thing. Palliative care is exactly what it sounds like—palliation of any pain or discomfort that a patient may be going through. Palliative care is always a part of the treatment of any animal with a disease for which we hope to achieve recovery. But palliative care also can be a part of hospice care, where recovery is not expected.

Hospice care is not just about keeping the patient comfortable. It is also about the changing relationship between pet and caregiver as the end of life approaches. For the patient, at a time when his body starts to fail him and he suffers shame and guilt as he becomes unable to deal with issues such as mobility and elimination, he can feel reassured as his caregiver helps him with those activities. For the caregiver, it is a chance to explore the changing relationship. Many caregivers who provide hospice for their dog describe a strengthening of their bond to their pets as they become not only the caregiver but also the caretaker. Many people also describe a sense of relief after letting go of the feeling that they need to "fix" their dog's problem and instead accept that their role is only one of maintaining his quality of life.

Hospice care is *not* about keeping an animal alive at any cost of time, money, or effort in order for him to die a "natural" death. Many animals do die of their own accord during hospice, but for many that end can be too full of agony and suffering, and so veterinary intervention becomes necessary.

An article in the 2014 issue of the American Animal Hospital Association (AAHA) magazine *Trends* discusses hospice care. It points out that there is no single consensus among veterinarians about guidelines and definitions of hospice care. Some hospice veterinarians have an extreme view (in my mind) that no animal should ever be euthanized. Other hospice veterinarians insist on treating the underlying disease as a means of controlling the pain. Despite these and other differences in philosophy, AAHA points out that "There are some basic tenets that pet hospice unquestionably shares with human hospice: a focus on comfort and quality of life—which includes the alleviation of the physical pain and emotional suffering of the entire family unit—when the decision is made to forgo aggressive treatment to extend a patient's life."

Everyone reading this will have a slightly different desire for what they want to get from hospice care for their dog, and that is okay. For this reason, allow me to provide an outline for how I think hospice should work and let you decide what parts of it you hope to engage. What I am not going to do is discuss every possible facet of hospice care. I encourage you to use my outline as a basis to discuss hospice care with your own veterinarian. I hope that your regular veterinarian is able to provide animal hospice. See Appendix A to help find a hospice care provider.

Hospice Plan

No hospice plan is going to be successful if both the veterinarian and caretaker don't have a complete medical picture of the patient's state of health. Diagnostics will vary depending on what is considered to be the primary issue at hand, despite the fact that in any gravely ill animal, especially aged ones, several medical issues are often occurring at the same time. Maybe you are considering hospice because of cancer. But what if there are other medical issues going on such as chronic kidney failure or anemia? These types of issues can affect the choices made for both the medical care and the at-home hospice care.

Utilization of X-rays, abdominal ultrasound, and blood panels are both reasonable and desirable as part of the standard of care for hospice patients. Only after completing this work can your veterinarian start to construct a treatment plan. Regardless, you should consider some things when starting any hospice plan.

Points that Must Be Part of Every Hospice Plan

No matter what path animal hospice may take for your pet, some specific areas *must* be met.

1. **The need of the animal is paramount.** Pain must be reasonably controlled, adequate nursing care must be provided, and the emotional needs of your pet must be considered.

2. **A veterinarian must be one of the core individuals providing animal hospice.** Only a veterinarian has the skills to properly assess an animal's physical state and suggest appropriate medical care.

3. **Outcome measures must be discussed at the very beginning.** In other words, all involved parties must agree upon realistic goals for the animal. This not only serves the needs of the pet but also prevents frustration on everyone's part because they will know in advance what is reasonable to expect during hospice care.

4. **Regular communication between all of the parties involved in hospice care is a must.** As I stated previously, patient assessments might take place at two-week intervals to start, but as the end approaches, these assessments might be made as often as every day. Only through effective communication can the actual needs of the animal be discovered and then met.

Points that Should Be Considered for Every Hospice Plan

Some parts of hospice care *should* receive strong consideration. Age-related pain issues and cancer are probably two of the more common reasons your dog might enter hospice. You need to consider the baggage these conditions often carry along with them.

1. **Mobility issues.** Whether it is because of pain, neurological problems, or mechanical issues, many dogs in hospice have issues related to moving around. Care must be taken to provide adequate bedding to prevent bedsores. Additionally, plans must be in place to help move dogs for purposes such as elimination, hygiene, and yes, even exercise. Your veterinarian

should be able to help you find not only proper bedding but also helpful devices, such as harnesses with handles.

2. **Emotional and mental issues.** If the same problem that has put your dog into hospice is also restricting his ability to move around, then you must take certain steps so that your dog does not feel socially isolated. Isolation may result in not only boredom but may also bring about anxiety and fear. And just like people, lack of mental stimulation can increase cognitive disorders in dogs, resulting in confusion and depression, which makes his life even more miserable. Keep your dog in the most active or populated area of your home, moving him around as necessary. Find some semi-sedentary games to play, be it tug-of-war, catch, or a modified version of what might once have been some part of his favorite game. Even a relatively immobile dog can play. And don't forget, your time left with him is limited. Take your place next to him as you read or watch television, and petting or even just touching him can be a lot of comfort to both of you.

3. **Other issues.** Don't forget that sick animals often have issues other than their main problem. These problems, or as they are called in the medical community, comorbidities, can easily be given less attention than they demand, or might even be forgotten. Problems that your dog may have had her entire life, such as allergies, ear infections, or anal sac impactions don't stop just because she might be dealing with cancer. In addition, age-related problems such as reduced kidney function may become a larger issue than you realize as she becomes more unable to demonstrate behaviors that are associated with different illnesses. I have found with many of my hospice patients that paying attention to many of the smaller details, in addition to the main problem, vastly improves the patient's

quality of life. It is not your responsibility to recognize these problems, but it is your responsibility to have regular contact with your hospice veterinarian through conversation, examinations, and blood work in order to be on top of these possibly emerging issues.

4. **Sanitary issues.** Especially as the end nears, it is much more likely that your ailing pet might have problems with urine and bowel control. If urinary incontinence, even partial incontinence, is an issue then you must take action. Urine that remains in prolonged contact with the skin can result in irritation, scalding, and skin infection, not to mention feelings of discomfort and guilt that your pet might experience. The same is true for fecal incontinence. This is not only distressing to your pet, it also can lead to medical issues if it is not handled promptly. Your veterinarian should have some suggestions for modifying bedding and for medications to protect the skin.

5. **Read the signs.** It is easy to ignore or misread many of the signs of decreasing body function. Just as easy to overlook is your dog's decreasing will to live. I was taught a valuable insight early in my career while treating a cat in chronic renal failure. The cat's caretaker told me that his cat always had loved to play with the buttons on whatever article of clothing he was wearing. In fact, when he first brought his outwardly healthy-looking cat to me he tried to entice his cat to play while saying, "Look, she won't swipe at the buttons on my coat." During the cat's lengthy treatment, we were always able to tell the current state of this cat's kidney function, almost as reliably as lab work, by the button test. When a week had gone by and none of our treatments could make him play with the buttons again, we agreed that although we could keep him going for a while, his interest in life had faded. Quickly there-

after the decision to end his suffering was made. Few pets have such a great measurement for determining happiness. But with a little effort and watchfulness, you should be able to help track your pet's emotional state.

6. **Take care of yourself.** Providing end-of-life care for your pet is both physically and mentally exhausting. In addition to the strains it might put on you, consider the strains it might put on your relationships, especially if there is not a consensus of opinion about what should be done and when. Maybe a good friend to lean on is all that is needed. But don't discount social workers, ministers, rabbis, and grief counselors. I have always thought of this as my airplane rule: In the case of loss of cabin pressure, put your own mask on before helping others. In other words, if you don't take care of yourself first, both you and your dog will suffer.

Take Stock of Your Own Limitations

One of my favorite quotes is by Anaïs Nin: "We do not see things as they are, we see them as we are." In other words, in any life experience we reference that experience through our own experiences. In the case of pain, dying, and death, the references we draw upon may be too limited to be effective in accomplishing what is best for our pets and us. It is essential that we look to others for help and guidance.

AFTERWORD

No statistics have been collected or studies done that outline the difficulties a caregiver must go through in order to find help for treating their dog's pain. It is an almost weekly event that someone tells me I am the fourth, fifth, sixth . . . etc. veterinarian they have come to before they found pain relief for their dog. It is my sincere hope that this book changes that for everyone. I have given you the tools to find veterinarians competent in various areas of pain management (see Appendix A) and have empowered you with the knowledge of what to ask, what to expect, and frankly what to demand for the care of your dog. You also have some basic tools to improve your dog's home environment and to provide him with some pain-relieving measures of your own in the form of things such as massage and mobility assistance.

More often than not, when you are the caregiver of a dog in pain, and your role increases such that you are caring for his daily needs that are now impossible for him to do on his own, it results in a change in that relationship. For the majority of people, the intimacy and the close daily, sometimes hourly, interaction with their painful and aging pet brings about a positive change. For any dog, the caregiver embodies his or her world, and this is especially true for an animal in pain. Your dog depends on you to help navigate the world and to provide the treatments he or she needs. Time and again I have seen illness and pain interposing itself between human and dog, exponentially tightening their bond. The result can be a level of companionship, love, and understanding that might otherwise never have been attained. I wish all of this for you and your dog, and I believe in your ability to achieve it.

—*Michael C. Petty*

PAIN-MANAGEMENT RESOURCES

Listed below are reputable organizations that provide advanced training and education to their members. Unfortunately, some businesses offer "certifications" after only a few hours of instruction. I have not included those places here. This list also contains resources for finding reputable prosthetic makers and quality-of-life scales.

In an effort to keep up with new organizations that might come to light after the printing of this book, I will provide an up-to-date list on my own website, www.drmikepetty.com. The website contains both organizations dedicated to pain management and veterinary practitioners who are experts in pain management. Visit my website prior to exploring the following websites to obtain the most current information available.

www.drmikepetty.com

Up-to-date resource for pain organizations and veterinarians certified in various forms of pain management.

Acupuncture

www.onehealthsim.org/grad-search

Hospice Care

www.iaahpc.org/for-pet-parents/public-directory.html

Pain Practitioners

ivapm.org/membership/find-a-member

All IVAPM members have a special interest in pain management. If you are looking for an IVAPM member who is also a Certified Veterinary Pain Practitioner, then check the box prior to conducting your search.

Prosthetics

www.k-9orthotics.com in Canada (also serves U.S. market); (902) 865-5596

www.orthopets.com (303) 653-9555

Quality of Life

www.newmetrica.com

aplb.org

Rehabilitation

ccrp.utvetce.com

www.caninerehabinstitute.com/find_a_therapist.html

rehabvets.org/Referrals.lasso

Appendix B

COMMON PAINFUL CONDITIONS BY BREED

Following is a list of diseases that cause pain in some of the most common breeds in the United States. This is neither an all-inclusive list of genetic diseases nor even a list of those genetic diseases that cause pain. For example, the only cancer I list is osteosarcoma, but some breeds are prone to various different cancers, all of which have the strong potential of causing pain. Consult Appendix C for a glossary that includes a very brief description of the common painful conditions noted here.

I have not included three conditions here—elbow arthritis, hip dysplasia, and patellar luxation—because it is possible for almost every breed to develop these problems. These conditions are, however, noted in Appendix C.

For those readers who wish to look into more diseases by breed, many sources are available to you.[79 80 81 82 83] There is also an ever-expanding list of genetic tests for some of the diseases mentioned here. I did not make an attempt to list the tests in this appendix because their number is increasing so rapidly that any listing would be out of date by the time this book is published.

Alaskan Malamute
Dwarfism, osteochondromatosis

American Eskimo Dog
Degenerative myelopathy

American Staffordshire Terrier
Cranial cruciate disease, stomach cancer

Australian Shepherd
Legg-Calvé-Perthes disease, panosteitis, various skeletal abnormalities

Basset
Panosteitis, intervertebral disk disease

Beagle
Dwarfism, intervertebral disk disease

Bernese Mountain Dog
Cranial cruciate disease, degenerative myelopathy, osteoarthritis, osteochondritis dissecans, panosteitis

Bichon Frise
Legg-Calvé-Perthes disease

Bloodhound
Degenerative myelopathy

Border Collie
Osteochondritis dissecans

Boston Terrier
Legg-Calvé-Perthes disease

Boxer
Cranial cruciate disease, osteochondritis dissecans, pancreatitis, various cancers including osteosarcoma

Brittany

Osteochondritis dissecans

Bulldog

Osteoarthritis, osteochondritis dissecans

Bullmastiff

Osteoarthritis

Cairn Terrier

Legg-Calvé-Perthes disease, cranial cruciate disease, osteochondritis dissecans, pancreatitis

Cavalier King Charles Spaniel

Legg-Calvé-Perthes disease, fibrocartilagenous embolism, intervertebral disk disease, pancreatitis, syringomyelia

Chesapeake Bay Retriever

Cranial cruciate disease, degenerative myelopathy, osteochondritis dissecans

Chihuahua

Legg-Calvé-Perthes disease, osteochondritis dissecans

Chow Chow

Cranial cruciate disease, osteochondritis dissecans

Cocker Spaniel

Very prone to patellar luxation

Collie

Degenerative myelopathy, dermatomyositis, osteochondritis dissecans, pancreatitis

Corgi

Degenerative myelopathy, intervertebral disk disease

Dachshund

Cellulitis, Legg-Calvé-Perthes disease, intervertebral disk disease

Dalmatian

Wobbler syndrome

Doberman Pinscher

Osteochondritis dissecans, panosteitis, wobbler syndrome

English Setter

Osteochondritis dissecans

French Bulldog

Degenerative myelopathy, hemivertebra, intervertebral disk disease

German Shepherd

Cauda equine syndrome, cranial cruciate disease, degenerative myelopathy, osteochondritis dissecans, panosteitis

German Shorthaired Pointer

Hemivertebra, osteochondritis dissecans

Golden Retriever

Cellulitis, cranial cruciate disease, hypertrophic osteodystrophy, osteochondritis dissecans, panosteitis

Great Dane

Hypertrophic osteodystrophy, osteochondritis dissecans, osteosarcoma, panosteitis, wobbler syndrome

Greyhound
Avulsion of the tibial tuberosity, avulsion of ligaments of the foot, cauda equine syndrome, cranial cruciate disease, osteoarthritis, osteochondritis dissecans, osteosarcoma

Havanese
Osteochondrodysplasia

Irish Setter
Degenerative myelopathy, dwarfism, hypertrophic osteodystrophy, osteosarcoma

Italian Greyhound
Legg-Calvé-Perthes disease

Jack Russell Terrier
Legg-Calvé-Perthes disease, osteoarthritis

Labrador Retriever
Cauda equine syndrome, cranial cruciate disease, hypertrophic osteodystrophy, osteochondritis dissecans, panosteitis

Lhasa Apso
Intervertebral disk disease

Mastiff
Cauda equine syndrome, cranial cruciate disease, osteochondritis dissecans, osteosarcoma, panosteitis, wobbler "syndrome"

Miniature Pinscher
Legg-Calvé-Perthes disease

Miniature Schnauzer
Legg-Calvé-Perthes disease, fibrocartilagenous embolism, pancreatitis

Newfoundland
Cranial cruciate rupture, osteochondritis dissecans, osteosarcoma

Papillion
Legg-Calvé-Perthes disease

Pekingese
Legg-Calvé-Perthes disease, hemivertebra, intervertebral disk disease

Pomeranian
Legg-Calvé-Perthes disease, intervertebral disk disease

Poodles (all)
Degenerative myelopathy, dwarfism, Legg-Calvé-Perthes disease

Pug
Degenerative myelopathy, hemivertebra

Rottweiler
Cranial cruciate disease, intervertebral disk disease, osteoarthritis, osteochondritis dissecans, osteosarcoma, panosteitis, wobbler syndrome

Saint Bernard
Cranial cruciate disease, osteochondritis dissecans, osteosarcoma, panosteitis

Shar-pei
Osteochondritis dissecans

Shetland Sheepdog
Dermatomyositis, distal tibial valgus formation

Shih Tzu
Legg-Calvé-Perthes disease

Siberian Husky

Cranial cruciate disease

Silky Terrier

Legg-Calvé-Perthes disease

Vizsla

Osteochondritis dissecans

Weimaraner

Wobbler syndrome

West Highland White Terrier

Legg-Calvé-Perthes disease

Yorkshire Terrier

Legg-Calvé-Perthes disease

Appendix C

DEFINITIONS OF DISEASES

A list of common diseases and a very brief description of each.

Avulsion of the Tibial Tuberosity—A fracture of the tibia or "shinbone" at the attachment point of the kneecap

Cauda Equina Syndrome—A neurological disease at or near the junction of the lower back and pelvis, causing pain and muscle weakness

Cellulitis—A juvenile skin disorder that causes acne-like eruptions, which is very painful

Cranial Cruciate Disease—A gradual degradation of an important ligament in the knee, usually resulting in rupture of the ligament unless diagnosed and treated early

Degenerative Myelopathy—A disorder of the spinal cord, which can be painful and causes gradual paralysis

Dermatomyositis—A painful muscle disorder, which also exhibits skin problems as well

NOTES

1. K. Mathews, P. Kronen, D. Lascelles, et al. "Guidelines for Recognition, Assessment and Treatment of Pain," *Journal of Small Animal Practice* (June 2014), E14.

2. L. Horn, F. Range, and L. Huber. "Dogs' Attention Toward Humans Depends on Their Relationship, Not Only on Social Familiarity," *Animal Cognition* (May 2013), 435–43.

3. J. Niu, L. Ding, J. J. Li, et al. "Modality-Based Organization of Ascending Somatosensory Axons in the Direct Dorsal Column Pathway," *Journal of Neuroscience* (November 2013), 17691–709.

4. A. Taddio, M. Goldbach, et al. "Effect of Neonatal Circumcision on Pain Responses During Vaccination in Boys," *The Lancet* (February 1995), 291–92.

5. G. Weber, J. Morton, and H. Keates. "Postoperative Pain and Perioperative Analgesic Administration in Dogs: Practices, Attitudes and Beliefs of Queensland Veterinarians," *Australian Veterinary Journal* (May 2012), 186–93.

6. Pfizer Animal Health Proprietary Market Research. Survey of 200 Veterinarians, 1996.

7. S. Fox. *Chronic Pain in Small Animal Medicine* (London: Manson Publishing Ltd, 2010), 75.

8. K. M. Vernau. "Cauda Equina Syndrome in Dogs and Cats," Western Veterinary Conference, 2006.

9. University of Pennsylvania School of Veterinary Medicine. "Cranial Drawer Movement," http://cal.vet.upenn.edu/projects/orthopod/oldsite/cruciate/crucmov01.htm.

10. B. Hart, L. Hart, et al. "Long-Term Health Effects of Neutering Dogs: Com-

parison of Labrador Retrievers with Golden Retrievers," *PLoS One* (July 2014), eCollection.

11. M. Atherton and G. Arthurs. "Osteosarcoma of the Tibia 6 Years After Tibial Plateau Leveling Osteotomy" (May–June 2012), 188–93.

12. P. Bajaj, T. Graven-Nielsen, et al. "Trigger Points in Patients with Lower Limb Osteoarthritis," *Journal of Musculoskeletal Pain* 9(3), (2001), 17–33.

13. M. C. Zink and J. B. Van Dyke, eds. "What Is a Canine Athlete," *Canine Sports Medicine and Rehabilitation* (Ames, IA: John Wiley and Sons, 2013), 15–17.

14. K. Mathews. "Neuropathic Pain in Dogs and Cats: If Only They Could Tell Us if They Hurt," *Veterinary Clinics of North America: Small Animal Practice-Update on Pain Management* (November 2008), 1365–1404.

15. WebMD. "Recognizing Caregiver Burnout," http://women.webmd.com/caregiver-recognizing-burnout.

16. P. Imperato. *Medical Detective* (New York: R. Marek, 1979), 13.

17. M. Papich. "An Update on Nonsteroidal Anti-Inflammatory Drugs (NSAIDS) in Small Animals," *VCNA Small Animal Practice* (2008), 1243–66.

18. C. Svensson. In *Synaptic Plasticity in Pain*, Marzia Malcangio, ed. (New York: Springer, 2009), 403–23.

19. A. Autefageet et al. "Long-Term Efficacy and Safety of Firocoxib in the Treatment of Dogs with Osteoarthritis," *Veterinary Record* (June 2011), 617.

20. Jill Maddison. The Royal Veterinary College, https://vimeo.com/65164382.

21. E. Epstein, I. Rodan, et al. "AAHA/AAFP Pain Management Guidelines for Dogs and Cats," *Journal of Feline Medicine and Surgery* (2015), 17, 257.

22. Wendy Brooks. "Gadapentin (Neurontin)," VeterinaryPartner.com, www.veterinarypartner.com/Content.plx?A=2764&S=1.

23. Wendy Brooks. "Amantadin," VeterinaryPartner.com, www.veterinarypartner.com/Content.plx?A=2781&S=2.

24. Megan Richardson. "The Side Effects of Amitriptyline for Cats," eHow.com, http://www.ehow.com/list_6653680_side-effects-amitriptyline-cats.html.

25. B. Kukanich and M. Papich. "Pharmacokinetics and Antinociceptive Effects of Oral Tramadol Hydrochloride Administration in Greyhounds," *American Journal of Veterinary Research* (February 2011), 256–62.

26. Jane Meggett. "Side Effects of Tramodol in Dogs," eHow.com, www.how.com/about_5422031_side-effects-tramadol-dogs.html.

27. M. Silverman, M. Lydecker, and P. Lee. *Bad Medicine: The Prescription Drug Industry in the Third World* (Stanford University Press, 1992), 88–90.

28. G. Hagg. "New Explanation for Muscle Damage as a Result of Static Loads in the Neck and Shoulder," *Arbete Manniska Miljo* (1988), 260–62.

29. J. Dommerholt and P. Huijbregts. *Myofascial Trigger Points* (Burlington, MA: Jones and Bartlett, 2011), 159–80.

30. F. Cevikbas, M. Steinhoff, et. al. "Role of Spinal Neurotransmitter Receptors in Itch: New Insights into the Therapies and Drug Development," *CNS Neuroscience & Therapeutics* 17 (2001), 742–49.

31. Z. Q. Zhao et al. "Descending Control of Itch Transmission by the Serotonergic System via 5-HT1A-Facilitated GRP-GRPR Signaling," *Neuron* (2014), 821–34.

32. J. Budginand and M. Flaherty. "Alternative Therapies in Veterinary Dermatology," *Veterinary Clinics of North America: Small Animal Practice* (2013), 189–204.

33. R. Marsella, C. Nicklin, and C. Melloy. "The Effects of Capsaicin Topical Therapy in Dogs with Atopic Dermatitis: A Randomized, Double-Blinded, Placebo-Controlled, Cross-Over Clinical Trial," *Veterinary Dermatolology* (2002), 131–39.

34. N. Dodman, L. Shuster, et al. "The Use of Dextromethorphan to Treat Repetitive Self-Directed Scratching, Biting, or Chewing in Dogs with Allergic Dermatitis," *Journal of Veterinary Pharmacology and Therapeutics* (2004), 99–104.

35. R. Marsella, L. Messinger, et al. "A Randomized, Double-Blind, Placebo Controlled Study to Evaluate the Effect of EFF1001, an Actinidia Arguta (Hardy Kiwi) Preparation, on CADESI Score and Pruritus in Dogs with Mild to Moderate Atopic Dermatitis," *Veterinary Dermatology* (2010), 50–57.

36. K. Wucherer et al. "Short-Term and Long-Term Outcomes for Overweight Dogs with Cranial Cruciate Ligament Rupture Treated Surgically or Nonsurgically," *Journal of the American Veterinary Medical Association* (May 15, 2013), 1364–72.

37. *Nature.* "Hard to Swallow" (2007), 105–106.

38. S. Forsyth, W. Guilford, et al. "Endoscopic Evaluation of the Gastroduodenal Mucosa Following Non-steroidal Anti-inflammatory Drug Administration in the Dog," *New Zealand Veterinary Journal* (October 1996), 179–81.

39. S. Reed. "Nonsteroidal Anti-inflammatory Drug-Induced Duodenal Ulceration and Perforation in a Mature Rottweiler," *Canadian Veterinary Journal* (December 2002), 971–72.

40. M. Moreau and J. Dupuis. "Clinical Evaluation of a Powder of Quality Elk Velvet Antler for the Treatment of Osteoarthritis in Dogs," *Canadian Veterinary Journal* (February 2004), 133–399.

41. J. Bauer. "Therapeutic Use of Fish Oils in Companion Animals," *Journal of the American Veterinary Medical Association* (December 2011), 1444.

42. J. Roush, C. Dodd, et al. "Multicenter Veterinary Practice Assessment of the Effects of Omega-3 Fatty Acids on Osteoarthritis in Dogs," *Journal of the American Veterinary Medical Association* (2010), 66.

43. J. Roush, A. Cross, et al. "Evaluation of the Effects of Dietary Supplementation

with Fish Oil Omega-3 Fatty Acids on Weight Bearing in Dogs with Osteoarthritis," *Journal of the American Veterinary Medical Association* (2010), 73.

44. P. Rialland, S. Bichot, et al. "Effect of a Diet Enriched with Green-Lipped Mussel on Pain Behavior and Functioning in Dogs with Clinical Osteoarthritis," *Canadian Journal of Veterinary Research* (January 2013), 66–74.

45. A. Hielm-Björkman, R. Tulamo, et al. "Evaluating Complementary Therapies for Canine Osteoarthritis, Part I: Green-Lipped Mussel (*Perna canaliculus*)," *Evidence-Based Complementary and Alternative Medicine* (September 2009), 365–73.

46. R. Gupta et al. "Comparative Therapeutic Efficacy and Safety of Type II Collagen Glucosamine and Chondroitin in Arthritic Dogs: Pain Evaluation by Ground Force Plate," *Journal of Animal Physiology and Animal Nutrition* (May 2011), 770–77.

47. S. Canapp et al. "Scintigraphic Evaluation of Dogs with Acute Synovitis After Treatment with Glucosamine Hydrochloride and Chondroitin Sulfate," *American Journal Veterinary Research* (December 1999), 1552–57.

48. M. Moreau et al. "Clinical Evaluation of a Nutraceutical, Carprofen and Meloxicam for the Treatment of Dogs with Osteoarthritis," *Veterinary Record* (March 15, 2003), 323–29.

49. R. Gupta et al. "Comparative Therapeutic Efficacy and Safety of Type-II Collagen (UC-II), Glucosamine and Chondroitin in Arthritic Dogs: Pain Evaluation by Ground Force Plate," *Journal of Animal Physiology and Animal Nutrition* (May 2011), 770–77.

50. A. Adebowale. "The Bioavailability and Pharmacokinetics of Glucosamine Hydrochloride and Low Molecular Weight Chondroitin Sulfate After Single and Multiple Doses to Beagle Dogs," *Biopharmaceutics and Drug Disposition* (September 2002), 217–25.

51. G. McCarthy et al. "Randomised Double-Blind, Positive-Controlled Trial to Assess the Efficacy of Glucosamine/Chondroitin Sulfate for the Treatment of Dogs with Osteoarthritis," *Veterinary Journal* (July 2007), 54–61.

52. L. Lippiello, S. Han, et al. "Protective Effect of the Chondroprotective Agent Cosequin DS on Bovine Articular Cartilage Exposed In Vitro to Nonsteroidal Antiinflammatory Agents," *Veterinary Therapeutics* (Summer 2002), 128–35.

53. D. Imhoff, W. Gordon-Evans, et al. "Evaluation of S-Adenosyl l-Methionine in a Double-Blinded, Randomized, Placebo-Controlled, Clinical Trial for Treatment of Presumptive Osteoarthritis in the Dog," *Veterinary Surgery* (February 2011), 228–32.

54. L. Deparle, R. Gupta, et al. "Efficacy and Safety of Glycosylated Undenatured Type-II Collagen (UC-II) in Therapy of Arthritic Dogs," *Journal of Veterinary Pharmacology and Therapeutics* (August 2005), 385–90.

55. M. D'Altilio, A. Peal, et al. "Therapeutic Efficacy and Safety of Undenatured

Type II Collagen Singly or in Combination with Glucosamine and Chondroitin Sulfate in Arthritic Dogs," *Toxicology Mechanisms and Methods* (2007), 189–96.

56. J. Lenz, D. Joffe, et al. "Perceptions, Practices, and Consequences Associated with Foodborne Pathogens and the Feeding of Raw Meat to Dogs," *Canadian Veterinary Journal* (2009), 637–43.

57. S. Lefebvre, R. Reid-Smith, et al. "Evaluation of the Risks of Shedding *Salmonellae* and Other Potential Pathogens by Therapy Dogs Fed Raw Diets in Ontario and Alberta," *Zoonoses Public Health* (2008), 470–80.

58. M. Kozak, K. Horosova, et al. "Do Dogs and Cats Present a Risk of Transmission of Salmonellosis to Humans?" *Bratislava Medical Journal* (2003), 323–28.

59. AmericanVeterinaryMedicalAssociation.com. "Raw or Undercooked Animal-Source Protein in Cat and Dog Diets," www.avma.org/KB/Policies/Pages/Raw-or-Undercooked-Animal-Source-Protein-in-Cat-and-Dog-Diets.aspx.

60. FDA.com. "Is It Safe for Me to Provide My Pet with a Raw Food Diet?" www.fda.gov/AboutFDA/Transparency/Basics/ucm206814.htm.

61. CDC.gov. "Q&A: Salmonella Outbreak. August 2007," www.cdc.gov/salmonella/schwarzengrund_faq.html.

62. P. Rialland, S. Bichot, et al. "Effect of a Diet Enriched with Green-Lipped Mussel on Pain Behavior and Functioning in Dogs with Clinical Osteoarthritis," *Canadian Journal of Veterinary Research* (January 2013), 66–74.

63. G. Singh and C. Atal. "Pharmacology of an Extract of Salaiguggal Ex-*Boswellia Serrata*, a New Non-steroidal Anti-inflammatory Agent," *Agents Actions* (1986), 407–12.

64. V. Kuptniratsaikul, P. Dajpratham, et al. "Efficacy and Safety of Curcuma Domestica Extracts Compared with Ibuprofen in Patients with Knee Osteoarthritis: A Multicenter Study," *Clinical Interventions in Aging* (March 2014), 451–58.

65. W. Becker, M. Kowaleski, et al. "Extracorporeal Shockwave Therapy for Shoulder Lameness in Dogs," *Journal of American Animal Hospital Association* (January/February 2015), 15–24.

66. M. Epstein, I. Rodan, et al. "2015 AAHA/AAFP Pain Management Guidelines for Dogs and Cats," *Journal of American Animal Hospital Association* (March/April 2015), 74.

67. Ibid.

68. D. O'Mathuna and R. Ashford. "Therapeutic Touch for the Healing of Acute Wounds," *Cochrane Database of Systemic Reviews* (June 2012).

69. G. da Silva, G. Lorenzi-Filho, et al. "Effects of Yoga and the Addition of Tui Na in Patients with Fibromyalgia," *Journal of Alternative and Complementary Medicine* (December 2007), 1107–13.

70. G. Ishikawa, Y. Koya, et al. "Long-Term Analgesic Effect of a Single Dose of

Anti-NGF Antibody on Pain During Motion without Notable Suppression of Joint edema and Lesion in a Rat Model of Osteoarthritis," *Osteoarthritis and Cartilage* (February 2015).

71. R. Webster, G. Anderson, et al. "Canine Brief Pain Inventory Scores for Dogs with Osteoarthritis Before and After Administration of a Monoclonal Antibody Against Nerve Growth Factor," *American Journal of Veterinary Research* (June 2014), 532–35.

72. M. Hochberg. "Serious Joint-Related Adverse Events in Randomized Controlled Trials of Anti-nerve Growth Factor Monoclonal Antibodies," *Osteoarthritis and Cartilage* (January 2015), S18–21.

73. AratanaTherapeutics.com. "Pain," www.aratana.com/for-veterinarians/pain.

74. D. Brown, K. Agnello, et al. "Intrathecal Resiniferatoxin in a Dog Model: Efficacy in Bone Cancer Pain," *Pain* (February 2015).

75. D. Brown and K. Agnello. "Intrathecal Substance P-Saporin in the Dog: Efficacy in Bone Cancer Pain," *Anesthesiology* (November 2013), 1178–85.

76. X. Yang, J. Liu, et al. "Reversal of Bone Cancer Pain by HSV-1 Mediated Silencing of CNTF in an Afferent Area of the Spinal Cord Associated with AKT-ERK Signal Inhibition," *Current Gene Therapy* (2014), 377–88.

77. F. McMillan. "A World of Hurts—Is Pain Special?" *Journal of American Veterinary Medical Association* (July 2003), 183–86.

78. P. Hellyer, I. Rodan, et al. "AAHA/AAFP Pain Management Guidelines for Dogs & Cats," *Journal of American Animal Hospital Association* (September/October 2007), 235–48.

79. University of Cambridge, Department of Veterinary Medicine. www.vet.cam.ac.uk/idid.

80. UPEI University of Prince Edward Island.com. "Canine Inherited Disorders Database," ic.upei.ca/cidd.

81. J. S. Bell, K. E. Cavanagh, L. P. Tilley, and F. W. K. Smith. *Veterinary Medical Guide to Dog and Cat Breeds* (Jackson, WY: Teton New Media, 2012).

82. A. Gough and A. Thomas. *Breed Dispositions to Disease in Dogs and Cats* (Hoboken, NJ: Wiley-Blackwell, 2010).

83. E. Cote, ed. *Clinical Veterinary Advisor* (Melbourne: Elsevier, 2011).

INDEX